SO-BYB-535

# KENTUCKY

# OFF THE BEATEN PATH™

## THIRD EDITION

## ZOÉ AYN STRECKER

### Edited by Teresa Day

*A Voyager Book*

The Globe Pequot Press

Old Saybrook, Connecticut

Cover map copyright © DeLorme Mapping
Illustrations on pages 19, 58, 62, 89, 103, 124, 136, 146, 158, 183, and
200 by Richard Gersony
Illustrations on pages 142, 155, and 195 by Julie Lynch

Off the Beaten Path is a trademark of The Globe Pequot Press.

**Library of Congress Cataloging-in-Publication Data**

Strecker, Zoé.
    Kentucky : off the beaten path / Zoé Strecker ; edited by Teresa
Day.  — 3rd ed.
      p. cm.  — (Off the beaten path series)
    "A voyager book."
    Includes index.
    ISBN 0-7627-0100-5
    1. Kentucky—Guidebooks. I. Day, Teresa. II. Title.
    III. Series.
    F449.3.S76  1997
    917.6904'43—dc21                                        97-22101
                                                                CIP

Manufactured in the United States of America
Third Edition/Second Printing

*To those Kentuckians who, with lots of love
and humor, continue to guide me
off the beaten path in all realms of life*

# KENTUCKY

EASTERN

NORTHERN

CENTRAL

SOUTH CENTRAL

WESTERN

# CONTENTS

*The prices and rates listed in this guidebook were confirmed at press time. We recommend, however, that you call establishments before traveling to obtain current information.*

# INTRODUCTION

In an age when *Vive la Différence!* is our cultural rallying cry, Kentucky should be a traveler's sheer delight. This forty-thousand-square-mile stretch of land is home to a greater variety of distinct cultures than any other rural state in the union. Our landscapes vary wildly, our accents fluctuate county to county, and we're downright contradictory, always have been. This contradictory nature is a quality that is both enjoyable and educational for locals as well as inquisitive outsiders. Despite being a longtime victim of simplified stereotypes, the Commonwealth of Kentucky doesn't include a single "typical Kentuckian." Where the edges of Kentucky's cultures overlap, delightful contrasts abound. Where else can you find hitching posts for horse and buggy rigs in a Druther's fast-food parking lot? Where else do you hear English spoken with a heavy German lilt and a thick Southern twang? or an Elizabethan dialect with a drawl?

Maybe the contradictions started with Daniel Boone (what didn't?), who was torn between settling the land he loved passionately and, not trusting his fellow pioneers, merging with the native people who loved and adopted him. Maybe Kentucky's contradictory nature proved itself in bearing both Civil War presidents into the world within a year and fewer than 100 miles apart. The same waters that produce the world's smoothest bourbon and worst bootleg also sustained the life of Carrie Nation and continue to fill the teetotalers' baptismal fonts. Stereotypes of illiteracy are at loggerheads with a remarkable history of erudition and fine literary accomplishments, and the lack of national recognition for Kentucky's contributions to the high arts is suspect upon examination of the state's almost unequaled tradition of music, dance, and fine craft.

Then there's our geography, as erratic as Colorado's, yet older and more diverse in terms of flora and fauna. Vast, big-sky country dominates the western regions where acre after fertile acre fan out, making a flat, midwestern horizon, ending in swampland and rich arable bottomland by the banks of the great Mississippi and Ohio Rivers. Central and northern Kentucky ride on a high, fertile plateau, where game has always grazed and where livestock continue to make the region wealthy and world famous for equine and bovine bloodlines. Eastern Kentucky's lush mountains are well-rounded with age, well-supplied with precious seams of coal and iron ore, and laced with clear, beautiful streams. The south central region has a touch of it all, including some of the world's most spectacular caverns.

In this book I'm just giving you leads to places that you may not have otherwise found. Your job is to immerse yourself and explore everything with fresh eyes and an open heart. The people here are so friendly, you'll get tired of smiling.

The pleasure of traveling in Kentucky begins with studying the map. Read the names of our towns and you'll begin to believe that Kentucky soil grows poets (and humorists) even better than tobacco: Bear Wallow, Horse Fly Holler, Cat Creek, Dog Town, Dogwalk, Dog Trot, Maddog, The Bark Yard, Monkey's Eyebrow, Possum Trot, Terrapin, Otterpond, Buzzard Roost, Pigeon Roost, Beaver Bottom, Beaver Lick, Rabbit Hash, Chicken Bristle, Chicken City, Ticktown, Scuffletown, Coiltown, Gold City, Future City, Sublimity City, Preacherville, Fearsville, Shuckville (population 7), Spottsville, Jugville, Blandsville, Pleasureville, Touristville, Wisdom, Beauty, Joy, Temperance, Poverty, Chance, Energy, Victory, Democrat, Republican, The Mouth, Mouth Card, Dimple, Nuckles, Shoulderblade, Big Bone, Back Bone, Wish Bone, Marrowbone, Cheap, Habit, Whynot, Pinchem Slyly, Mossy Bottom, Needmore, Sugartit, Hot Spot, Climax, Limp, Subtle, Geneva, Moscow, Bagdad, Warsaw, Paris, London, Athens, Versailles, Ninevah, Sinai, Buena Vista, Key West, Texas, Pittsburg, Omaha, Yosemite, Two Mile Town, Four Mile, Ten Mile, Halfway, Twenty-six, Seventy-six, Eighty-eight, Bachelor's Rest, Belcher, Brodhead, Oddville, Waddy, Wax, Dot, Empire, Embryo, Factory, Tidal Wave, Troublesome Creek, Vortex, Princess, Savage, Clutts, Decoy, Thousand Sticks, Gravel Switch, Quicksand, Halo, Moon, Static, Nonesuch, No Creek, Slickaway, Slap Out, Sideview, Nonchalanta, Fleming-Neon, Hi Hat, Go Forth, Alpha, Zula, Zoe, Zag, Zebulon, Zilpo, Yamacraw, Yeaddis, Yerkes, Uz (YOOzee), Wooton, Tyewhoppety, Kinniconic, Willailla, Whoopflarea, Symsonia, Smilax, Escondida, Cutshin, Cubage, Dongola, Nada, Nada (NAdee), Nebo, Slemp, Se Ree, Gee, Gad, Glo, Guy, Ono, Uno, Ino, Elba, Ulva, Ula, Ep, Eden, Devil's Fork, Paradise, Hell'n Back, Kingdome Come, Hell Fer Certain.

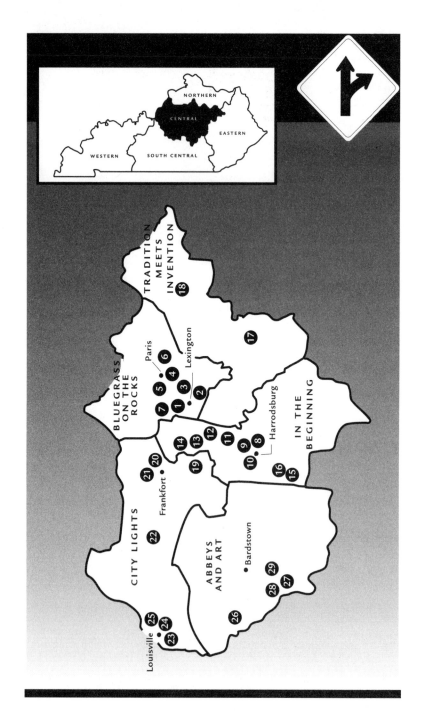

# CENTRAL KENTUCKY

1. Kentucky Horse Park
2. Keeneland Race Course
3. Kentucky Horse Center
4. Duncan Tavern
5. Amelia's Field Country Inn
6. Cane Ridge Meeting House Shrine
7. Cardome Centre
8. Old Fort Harrod State Park
9. The Beaumont Inn
10. Olde Towne Park
11. Shaker Village of Pleasant Hill
12. Irish Acres Antiques
13. Nostalgia Station Toy Train Museum
14. Labrot & Graham, The Bourbon Homeplace
15. Penn's Store
16. Perryville Battlefield State Historic Site
17. Berea
18. Ruth Hunt Candies
19. Wild Turkey Distilleries
20. Luscher's Farm Relics of Yesterday: Museum of the American Farmer
21. Shooting Star Nursery
22. Science Hill
23. J. B. Speed Art Museum
24. Kente International
25. Joe Ley Antiques
26. Bernheim Forest Arboretum and Nature Center
27. Abbey of Gethsemani
28. Kentucky Railway Museum
29. Rhodes Hall Art Gallery

# CENTRAL KENTUCKY

Like nowhere else in the world, central Kentucky seems to have been created for horses. For this we can thank the rocks. Water percolates through the limestone strata and brings phosphates into the soil that, in turn, enrich plants like bluegrass (actually green with a subtle blue tint), which give our Thoroughbreds strong, lightweight bones—perfect for racing. The same water is the magic ingredient in this region's world-famous bourbon whiskey.

Central Kentucky is also a kind of Mesopotamia of the South, a cradle of civilization west of the Allegheny Mountains. Modern buildings and businesses revolve around the region's direct links to the past. Antiques malls and bed and breakfasts in restored homes are ubiquitous in central Kentucky, and many of the humorous sites, like old country stores, are funny precisely because of their anachronisms. But there's nothing homogenous about an area that can comfortably be home to everyone from Trappist monks to soul food chefs, jockeys, millionaires, Amish farmers, sculptors, and yoga teachers. And there's no chance you'll be bored exploring it all.

## BLUEGRASS ON THE ROCKS

Wherever there is bluegrass, there are horse farms. To get a good long look at some of the world's best-known horse farms, start in Lexington. Take a drive on Harrodsburg Road, Old Frankfort Pike, Iron Works Pike, Paris Pike, Danville Road, or Versailles Road. Many of these and the smaller lanes that weave through them make wonderful bicycling routes. The miles of wooden plank fences are dizzying; these days most are sprayed with a black, creosote-based paint instead of the traditional white. Dotting the countryside are ostentatious mansions and lavish horse barns where handmade wainscoting and brass chandeliers are not unheard of.

Lexington is surrounded by hundreds of horse farms. The most famous are the Thoroughbred farms, where the top racehorses in the world are bred, born, trained, and retired. Amid those gangly legged foals you see romping in the fields in the spring may be a future Kentucky Derby—or Epsom or French Derby—winner.

Visitor policies on the farms vary widely. Some farms are open only to breeders and other industry insiders. Others, like the famous **Calumet Farm,** producer of a record eight Kentucky Derby winners, can be visited through local tour companies (Historic & Horse Farm Tours, Inc., 606–268–2906 for Calumet; or Blue Grass Tours, 606–252–5744 for other farms). Some Lexington-area farms do allow visitors by appointment, including **Three Chimneys** (606–873–7053), home of 1977 Triple Crown winner, Seattle Slew.

The best way to find out which farms are currently open is to call or stop by the **Lexington Convention and Visitors Bureau** (606–233–7299 or 800–845–3959), which keeps updated information. The bureau is in downtown Lexington at 301 East Vine Street. There's no admission charge to tour individual farms, but keep in mind that it's traditional to tip the groom who shows you around, at least $5.00 to $10.00.

While you're at the visitor center, pick up a free copy of the *Lexington Walk and Bluegrass Country Driving Tour.* Just driving around is a very enjoyable way to see horse farm country, and this guide offers direction and interesting narrative to your wanderings. The visitor center also has special guides on more than a dozen topics of special interest, from antiquing to area museums.

The ◈ **Kentucky Horse Park** (606–233–4303), located a few miles north of downtown on Iron Works Pike, is a great place to see all kinds of real horses, from Thoroughbreds to rare breeds. There are some lesser known aspects of this 1,073-acre park. Everybody stops at the Man o' War statue and grave, but take time also to visit the grave of Isaac Murphy. Here's a reminder of the important and largely unheralded role African Americans played in the early days of Thoroughbred racing. Fourteen of the fifteen

riders in the first Kentucky Derby were African American. Murphy, born in Lexington in 1861, remains the all-time most winning jockey, achieving victory in 44 percent of his races.

The Kentucky Horse Park is an education center as well as a tourist attraction. So in addition to watching the films, and looking at the antique carriages and other exhibits in the museum, be sure to walk through the Big Barn. You might find future horse trainers or veterinarians hard at work, or meet some members of the Mustang Troop, Lexington inner-city youngsters who come to the park to care for once-wild Western mustangs. The Mustang Troop rode in the 1997 Presidential Inaugural Parade. The Kentucky Horse Park is open 9:00 A.M. to 5:00 P.M. daily April through October and 9:00 A.M. to 5:00 P.M. Wednesday through Sunday November through March. There are many special shows and events throughout the year. Admission is $9.95 spring through fall, $7.50 in winter.

If you visit the Kentucky Horse Park, stop by the **Jot 'Em Down Store** at the intersection of Iron Works Pike and Russell Cave Road. Once called Terrell's Grocery, this little store has been a favorite hangout for horse farm employees. Owner Robert Terrell remembers the late 1930s when his father and uncle listened for fifteen minutes every night to a radio show called "Lum and Abner," a comedic series about two store owners much like themselves. Lum was tall and savvy, while Abner was short, dim-witted, and funny. The fictional characters ran a grocery called the Jot 'Em Down Store in Pine Ridge, Arkansas. The Terrells' customers got into the habit of calling them Lum and Abner and began adopting character names from the show, like Mousie and Grandpappy Spears. When the real Lum and Abner were in Lexington buying horses, they heard about the tradition at Terrell's Grocery, so they dropped in for a visit, bringing with them a sign that read JOT 'EM DOWN STORE. The rest is history. Come by for sandwiches and beers and you may coax Robert Terrell into playing a recording of the old show—he knows every line by heart.

To experience another important aspect of Kentucky's equine industry, go to the races or one of the big sales. Late April through May, and in late September and early October, Standardbred horses race at **The Red Mile Harness Track** (606–255–0752 or 800–354–9092), located off South Broadway, just a few blocks from the downtown business district. Great trotters and pacers have been racing this track and provoking bets since 1875. Tattersalls Sales holds a variety of Standardbred auctions at the track throughout the year.

Across the street from the Red Mile at 711 Red Mile Road

(606-252-3481) is a small riding apparel store called **Le Cheval Ltd.** Paige Kahn tailors custom-made riding apparel for clients from coast to coast. The store is open weekdays and Saturday mornings. Even if you're not in the market for a $1,500 riding suit, the fine designs are worth seeing.

About 43 percent of all the Thoroughbred horses sold in North America are sold at public horse sales in Kentucky. And the most prestigious horse sale in the world is the July Selected Yearling Sale at ◆ **Keeneland Race Course** (4201 Versailles Road; 606-254-3412 or 800-456-3412) in Lexington. This sale dates to 1943, and the horses sold must meet high bloodline and conformation standards. The bidders are an impressive group, too. From sheiks and film stars to international business moguls and Texas cowboys, you just never know who you'll see at the Keeneland sales pavilion. But you can bet that they will have one thing in common: the means and the desire to spend big bucks on horses. The world-record price for a horse ($13.1 million) was set at this sale. You don't have to be a millionaire to watch the sales from the pavilion lobby, or to walk through the barns while the horses are being shown to potential buyers, and it's a fascinating experience. Additional sales are held at Keeneland in January, September, and November.

**TRUE BLUE**

Kentucky has more than 1,500 miles of marked hiking trails.

Race meets at Keeneland are brief (just three weeks in April and three weeks in October), but they usually attract the top echelon of the Thoroughbred world. The spring meet includes the Blue Grass Stakes, an important preparatory race to the Kentucky Derby. The atmosphere is relaxed and genteel (until 1997, the track didn't even have a public address system), and this is one of the few tracks in North America where the public is allowed access to the barn areas. Keeneland is worth a visit at any time of year. The old stone buildings and grounds are lovely, and at the track's training center, you can catch early morning workouts year-round. Plan to have breakfast at the track kitchen.

Just west of Keeneland on Versailles Road is a **castle** surrounded by stone walls and mysterious rumors. According to the rumors a slew of celebrities have owned it, including actor Lee Majors, but the truth is that the original owner and builder, Rex Martin, still owns the property but is looking to sell it. He and his ex-wife had the castle built as a residence in 1969; inside the turreted wall is a 10,400-square-foot, six-bedroom house complete with a huge library and swimming pool. Add chickens, goats, and peasants and you'd have a medieval village fort.

Even in Lexington a castle is a rare sight, but the city does boast plenty of beautiful mansions, many dating to the early 1800s. One of the historic houses open for tour is **The Hunt-Morgan House** (201 North Mill Street; 606-253-0362). This lovely Federal-style brick house was built in 1814 by John Wesley Hunt, an early Lexington entrepreneur believed to be Kentucky's first millionaire. Later residents included Thomas Hunt Morgan, who won a Nobel prize for medicine in 1933. Civil War buffs will be interested in the collection of uniforms, weapons, pictures, and other items relating to its most flamboyant occupant, Confederate General John Hunt Morgan. The escapades of Morgan and his "Morgan's Raiders" are recounted to this day in many a Kentucky community. Tour guides tell visitors that Morgan is reputed to have ridden his horse into the front hall of the house, kissed his mother, and galloped out the back door, with Federal troops in hot pursuit. Morgan must have had a thing about riding his horse in the house, because there's a similar story attached to a house Morgan and his troops occupied in Lebanon, Kentucky. If you like old houses, you'll enjoy strolling in the surrounding Gratz Park neighborhood, Lexington's most posh address in the early 1800s.

Several historic Lexington homes operate as bed and breakfasts. At **The Brand House** (461 Limestone Street; 606-226-9464), you can enjoy nineteenth-century charm along with modern comforts such as whirlpools. Pam and Logan Leet bought the 1812 house at auction in 1994, then painstakingly renovated it into a luxurious city getaway. The house is within easy walking distance of most downtown attractions. The five rooms, each with private bath, start at about $80 per night. The five guest rooms at **A True Inn** (467 West Second Street; 606-252-6166 or 800-374-6151) are named for historic Lexingtonians, from statesman Henry Clay and First

Lady Mary Todd Lincoln to Belle Brezing, the city's most famous madam (thought to be the inspiration for the Belle Watling character in *Gone With the Wind*.) The inn itself, an 1843 Romanesque-style brick house, is named for owners Bobby and Beverly True. Rates start at about $65 per night.

Consider a man who was a jewelry designer known to drape diamond necklaces around the stubby red neck of his dachshund, Ernie, and then send the dog out to model them for potential clients who were sunbathing by the swimming pool at the Bel Air Hotel. Try to imagine what kind of museum this man would build. When you give up, take a drive west on the Old Frankfort Pike to the **Headley-Whitney Museum.** Originally the late George W. Headley, III, established the space at his home to privately display his jewel collection, but in 1968 he and his wife opened the place to the public. Headley died in 1985, but the legacy of his museum continued. In the

> ## TRUE BLUE
> In 1789 there were more horses than people in Lexington.

dramatic setting of the Jewel Room, visitors could marvel at Headley's unusual jeweled boxes and bibelots, ranging from a gold face mask and ruby-encrusted abalone horse head to a scene of the moon landing in semiprecious stones. Unfortunately, in a sensational 1994 heist, burglars made off with many of the pieces. Since the robbery, the museum has increased its focus on fine decorative arts, featuring changing exhibits of clothing, textiles, and furniture. There are still many Headley creations on display, loaned by private owners, and if you need further evidence of his eccentricity, you need only step into the Shell Grotto—an entire room encrusted with thousands of seashells. The museum is open from 10:00 A.M. to 5:00 P.M. Tuesday through Friday and from noon to 5:00 P.M. Saturday and Sunday. It's closed in January. The grounds are elegant for picnicking. Old Frankfort Pike is a great place for biking; part of it is an official national Scenic Byway.

For more art, the Lexington Art League has its headquarters and a small gallery in a strange castellated 1852 Gothic villa in downtown Lexington, one of five designed by the architect A. J. Davis. **Loudoun House** is an interesting place to explore and get a taste of the work of one group of visual artists in the area. From downtown, go north on North Broadway and turn right (east) on Loudon Avenue, then bear left when you reach a V in the road. Turn right onto Castlewood Drive. Hours are noon to 4:00 P.M. Tuesday through Friday and 1:00 to 4:00 P.M. on weekends (606-254-7024).

Despite being central Kentucky's second-largest tourist attraction (the largest is Kentucky Horse Park), the **Lexington Children's Museum** is something of a hidden treasure. It is hidden to adults because we might assume it's not for us. Think again. I found myself replanning my shower stall after playing in the "bubble area," where you stand in a funny little booth and pull a giant vertical bubble completely around you, watching it all in a fun house mirror. Being confronted with "kid" information is also humbling. The ever changing display areas range from cultural introductions to the Ukraine to a hands-on exhibit about how animation works. The professed favorite educational area is a walk-through human heart, a series of sculpted and marvelously painted plaster chambers representing ventricles and auricles, all vibrating to the constant beat of our most powerful muscle. This megaheart was designed and made in part by medical illustrator Rick Gersony, who is also the pen-and-ink illustrator for this book. This museum is an all-day treat at the price of $3.00 per person; under 2 admitted free. Downtown, take the pedway from the Lexington Civic Center on Main Street or enter through the Victorian Square on the corner of Vine and Broadway. Call (606) 258-3253 for more information.

Lexington is Kentucky's second largest city, so there are all manner of eateries and shops, but there are a few special places, oddballs, or old standbys that you may miss. **Flag Fork Herb Farm Gift Shop** (900 North Broadway; 606-252-6837 or 800-436-5083) is a little bit of country in the city. Mike and Carrie Creech started their business on a remote farm in Franklin County. In 1994 they moved, gardens and all, to the city. The shop is located in a carriage house dating to the 1790s. Out back are about one-half acre of herb, perennial, and everlasting gardens. Starting in the spring, tables of plants are set up in the front yard. The shop carries dried herbs and herb cooking mixes, jellies, potpourri and handmade soaps—all kinds of wonderful smelling and tasting things. You'll want to linger. The shop is open 10:00 A.M. to 6:00 P.M. Monday through Saturday. Plan to have lunch or afternoon dessert at The Garden Café, which overlooks the birdfeeding garden. The menu is a combination of healthy soups, salads, and quiches, with many vegetarian items, and delightfully rich desserts. Café hours are 11:00 A.M. to 2:00 P.M. for lunch and 2:00 to 4:00 P.M. for beverages and dessert Monday through Saturday.

**Buffalo and Dad's,** near the corner of North Broadway and Loudon Avenue, is a quirky little hangout famous for its Kentucky hot browns, BIG hamburgers, and sports- and horse-oriented decor. Frank Adams (Dad) opened the place in 1975 and runs it with his son Robert "Buff" Adams, a burly, bearded fellow who deserves his nickname. Hours are 8:00 A.M. to 11:00 P.M. on weekdays; on weekends food is served until midnight and the bar closes at 1:00 A.M. Call (606) 252-9325.

What Buffalo and Dad's is to carnivores, **Alfalfa Restaurant** is to vegetarians. Actually, Alfalfa is not purely vegetarian, but it does emphasize meatless health food and titillating desserts. Come hungry. Saturday nights include live music right by your table, ranging from jazz flute to Irish guitar. Alfalfa's is across from the main gate of the University of Kentucky, 557 South Limestone Street. Open daily for lunch and dinner (606-253-0014).

Another university-area eatery, **Joe Bologna's** (606-252-4933) has been a favorite Lexington hangout, and not just for students, since the early 1970s. A few years ago it moved across the street from its original location to a restored church building at 120 West Maxwell Street, putting the decor on a par with the Italian food. Joe B's is the place to go for sublime pizza, other Italian dishes, and famous breadsticks, served in a sinful pool of garlic butter. If you insist, they'll put the garlic butter on the side.

To get an unusually intimate look at the world of Thoroughbred training, plan to tour the ◆ **Kentucky Horse Center,** 3380 Paris Pike. From downtown Lexington, take North Broadway out of town, which becomes Paris Pike (or Highway 68 and 27). After a few miles, look for the horse center on your right. Since 1969 when this business was started, it has been one of the most prestigious privately owned Thoroughbred training centers in the world. More than 1,100 stalls are leased to individual horse owners who bring in their own trainers and riders.

The tour takes you through a barn, by the rail where you can talk to a trainer, and into the sales pavilion, where you'll be amazed at the complexity of yet another aspect of the business—horse sales. Tours take 1½ hours and cost $10.00 for adults, $5.00 for children. Available Monday through Saturday. Tour times are 9:00 A.M. and 10:30 A.M., with an additional 1:00 P.M. tour Monday through Friday. Call ahead because tour space is limited (606-293-1853). Either before or after the tour, stop by the extensive tack shop, where you may luck into an opportunity to watch leatherworkers in action.

## TRUE BLUE

Because of its many nineteenth-century houses and old-fashioned charm, Danville was chosen as the location for the 1956 film *Raintree County* starring Elizabeth Taylor and Montgomery Clift.

We all love to experience a time warp. Even if you don't like to bowl, stop by the **Bourbon Bowl,** just south of Paris on Highway 68. This place has not changed since it opened more than thirty years ago. Owner Sue White swears that she will never install automatic scoring or radically alter the decor. This place is super clean, and people say that the snack bar serves the best cheeseburgers in town. Saturday is "red pin night"—if the red pin comes up in your lane as the head pin and you get a strike, then you win a free game and the admiration of your fellow bowlers. Call (606) 987-3161.

**Van Hoose Steak and Tavern** is not only the most popular site for nightlife in Paris, but it also may be the best-loved steak house in the region. Owners James and Brenda Van Hoose serve fresh steaks only. The meat, which is never frozen, is cut in the kitchen, so it's as tender as a steak can be. There isn't a steak knife in the house, and their guarantee is, "If the steak's not tender enough to cut with a table knife, you get it free." Prices are fairly reasonable, and the variety is good. After 9:00 P.M. on weekends, there is live country music. Go to downtown Paris on Main Street and watch for it on the right. The bar is open from 4:00 P.M. to 1:00 A.M. and the dining room is open from 5:00 to 9:00 P.M. daily except Sunday (606-987-6180).

Van Hoose would have had a serious competitor in the late eighteenth century when the ◆ **Duncan Tavern** was in its heyday. Major Joseph Duncan built the huge inn out of native limestone on High Street in 1788, four years before Kentucky was a state. Everything else in town was built of logs, so the Tavern was an eye-catcher as well as a social catchall. Originally there was a ballroom, a bar, a billiards room, dining rooms, kitchens, and bedrooms. Today the Duncan Tavern and Anne Duncan House is a historic site owned by the Kentucky Society of the Daughters of the American Revolution, which has acquired enough period furniture and significant artifacts to fill the huge building gracefully. Much of the original large furniture was built on site. They maintain its tradition as a tavern by keeping it active as a party place. People use the Duncan Tavern for parties and receptions. The D.A.R. hosts small events in the original dining room and serves meals on a long cherry boardinghouse-style table, valued at $30,000. The tavern and genealogy library are open to visitors Tuesday through Saturday, 10:00 A.M. to noon and 1:00 to 4:00 P.M. Call (606) 987–1788.

Another historic building being kept alive by means of regular use is the L&N Depot, between tenth Street and Winchester Road. Built in the early 1800s, this station saw lots of Civil War action, and Theodore Roosevelt is said to have made a whistle-stop speech here. Today it houses the very popular **Iron Rail Restaurant,** self-proclaimed "Home of Home Cooking." For $5.30 you can help yourself to a large lunch buffet loaded with home-style foods. Closed Monday. Call (606) 987–4422.

Another way to travel into the past and yet satisfy the desires of your contemporary senses is to spend some time at ◆ **Amelia's Field Country Inn,** 2 miles north of downtown Paris on Highway 27. First, you should know that the farm functions as an all-organic CSA (community supported agriculture) project, basically a massive kitchen garden that supplies nongardening members with fresh produce on a weekly basis for a set rate, paid in advance at the beginning of the season. In this way, the customers are intimately connected with the grower, even taking the seasonal financial risk. The risk is small, however, and the rewards great in this and other such operations. You may be taking a greater risk by buying produce at the grocery store that may have been sprayed with unspeakable chemicals or irradiated, and probably grown in ways that are detrimental to the land.

Amelia's Field is co-owned by Joseph Clay and chef Mark May. It makes wonderful use of the fresh produce and free-range chickens by serving classy, beautiful French Provençal meals either indoors or outdoors on the garden terrace. You must make reservations to dine, or you might just miss out on the chance to savor poached shrimp in spiced carrot juice or grilled salmon with wild mushrooms. The inn is also a lodging, offering four traditionally appointed rooms in the 1936 Georgian-style country mansion. Rates are $75 or $100 per night. Call (606) 987–5778 for reservations or write Amelia's Field at 617 Cynthiana Road, Paris 40361-8859.

Bourbon County has more than eighty-five horse farms, but very few allow visitors. One fine exception is **Claiborne Farm,** home and burial place of the celebrated Triple Crown winner, Secretariat, which generously welcomes visitors, by appointment only. Call (606) 233-4252 or 987-2330. From downtown Paris, go south on Highway 627 (also called Winchester Road) beyond the edge of town. Watch for the farm entrance on your left.

◆ **Cane Ridge Meeting House Shrine** is the site of some powerful events and the source of some wild stories. Follow Main Street (Highway 68) north from downtown Paris and go east on Highway 460 to Highway 537 North. Take the latter for 5.6 miles and look left (west) for the shrine. Said to be the the largest one-room log structure in the state, the church is impressive.

Two events make this church significant. The first was the Cane Ridge Revival, which took place August 7–12, 1801. It was one of the nation's largest revivals during a period of big ones. Preachers stood on stumps and hay bales all over the yard, talking simultaneously to 30,000 people for seven days and six nights. As the story goes, women's hair stood straight out and crackled like fire; people spoke in tongues, barked, shook, danced, and were moved every which way by the Holy Spirit. The excitement ended only when the food ran out. The second event occurred in 1804 when the new Cane Ridge preacher, Barton Warren Stone, led the people away from the Presbyterian Church and started a new, nondenominational movement that, after linking with the Campbell movement in Virginia, became the Christian Church, Disciples of Christ. Today the denomination (which numbers nearly 2 million) owns and manages the shrine. In 1957 they erected an enormous limestone superstructure to protect the log building. Later a museum was built nearby. From April through October the whole place is open daily, 9:00 A.M. to 5:00 P.M. Donations are accepted. Call (606) 987-5350.

Near Millersburg, the next town to the north on Highway 68, there is an old but functional covered bridge called **Colville Bridge** that crosses the Hinkston Creek. Just before entering Millersburg from the south, take Highway 1893 to the west for 3.1 miles, where you'll find an unmarked road going north (there are natural gas pipes on each side next to stone walls). Turn right and drive 1 mile to the bridge. If you tromp down the creek banks far enough, you can take pictures in which the graffiti doesn't show.

You'd better sit down for this one: The father of bourbon whiskey was a Baptist preacher. According to legend, the good Reverend Elijah Craig ran a distillery, a hemp rope walk, and a paper mill (the first in the state). According to legend, a fire swept through a building where barrels were being stored. Being something of a tightwad, Reverend Craig decided to put new corn whiskey into the charred barrels despite the damage. The color of the whiskey changed, the flavor mellowed, and a tradition was born. Eventually this new sour mash was named *bourbon* because large quantities were made in nearby Bourbon County. Bap-

## TRUE BLUE

The Vest-Lindsay Home in Frankfort was the boyhood home of U.S. Senator George Graham Vest, credited with the immortal phrase "Dog is man's best friend."

tists, don't despair. In the late eighteenth century, Baptists were not as concerned with temperance. Drunkenness among preachers was prohibited, but drinking was not. In fact, clergy often were paid in whiskey. Gambling, dancing, and going to barbecues, on the other hand, were considered serious crimes.

Elijah Craig's sundry enterprises were all built near the **Royal Spring,** a huge limestone spring discovered in 1774. **Georgetown** was built around the spring, and the city still gets its water from it. A small park around the spring is the site of an 1874 log cabin built by a former slave, Milton Leach, and a 1997 wooden statue of Elijah Craig by Georgetown artist Sandy Schu. This is no typical wood-carving; it was created using a chainsaw from a tree still rooted in the park grounds. Other examples of Schu's noisy yet surprisingly detailed work can be seen throughout the area. He created the buffalo on display at Cardome Centre, north of downtown. His 20-foot eagle inspires golfers at the twelfth hole of Kearney Hill Links golf course in Lexington. For more information about Royal Spring and other Georgetown attractions, call the Scott County Tourism Commission at (502) 863-2547.

Downtown Georgetown is chock-full of history. It's a good place for a walk. **Fava's Restaurant,** established in 1910 on East Main Street (502-863-4383), is the place to eat lunch or have three o'clock coffee and argue local issues with politicians and merchants.

If you're more interested in antiques, look in any direction. In a state as obsessed with old stuff as Kentucky, any town that dares call itself the "Antiques Capital of Kentucky" better be able to back up that claim with something substantial. Georgetown does, with seven malls all within easy walking distance of the courthouse. If it's old, you probably can find it at the **Central Kentucky Antique Mall, Wyatt's Antique Center,** the **Den of Antiquity, Trojan Antique Mall, The Vault** (housed in an old bank building), **Pooh's Place,** or the **Georgetown Antique Mall**. In addition to its Main Street entrance, the latter has an entrance at 119 South Broadway, which leads to another aspect of the business. Liz Cox does picture framing, custom leaded- and stained-glass work, and what she calls family heirloom bears. The bears are made from vintage clothing, fabric, or fur that the customer supplies. Say your great-grandmother wore a fur coat, but it's been partially destroyed. You can take the scraps to Liz Cox, and she'll transform them into well-made Mama, Papa, or Baby bears. Call her at (502) 863-2538.

The **Log Cabin Bed and Breakfast** at 350 North Broadway is a fully restored 1809 log cabin, rustic on the outside, modern within. The large fieldstone fireplace is always ready with firewood for winter guests, and the porch swing is an enticing summertime object. The cabin is equipped with a small kitchen, so that extended stays are possible. (Pets are allowed.) Call Clay and Janis McKnight for reservations at (502) 863-3514.

From downtown Georgetown, take Highway 25 North out of town and watch for signs to ◆ **Cardome Centre** (602-863-1575), a property that has played a significant role in Kentucky history for hundreds of years. After having been a major hunting ground for Choctaw, Mingo, and Shawnee Indians, it was one of the first areas deeded and settled west of the mountains. It was home to a number of early prominent white families during the 1800s, including James F. Robinson, a Kentucky governor, who gave the place its name, Cardome, after the Latin phrase *cara domus,* or "dear home." The Sisters of Visitation, a cloistered sect, bought Cardome in 1896 and ran an academy there until 1969. Now Cardome belongs to the City of Georgetown and operates as an educational center and historic site, open for tours Monday through Saturday from 9:00 A.M. to 4:00 P.M. Visitors can tour the original academy and monastery buildings as well as a science classroom and a "dream house," where the senior girls were finally allowed to have outside visitors and even to smoke. Cardome's pride and joy is the school chapel, which features some gorgeous woodwork, Romanesque vaulted ceilings, stained-glass windows, and a classic bell tower. The whole property can be rented for huge company picnics, or smaller areas can be used for weddings, seminars, meetings, and so forth.

On the lower level of the main building is the **Georgetown/Scott County Museum,** which is developing displays about county history. The museum sponsors an interesting monthly program (with corresponding exhibits) called Mondays at the Museum, topics for which range from Elkhorn Creek to the World War I invasion of Europe to early paper mills in Kentucky, the latter a lecture that also involves a demonstration.

One of the best-selling family sedans in America, the Camry, along with Toyota Avalons and Sienna minivans, are made in Georgetown at **Toyota Motor Manufacturing, Kentucky, Inc.,** on Cherry Blossom Way (exit 129 from I-75). Hour-long guided tours of the plant are given several times a day on Tuesdays and Thursdays, by reservation. Call (502) 868-3027. No shorts, cameras, or children under eight are allowed. You'll don a hard hat and safety goggles and ride an electric tram through the stamping, bodyweld, and assembly areas of the plant. The recipient of numerous national industry awards for quality, the plant is a big—about 8 million square feet under roof—bright and noisy place, all the more mind-boggling when you consider that nearly 400,000 vehicles and 500,000 engines are made here each year. Plant tours usually get booked far in advance, but you can stop by and look at the cars and manufacturing exhibits at the Visitor Center anytime between

10:00 A.M. and 4:00 P.M. Monday, Wednesday, and Friday or between 8:00 A.M. and 7:00 P.M. Tuesday and Thursday.

## MORE GOOD LODGING

Ask about lower priced weekend specials and other special rates.

LEXINGTON

**Camberley Club Hotel at Gratz Park,** 120 West Second Street; (606) 231-1777 or (800) 555-8000. An historic downtown hotel complete with a ghost or two. About $129 per night.

**Cherry Knoll Inn,** 3875 Lemons Mill Road; (606) 253-9800 or (800) 804-0617. A handsome 1850s mansion in a country setting. Dinner served. About $100 per night.

**Hilton Suites of Lexington Green,** Nicholasville Road at New Circle Road; (606) 271-4000 or (800) 445-8667. Deluxe two-room suites. $105 and up.

**Holiday Inn North,** Newtown Pike at I-75/64 exit 115; (606) 233-0512 or (800) HOLIDAY. A great place for families, with a basketball court and a Funtronics virtual reality and video game center. About $100 per night.

**Marriott's Griffin Gate Resort,** 1800 Newtown Park; (606) 231-5100 or (800) 228-9290. Eighteen-hole championship golf course, plus tennis courts and an excellent restaurant, The Mansion. About $139 per night.

## MORE FUN PLACES TO EAT

LEXINGTON

**Dudley's,** 380 South Mill Street; (606) 252-1010. A Continental menu and a cozy bar; the restaurant is located in an historic former school building downtown.

**Ed and Fred's Desert Moon,** 164 Southeastern Avenue; (606) 231-1161. An eclectic blending of Southwestern and nouvelle cuisine.

**Merrick Inn,** 3380 Tates Creek Road; (606) 269-5417. Regional cuisine in a traditional setting. Dine formally or more casually on the patio.

**Parkette Drive-In,** 1216 New Circle Road NE; (606) 254-8723. Drive-thru? No, a real drive-in, with sign, service, and menu much the same as when it opened in 1952.

**Ramsey's Diner,** Woodland and High Streets in downtown Lexington, (606) 259-2708; 4053 Tates Creek Road, (606) 271-2638; and 1660 Bryan Station Road, (606) 299-9669. Casual homey atmosphere and a down-to-earth menu of "classy comfort food."

## IN THE BEGINNING

In the beginning there was **Harrodsburg.**

A friend of mine swears that it takes a Harrodsburg resident less than four minutes of any conversation to bring up the fact that the genesis of the American West is Harrodsburg, Kentucky. On June 16, 1774, James Harrod and his company took a great leap of faith and of foot when they chose to settle the fertile strip of land between the Kentucky and Salt Rivers, the "Big Spring"—more than 250 miles of wilderness and mountains away from the nearest Anglo-Saxon settlement to the east. Today Harrodsburg sports a full reproduction of the 1775 fort in the ◆ **Old Fort Harrod State Park,** at the intersection of Highways 68 and 127, a good place to begin your exploration of one of the state's significant historic areas.

Inside the park's entrance is the **Mansion Museum,** featuring Civil War artifacts, and the **Lincoln Marriage Shrine,** a red brick building that houses the log chapel where Abraham Lincoln's parents "got hitched." Inside the fort's walls people in period costumes demonstrate pioneer crafts during the summer. The fort is open to the public year-round, and from March 16 to November 30 the museum is also open from 10:00 A.M. to 6:30 P.M. daily. Admission is charged. Call (606) 734-3314.

Behind the fort in the James Harrod Amphitheater, "The Legend of Daniel Boone," a high-adventure drama, is performed under the stars from mid-June to the first of September, Monday through Saturday beginning at 8:30 P.M. For those with children, rest assured that this colorful drama easily qualifies as family entertainment. Call (606) 734-3346 for further information.

Follow Chiles Street south to Kentucky's first row house, circa 1800, known as **Morgan Row,** after the builder, Joseph Morgan. The street is named after Morgan's son-in-law, John Chiles, who ran a famous tavern on the site. In front of Morgan Row, Uncle Will of

Wildwood, a prominent Mercer County farmer, is said to have been cited for speeding in his one-horse buggy. When Uncle Will went to pay his ticket, he paid double the amount, telling the clerk in a voice loud enough for the whole courthouse to hear, "I'm paying you double 'cause I plan to leave the way I came." Today Morgan Row houses, among other things, the **Harrodsburg Historical Society Museum** and office (606–734–5985).

Another of Harrodsburg's claims to fame is ◆ **The Beaumont Inn.** The graceful brick Greek Revival building, constructed in 1845, was once a finishing school called the Greenville Institute, then Daughter's College, and later Beaumont College. It was converted into an inn in 1919 by Annie Bell Goddard and her husband, Glave. The inn has remained in the family and is now managed by Annie Bell's great-grandson, Chuck Dedman. The dining room serves traditional Kentucky-style meals that include dishes such as two-year-old cured country ham (smoked and cured by the proprietor himself), fried chicken, corn pudding, and Robert E. Lee Orange-Lemon Cake. Be ready for a feast! The antiques-filled sleeping quarters embody the extravagant beauty of the Old South, with a few modern conveniences. Swimming pool, tennis courts, and a gift shop are also on the premises. Reservations are advisable for meals and lodging. Closed late December though early March. Call (606) 734–3381.

Acting as a business-savvy alchemist, the City of Harrodsburg transformed an unsightly lot where an old building burned down in the first block of South Main Street into a city park, called ◆**Olde Towne Park,** which includes a stage for civic events and a 14-foot-high by 35-foot-wide sculptural, wall water fountain designed and made by me, Zoé Strecker, your author with a double life. The fountain sculpture is a lyrical representation of the historic limestone palisades that line the Kentucky River on the eastern border of Mercer County. This work is made of nearly 700 large,

**Olde Towne Park—Palisades Fountain**

high-fired ceramic tiles, all molded or directly sculpted by hand, featuring high-relief plants, vines, reptiles, and rocklike textures for the falling water to play over. For more information, call (606) 734-6811.

One of the most unique historical buildings in Mercer County is the **Old Mud Meeting House,** built in 1800 by members of the Dutch Reformed Church. As early as 1781 a group of Dutch settlers immigrated here and formed a community where they spoke Dutch and worshiped as they did in the Old World. The church they built became known as the Mud Meeting House because massive timber walls are chinked with clay, straw, twigs, roots, and gravel. The handsome structure, constructed "for the sole Benefit & use of the said Reformed Church forever," has long outlasted its little congregation. The church was restored to its original form in 1971. To visit the site, drive south from town on Highway 127 to the junction of Highway 68 (Moreland Avenue) and turn right. Follow Highway

68 until you reach Dry Branch Pike; turn left and look for the historical marker. Getting there can be confusing. Here's an even better idea: Call the Historical Society office at (606) 734-5985 to arrange a guided tour.

If you leave town going northeast on Highway 68, toward Lexington, you will pass my alma mater, Harrodsburg High School, affectionately known as "Hog Town." This nickname harks back to the late 1820s, when hogs outnumbered county residents two to one and there were huge hog corrals, sales rings, and auction blocks. Our official high school sports mascot was a pioneer with a coonskin cap, but our proud rallying cry was *SOOOOOOEYYY!!!*

Exactly 1 mile outside the city limits, look on the right for **Harrodsburg Pottery and Crafts,** a picturesque 1866 Victorian-style farmhouse surrounded by colorful flower and herb gardens. The shop features a wide variety of works by regional craftspeople, hand-dipped candles made right in the shop, and herbal and floral wreaths made by the owner, Nancy Washington. Between scented candles and herbs, the showroom is always permeated by a wonderful aroma. This place is best known for hand-thrown, functional pottery by Chris Strecker (my mother) and other regional potters. Whether you need dinnerware, wedding gifts, or just an opportunity to handle fine workmanship, this shop is a delight and a real find. Open daily. In January and February, hours are by chance. Call (606) 734-9991.

Heading east, you pass the world's most beautiful house of mechanic work, **The Stringtown Garage.** Father and son, Big Jack and Lil' Jack Pearson, have transformed a cement-block eyesore into a little paradise. If you like their vibrant flowers, stop and see Big Jack's antiques and James Dean memorabilia inside, or just honk and wave.

You are now entering real saddlebred horse country. Driving Highway 68 will give you an opportunity to fall in love with the miles of hundred-year-old mortarless fieldstone walls visible on both sides of the road.

◆ **Shaker Village of Pleasant Hill** is one of Kentucky's most significant historic sites, located 8 miles east of Harrodsburg off Highway 68. The whole restored village is a museum featuring thirty original Shaker buildings and more than 2,700 acres of manicured farmland (about half of what the Shaker community farmed in its prime). "The United Society of Believers in Christ's Second Appearance" was originally founded by an English Quaker woman, Mother Ann Lee, who came to America in 1774 and claimed to be Christ incarnate (this time as a woman) to herald the prophesied millennium preceding the total destruction of the earth. The most publicized doctrine of the sect was that Believers should remain pure by avoiding the World (non-Shakers) and all its ways, including the "disorderly" state of matrimony. Instead of procreating, the Shakers adopted orphans and received converts, who were plentiful during America's "Great Revival" period of Protestant faiths in the early nineteenth century. Shakers also avoided "the World" by remaining economically self-sufficient; their products were always of the highest quality, from seeds to silk, and continue to influence modern design. The Shakers' Utopia at Pleasant Hill lasted more than one hundred years, until the death of the village's last resident in 1923.

The village admission fee enables you to take a self-guided tour through the buildings, which, like Shaker furniture, are renowned for their graceful, functional aesthetic simplicity. (The song "Simple Gifts" is associated with the Shakers.) Be sure to visit the newly added Interpretive Center, where an excellent video and other exhibits give you moving insight into the Shakers and their tenure at Pleasant Hill. The village offers fine Southern dining and overnight accommodations in original buildings. Call (606) 734–5411 for more information, special programs, and reservations.

The Shakers traded goods with "the World" in large part by river. The road built by the Shakers in 1861 still accesses one of the most spectacular stretches of the Kentucky River, known as **The Palisades,** where high Ordivician limestone bluffs change color with the time of day. Go east about ⅛ mile from Shakertown's entrance and turn right where a sign indicates RIVER EXCURSIONS. Shaker-

## TRUE BLUE

Jesse James's mother, Zerelda Cole, once lived in the Offutt-Cole Tavern, located at the intersection of U.S. 62 and KY 1981 between Versailles and Midway.

town offers one-hour trips on a paddle wheel boat called *The Dixie Belle.* From the boat you have a perfect view of **High Bridge,** the first cantilever bridge in the United States, a miracle of engineering at the time of its completion in 1877. High Bridge stretches 1,125 feet and stands 280 feet high; it is still the highest two-track railroad pass in North America.

Heading east on Highway 68, there is a sign on the left for **Canaan Land Farm Bed and Breakfast.** Be kind to your shock absorbers and drive the gravel road slowly to the 1795 Benjamin Daniel House and recently relocated log cabins. The farmers and hosts are Fred and Theo Bee and a varying number of cats, sheepdogs, goats, and a large herd of sheep. If you're willing to help, you can try milking the goats or pulling a few weeds in the garden. Call (606) 734-3984 for reservations.

If you're traveling toward Lexington or the Versailles area, continue east on Highway 68. The road begins to wind dramatically as it descends into the river gorge, crosses the Kentucky River on Brooklyn Bridge, and begins another curvy climb. About a mile up you'll come to a narrow "holler" that contains the **Shanty Hill Market**—you won't miss it, and you shouldn't. Years ago I stopped to buy a watermelon. The old proprietor proceeded to tell me "how God intended watermelons to be et. You cut yursilf a tiny little plug, fill 'er up with a pint of Evercleer [tasteless, 200 proof, grain alcohol], wait an hour, and slice 'er up. Lordamercy!" Don't worry, today you will find a mother-and-son team who sell seasonal fruits, antique junk, grapevine for wreaths, bunches of deep orange bittersweet, and scrumptious homemade sorghum.

Traveling north on Highway 68, turn west or left onto Highway 33 and follow the signs to ◆ **Irish Acres Antiques** in Nonesuch (population 343), a "downtown" comprised of the smallest freestanding voting building you'll ever see and a cluster of houses, one of which has the greatest number and variety of purple martin houses known to humanity (the owner must be a frustrated urban housing planner). Irish Acres Antiques is a not-to-be-missed 32,000-square-foot antiques gallery and tearoom founded by Bonnie and Arch Hannigan and now run by their daughters Emilie Hannigan McCauley and Jane Hannigan. Two floors of what was once the Nonesuch School are gracefully crammed with antiques, which range from affordable early American primitives to pricey Asian art, fifteenth-century Chinese lacquered boxes, and nineteenth-century French country furniture. An ornate $38,000 French palace bed is among the treasures.

**TRUE BLUE**

Transylvania University in Lexington was the first university west of the Alleghenies.

The old cafeteria has been converted into an elegantly whimsical tearoom called "The Glitz." Amid a fantasia of lights, grapevines, iridescent paper, and silver cherubim, you can enjoy a lavish four-course meal for $13.95. It's a good place to take your time and not the best place to take your kids. Reservations are required. Lunch is served from 11:00 A.M. to 2:00 P.M. when the gallery is open. Gallery hours are 10:00 A.M. to 5:00 P.M., Tuesday through Saturday. Irish Acres and The Glitz are closed in January and February. Call (606) 873-7235.

Get back onto Highway 33, which winds through lush horse farm country to **Versailles** (pronounced *Ver-SALES*). You can also get to Versailles by way of Highway 60 or Highway 62, once one of the largest buffalo trails in the United States. From the landscaping and architecture in town, one senses an aura of the wealth and deliberate pace of the Old South. Downtown Versailles is full of well-preserved old Federal and Beaux Arts homes, beautiful churches, and antiques stores, one of which is **Farm House Antiques** (606-873-0800), 175 North Main Street. A lunch place a couple of blocks away called **Cafe on Main** (606-873-2265) serves soups, quiche, and country-style specials Monday through Friday from 11:00 A.M. to 2:00 P.M.

For the toy train enthusiast, Versailles offers a once-in-a-lifetime opportunity to pore over the collection of Wanda and Winfrey Adkins, who have converted an old (1911–1932) Louisville and Nashville (L&N) railroad station into the ◆ **Nostalgia Station Toy Train Museum,** located at 279 Depot Street, a one-way street on the east side of Main. The Adkinses, who do repairs and will find rare parts, can tell you just about anything there is to know about model trains and antique cast-iron and mechanized toys. I didn't realize that there are modern versions of the 1950s

# FASCINATING FACADE

One of Louisville's most fascinating house tours isn't really a house; it's just the front of a house. Like a piece of a movie set, the front of the **Charles Heigold House** sits forlornly in Thruston Park, off River Road east of downtown Louisville. If this were a movie it would be a historical drama, set in the mid-1800s, when Heigold, a German immigrant and stonemason, decided to carve his political feelings in stone—on the front of his house. "The Union Forever, All Hail To This Union, Let It Never Desolve It" is among the sayings and figures elaborately carved into the facade in exuberant fashion. The rest of the house was razed when the street on which it originally stood became part of the city landfill. Luckily, city officials decided to save this face for visitors and future residents to ponder and enjoy.

locomotives, boxcars, switches, coal cars, and crossing lights that we played with every Christmas. Wanda likes to point out a wind-up Mickey and Minnie Mouse hand-pump car, one of L&N's forgotten "cheap" toys from the 1930s, when the company was struggling, and a regular engine and coal car that cost at least $32. Hours are Wednesday through Saturday, 10:00 A.M. to 5:00 P.M., and Sunday, 1:00 to 5:00 P.M. Admission is $3.00. Call (606) 873-2497 for more information.

For enthusiasts of full-size railroad artifacts, follow Highway 62 west to the **Bluegrass Railroad Museum, Inc.** in Woodford County Park. On weekends from mid-May to early November, you can take a 5$^{1}/_{2}$-mile train ride on the Old Louisville Southern Mainland through quintessential Bluegrass country, including a hawk's view of the Kentucky River palisades, Wild Turkey Distilleries, and Young's High Bridge. The museum is an actual train car with historic railroad displays. A recent addition to the collection is an original L&N railroad bay-window caboose. For times, rates, and special events, call (606) 873-2476 or (800) 755-2476.

"Here's to Old Kentucky, The State where I was born, Where the corn is full of kernels and the Colonels full of corn," goes an old Kentucky toast. The abundant corn crops of early Kentucky settlers played an important role in the creation of bourbon whiskey.

Though when and how and by whom bourbon was first made remains a matter of debate that may never be settled (Georgetown claims it was Baptist minister Elijah Craig; nearby Bourbon County credits Jacob Spears), there's no disagreement that by the early 1800s whiskey-making was a fine art in the Bluegrass. Elijah Pepper started making whiskey near Versailles in 1797; in 1812, in search of a more abundant water supply, he moved his operation to a spot along Glenn's Creek. Today, whiskey is still made at the site of Pepper's early distillery, under the name ❦ **Labrot & Graham, The Bourbon Homeplace** (7855 McCracken Pike; 606–879–1812).

**TRUE BLUE**

Louisville is second only to Boston in number of registered historic sites.

Brown-Forman, an international beverage company based in Louisville, renovated the property as a showplace of the "old ways" of making premium bourbon whiskey. The quaint old stone buildings nestled against the creek, the fascinating aromas from the mash tank, the 25-foot-tall copper stills (unique in modern American distilling), and the lively and colorful presentations by the tour guides certainly make it a premium tour. Your visit ends with a taste of bourbon ball candy at the "bar" in the visitor center. (This would certainly be a fattening place to work!) By the way, the bourbon that's being distilled the day you visit won't be available in a bottle for about seven years. The free tours are given at 10:00 and 11:00 A.M. and at 1:00, 2:00, and 3:00 P.M. Tuesday through Saturday April through October, and Wednesday through Saturday November through March. The distillery is about 6 miles from Versailles (so far out that it has its own lake as a source of water in case of a fire). If you're in Versailles, take Highway 60 toward Frankfort, turning left onto Grassy Spring Road, then right on McCracken Pike. Or take Elm Street out of downtown Versailles. Either way it's a scenic and winding drive through classic horse farm country.

For another worthwhile excuse to take a country drive, visit the restored **Jack Jouett House,** circa 1797. This home was built by folks who believe, like Mies van der Rohe, that "God hides in details." From Versailles, go 5 miles west on McCowans Ferry Road and turn on Craig Creek Pike. It is open on Saturday and

Sunday from noon to 5:00 P.M. and by appointment. The house is closed November through March. Call (606) 873-7902.

From **Shepherd Place Bed and Breakfast** (31 Heritage Road, off Highway 60, Versailles; 606-873-7843), it's easy to head into Lexington or into Versailles and other surrounding Bluegrass communities. You might just want to stay put, however, and sit on the great front porch of this 1815 house and watch the pet sheep, Abigail and Victoria, graze. You can even commission hostess Sylvia Yawn to hand-knit you a sweater, hat, or mittens from hand-spun yarn. The spacious **Sills Inn** (270 Montgomery Avenue in downtown Versailles; (606- 873-4478 or 800-526-9801) is known for its gourmet breakfasts and whirlpool suites.

From Versailles, take Highway 62 north to **Midway,** a town midway between Frankfort and Lexington and the first town in Kentucky built by a railroad company. These days it is a quaint college town full of antiques shops, beautiful historic homes, and a few surprises. One such gem is an operative, century-old, hydropower grain mill on the South Elkhorn Creek. The **Weisenberger Mill** is the oldest continuously operating mill in Kentucky and one of the few in the nation to remain in the same family. In 1866 a German steamboat and mill specialist named August Weisenberger bought the mill that had been built on the site in 1818. He revamped the entire system and began grinding all manner of grain at the rate of 100 barrels a day. His great-grandson Philip J. Weisenberger and his son, "Mac," have modernized some of the methods and now grind about 3,000 tons of grain a year. The Weisenbergers introduced the use of the mill's electricity-making capacity by having Kentucky's alternative energy whiz, Dave Kinlock, rebuild the mill's hydropower turbines and add an efficient generator. Now most aspects of the business are water powered, even the computers. Although visitors are not allowed inside the work area, you can walk around the property. Everything Weisenberger mills is sold by the package in the front office (the fifty-pound bags are a very good buy). As an addicted breadmaker, I can attest to the excellent quality of their products. Call (606) 254-5282 for more information.

There are several eateries around Midway. There has been a restaurant in the building at 128 Railroad Street (so named because the tracks run right down the middle of it) since 1840. It was known as The Depot then, and it's known as **The Depot** (606-846-4745) now. Crab cakes are a traditional feature, but try the delightful daily specials made with local, organic produce and other fresh ingredients. Lunch and dinner are served Tuesday through Saturday.

The nature of "home-style cooking" depends upon what kind of place you call home. For those with a grander upbringing, lunch at the **Holly Hill Inn** may be "just like Mom used to make it." From Main Street turn east on Highway 62, also called Winter Street, veer to the right at the Corner Grocery, and go about $^1/_4$ mile. The Holly Hill Inn, a Greek Revival home, circa 1830, was restored earlier this century in Victorian style and recently restored again and decorated in the original Greek Revival colors and styles. Two double rooms are available, each for $50 per night, breakfast included. The hosts and cooks are Rose and Rex Lyons. Open year-round, Tuesday through Saturday for lunch from 11:30 A.M. to 2:00 P.M. and Thursday through Saturday for dinner from 5:30 to 9:00 P.M. Call (606) 846-4732 for reservations.

## TRUE BLUE

Kentucky became a state in 1792, as the fifteenth state.

**Danville** is a handsome little college town just south of Harrodsburg. From town, take Highway 127; from Shakertown, take Highway 33 through Burgin. Drive or walk around Danville and the Centre College campus to admire the architecture. For arts and cultural events, check the gallery and schedule of performances at the Frank Lloyd Wright-style **Norton Center for the Arts** (606-236-4692) on campus.

You know an Italian place is good when there's always a customer at the counter reading an Italian newspaper. **Freddie's Restaurant** (126 South Fourth Street; 606-236-9884) serves quick, primo cuisine for lunch and dinner Monday through Saturday. If you're bicycling, this is a fantastic place to actually enjoy stocking up on your "carbs." Stop by **Dave's Cycle Shop** (130 South Fourth Street; 606-236-9573), near Freddie's, for parts, water bottles, and directions to the lovely bike routes in this area.

The hospital in Danville was named for a local medical hero, Ephraim McDowell, who performed the first successful removal of an ovarian tumor in 1809. Something should be named for his patient, Jane Todd Crawford, who survived the surgery without the aid of antisepsis or the comfort of anesthetic. The site of the operation, the **Ephraim McDowell House and Apothecary** at 125 South Second Street, has been accurately restored and is open Monday through Saturday from 10:00 A.M. to noon and 1:00 to 4:00 P.M., Sunday from 2:00 to 4:00 P.M. From November through February, it is closed Monday. Admission is $3.00. Call (606) 236-2804.

Across the street is **Constitution Square State Park,** a reproduction of the state's first courthouse square and the site of the first post office in the West, circa 1792. All the buildings are log replicas, and most have recorded interpretations (kids like to push the buttons and run when the voice begins to drone). The lawn is a good place for a downtown picnic, and dessert is right across the street at **Burke's Bakery,** 116 West Main (606-236-5661). Burke's is in its fourth generation of owners and customers. They make good old sweet pastries for those times when you just don't want whole grains and carob powder.

**The Tea Leaf** (230 West Broadway; 606-236-7456) is strictly for lunch, tea, and gift buying. Rosemary Hamblin and Jane Stevens have specialized in children's books and adult aromas—it's easy to get carried away sniffing teas. The **Antique Mall of Historic Danville** (158 North Third Street; 606-236-3026) is housed in a large brick Presbyterian Church, circa 1867, across the street from the public library. The booths are full of old goodies—a great place for poets. Hours are Tuesday through Saturday, 10:00 A.M. to 5:00 P.M., and Sunday, 1:00 to 5:00 P.M.

If you're like me, your favorite nights during childhood were spent in a great aunt's squeaky old cherry bed with tall, curving posts topped with balls or acorns. Brenda Lovett Phillips's passion for traditional furniture goes beyond mere nostalgia; her Junction City store, **Lovett's Cherry Shop,** is chock-full of walnut and cherry reproductions. People come great distances to pick up furniture orders from Lovett's. You'll see why if you run your fingers over the satiny finish of a cherry lingerie chest. Follow Highway 127 south (Fourth Street) of Danville to Old Highway 127 and into Junction City. A few hundred yards past the road to the airport, Lovett's is on the left. Hours are Monday through Saturday, 10:00 A.M. to 5:00 P.M. Call (606) 854-3857.

Get apples as big as a giant's fist, fifty-pound bags of sweet Vidalia onions 5 inches in diameter, or tender green beans *any* season of the year at **Lear's Produce,** south of Lovett's on Highway 127 at the junction with Highway 300. Look for the sign that says LEAR'S PRODUCE: MATERS, TATERS, NANNERS & SECH, APPLES, KUNTRY SARGUM, PUR-HONEE. This place is a joy to behold in a world where the produce managers in big-time gro-

**TRUE BLUE**

Zachary Taylor grew up and is buried in Louisville.

cery stores seem to have been taught that repetition is the spice of life. Open Monday through Saturday from 9:00 A.M. to 6:00 P.M.

Leave Junction City on Highway 37 south. You have suddenly entered "the knobs," a narrow belt of fairly isolated, wooded hills that encircles the Bluegrass region. (Rock lovers, the creeks here are loaded with geodes.) In the heart of this alluring terrain is a little town called Forkland, where there's a good little country festival the second weekend of October at the **Forkland Community Center.** Notice the huge, round piece of sandstone in the yard. It measures 51 inches in diameter, is 18 inches thick, and probably weighs over a ton. What the tarnation is it? No one knows. Sandstone is never used for grinding grain, so a millstone is out. Archaeologists say it's not prehistoric. The best guess is that it was a "hemp brake," a heavy rock rolled by hand or by oxen over hemp stalks to break the fibers apart for making rope.

Near Forkland, ◆ **Penn's Store** may be the oldest continuously operated one-family-owned store west of the Alleghenies, and it looks like it. Everyone falls in love with the wise, tumbledown appearance of the general store opened in 1852 by Dick Penn. The original building burned, and this replacement is more than a hundred years old. In the winter, the little potbellied is cranked up high and at least three men are playing checkers on a barrel in the middle of the room at all times. (It takes two to play and one to shake his head and chew on his toothpick.) In the summer there's no better place in the world to have a Dr. Pepper than on Penn's front porch, where you can hear the creek rumble by. Now Dick Penn's twin great-great-granddaughters, Dava and Dawn, who sing perfect harmonies, organize frequent Sunday music jams with regional musicians. Call Dava Osborn for dates and times at (606) 336-3701. The store phone number is (606) 332-7715. From Forkland, continue on Highway 37 south to Highway 243, turn right, then right again just after crossing a concrete bridge. When you see the store by the creek, cross the new bridge and come on in! The store is open Monday through Saturday from 8:00 A.M. to 5:00 P.M.

Leaving Danville to the west, Main Street becomes Highway 150 (or 52) and leads to the historic town of Perryville. Under the shade of massive maple and sweet gum trees on the banks of the Chaplain River is a quiet haven made ready for rest and high tea. The **Elmwood Inn** is a well-preserved Greek Revival home that has been over the years a hospital (during the Battle of Perryville), a private school, a music academy, and a restaurant. (Stains on my prom dress remind me of my first meal in the building as a nervous adolescent eating fried chicken.) The inn is now a stately tearoom. Owners Bruce and Shelley Richardson have added a creative twist to traditional English tea. Each month, the tea and pastries served reflect a different theme. Past themes have included Irish tea (in March) and Shakespeare. Art exhibits at the tearoom often complement the monthly theme. Whatever the theme, count on it to be delicious, and make sure you make reservations by calling (606) 332-2400. Tea time is 1:00 and 3:00 P.M. Thursday, Friday, and Saturday.

Across the river from the Elmwood Inn, you can see the back of **Merchants' Row,** a small row of renovated buildings that house antiques and gift shops, a pizza place, a dry goods store, and an active saddlery. Moving away from creature comforts, proceed in an appropriately somber spirit to the ◆ **Perryville Battlefield State Historic Site.** Go north on Highway 1920 for 3 miles and follow the signs. Forty thousand men fought for one bloody day on this site on October 8, 1862, when Confederate soldiers in search of water accidentally encountered Union troops who were guarding nearby Doctor's Creek. More than 6,000 soldiers were killed, wounded, or missing by sunset. There's a small museum with artifacts and battle displays on the grounds, which also offer plenty of room for picnicking. The best time to visit is during the first weekend of October for a massive annual reenactment of the battle when people in full period costume, with weapons and horses, stage a long, gory battle. The park is open from April through October, daily from 9:00 A.M. to 5:00 P.M. Call (606) 332-8631 for more information.

The **William Whitley House State Historic Site** is southeast of Stanford on Highway 150. Famous "Indian Fighter" (a dubious claim to fame) William Whitley built the elegant brick house in the mid-1780s, making it one of the oldest brick buildings west of the Alleghenies. It was called "a guardian of the Wilderness Road" because it stood next to the important overland route and served as a place of refuge for white travelers. The high upper windows and barred lower windows, the gun ports, and a hidden staircase were built as precautions against Indian attacks.

Whitley's big contributions to Kentucky (and American) culture were building the first track in the state and racing the horses counterclockwise, a practice he encouraged to defy the British custom of racing clockwise. Having served as a colonel in the Revolution, Whitley was passionately anti-British. (I'm sure he hated crumpets and tea.) Whitley died in the 1813 Battle of the Thames River after he supposedly killed the great chief Tecumseh. Tours of the house are given from June through August daily, from 9:00 A.M. to 5:00 P.M. From September through May the home is closed on Monday. Call (606) 355-2881 for further information.

Just north of Lincoln and east of Boyle counties is Garrard County, birthplace of a radical antiliquor activist oft neglected by history books. From Lancaster, take Highway 27 north to Highway 34 and go east to its junction with Fisher Ford Road to find **Carrie A. Nation's birthplace** at "the jumping off place," as local folks call it. The house was built about 1840, and Carrie was born there in 1846. In 1900, after a short, disastrous, and life-changing marriage to a severe alcoholic, Carrie single-handedly wreaked havoc on the saloon at the Hotel Casey in Wichita, Kansas, and, consequently, spent seven days in jail, her first of more than thirty jail sentences on similar charges. I've seen fearsome pictures of Ms. Nation in her prime: hatchet in hand, Bible in the other, purse to the front (the way one wears a pouch-wallet in Manhattan today), and a glare that would make any bartender's blood run cold.

## MORE GOOD LODGING

Bluegrass Bed and Breakfast Reservation Service (606-873-3208). Information about twenty private bed and breakfasts that do not advertise.

### HARRODSBURG
**Bright Leaf Golf Resort,** 1742 Danville Road; (606) 734-5481. About $70 to $80 per night.

### DANVILLE
**Days Inn,** Highway 127; (606) 236-8601. About $55 per night.

**Twin Hollies Retreat,** 406 Maple Avenue; (606) 236-8954. An antebellum house updated with whirlpool baths, in a quiet historic neighborhood. About $75.

## MORE FUN PLACES TO EAT

### MIDWAY
**Main Street Café,** 117 Railroad Street; (606) 846-4233. Contemporary versions of traditional regional foods. Open daily for lunch and dinner.

### HARRODSBURG
**Old Happy Days Diner,** 122 East Lexington Street; (606) 734-4607. Famous for its barbecued baby back ribs and homemade pies. Closed Sunday.

### VERSAILLES
**Tamara's,** 197 South Main Street; (606) 879-1697. Pasta dishes and grilled steaks for lunch and dinner. Closed Sunday.

## TRADITION MEETS INVENTION

◆ **Berea** is a nationally known folk arts and crafts center located in southern Madison County just off I-75. Stop by the Tourist Commission, 201 North Broadway, for brochures about all the craft businesses. You can also call (606) 986-2540 or (800) 598-5263. You'll find more than thirty craftspeople—chair makers, potters, leathersmiths, blacksmiths, stained-glass artisans, weavers, spoon-makers, basket weavers, quilters, and on and on—whose studios and salesrooms are open to the public. Also ask about the big outdoor fairs at the Indian Fort Theatre sponsored by the Kentucky Guild of Artists and Craftsmen.

You'll definitely want to stop at **Warren A. May's Woodworking Shop** (110 Center Street; 606-986-9293). May is one of the nation's foremost crafters of dulcimers—graceful wooden stringed instruments so beautiful that many people buy them not as musical instruments, but as artwork to hang on the wall. May's shop is open Monday through Saturday. At **Churchill Weavers** (Lorraine Court at Highway 25; 606-986-3127), you can walk through the loom-house and see master weavers hard at work creating shawls, throws, and blankets. A Churchill Weavers receiving blanket in pastel shades is the classic Bluegrass baby shower gift.

An elegant place for fine regional foods and downtown lodging is the **Boone Tavern Hotel and Dining Room** (606-986-9358), owned and run by Berea College. There's even a dress code for evening meals. It's open daily for all meals. Berea College is a highly acclaimed liberal arts college that serves primarily low-income students from Southern Appalachia. Students pay no tuition but work ten to fifteen hours a week at any of 138 college-owned businesses, which include the Boone Tavern and studios for pottery, weaving, woodworking, broommaking, and other crafts. The student-made crafts are sold at the **Log House Sales Room** on Jackson Street. The college also runs the **Appalachian Museum** near the tavern, which features a massive, fascinating collection of mountain life artifacts. Call (606) 986-9341, extension 6078, for hours and information.

North of Berea is Richmond, home of Eastern Kentucky University and very much a university town, full of restaurants, bars, hotels, and shops. If you plan to be downtown at night, check the **Phone 3 Lounge** on First Street (606-624-2556) for live music every night, everything from blues to heavy metal. For the stargazer, the **Hummel Space Theater** on Kit Carson Drive on campus is totally cosmic. This is the tenth largest planetarium in the nation, and it feels even larger as you crane your neck in the dark dome to catch a view of the galaxy from 9.3 billion miles away from Earth. Shows are Wednesday through Saturday nights at 7:30 and Saturday and Sunday afternoons at 3:30. Call (606) 622-1547.

Five generations of Cornelisons have kept **Bybee Pottery** thriving since at least 1845, making it the oldest existing pottery west of the Alleghenies. If you're from this region, you've probably seen Bybee's pots in homes of all kinds. The wheel-thrown, slip-cast (molded), and jiggered stoneware pots are based on traditional designs. The charming droop of the studio building itself reflects the age of the pottery. The clays used in all of Bybee's pieces (more than 125,000 annually) come from a small, remarkably pure clay mine less than 2 miles away. Visitors are welcome to mosey around the entire work area. Take Highway 52 east from Richmond for 9 miles. Bybee salesroom and workshop are open on weekdays, from 8:00 A.M. to noon and from 12:30 to 3:30 P.M. There's often a crowd waiting outside at 8:00 A.M. Monday, Wednesday, and Friday when the salesroom shelves are stocked, but that is the best time to grab the colors and styles you're looking for at low "factory" prices. Call (606) 369-5350.

The **White Hall State Historic Site** is accessible from I-75 (exit 90) or directly from Richmond. Take Highway 421/25 and follow the signs to the restored home of one of Kentucky's best-loved big mouths and influential abolitionists, Cassius Marcellus Clay, the "Lion of White Hall." White Hall is well fortified in part because Clay's ideological and political opponents were not beyond attempts at physically sabotaging his basement press where he produced his radical paper, *The True American*. After a failed political career, Clay served under President Lincoln as minister to the court of Czar Alexander II at St. Petersburg, Russia, then retired and lived bankrupt at White Hall until his death in 1903. The building is open from April to Labor Day daily and from Labor Day to October, Wednesday to Sunday, 9:00 A.M. to 5:00 P.M. Call (606) 623-9178.

**Fort Boonesboro State Park** is on the beaten path and self-explanatory. From I-75, take exit 95 on Highway 627 and follow the signs. The reconstructed fort is at the site of Kentucky's second settlement. Interpreters at the park dress in period clothing and demonstrate pioneer crafts, such as lye soapmaking. Hours from April to Labor Day are 9:00 A.M. to 5:30 P.M. Labor Day through October 31, the fort is open only Wednesday through Sunday, and it is closed November through March. Call (606) 527-3131.

The Virginia Assembly granted the **Valley View Ferry** a "perpetual and irrevocable franchise" in 1785. Let me emphasize the word *perpetual*. More than two hundred years later, the little boat is still carrying anyone and anything that needs to cross the Kentucky River on Highway 169 between Madison and Jessamine counties. The strangest passengers of late have been two wolves and a bear (nonunion movie stars). The governments of Jessamine, Madison, and Fayette counties recently decided to purchase and jointly operate this sole functioning ferry on the Kentucky River.

## TRUE BLUE

In 1893 a pair of Louisville sisters penned a kindergarten greeting song, "Good Morning to You," which later became the most-sung song in the world rewritten as "Happy Birthday to You."

For a dizzying view of High Bridge and the junction of the Kentucky and Dix Rivers, drive from Nicholasville south on Highway 29 about 4 miles. Notice how the Dix's water is greener than the brown of the Kentucky's. There may also be a thick layer of mist over the Dix due to the fact that the water is released from the bottom of Herrington Lake at Dix Dam.

Lower your canoe from the bluffs by High Bridge and paddle upriver all day. When you reach **Hall's on the River** restaurant (606-527-6620), you'll be hungry enough to finish one of their mouth-watering seafood entrees. Hall's is also famous for take-home foods like beer cheese. If you're a die-hard landlubber, go by road. From I-75, take the Athens-Boonesboro Road exit. From Winchester, take Highway 627 down to the river. On the way down, you may want to veer to the right where the road intersects Old Boonesboro Road; watch for Old Stone Church Road and the lovely little church by the same name. This was supposedly the first church established west of the Appalachian Mountains. It still has an active congregation, but they don't mind visitors as long as you don't leave trash.

Though the telephone has radically altered our society and world, it is seldom commemorated. Winchester's **Pioneer Telephone Museum** is one of a kind. The collection of antique phones, phone booths, switchboards, and memorabilia is housed in the phone company's maintenance building at 203 Forest Avenue. From Winchester, go west on Highway 60 past the cemetery; turn right at the first light onto Bloomfield, then go 1 block to Forest Avenue and look for a building with South Central Bell phone trucks parked in front. The museum is open only on Monday from 1:00 to 4:00 P.M. Call (606) 745-5131 or 745-5400 to make arrangements to visit.

You've probably heard that Indians did not have permanent habitations in Kentucky because it was a commonly owned hunting ground. Not true. Thirty-five hundred acres in southeastern Clark County were occupied, farmed, kept clear, and hunted by Shawnee Indians. Archaeologists are in search of the Shawnee village called Eskippakithiki, meaning "blue lick place" because of salt-sulphur springs in the area that attracted game. So if you happen upon a passel of arrowheads while walking across a plowed field here, call the archaeologists.

If you are driving near the Mount Sterling Plaza on the bypass, stop at Arby's. Don't eat. Just get out of the car and look for a rather abrupt grassy knob. That's the **Gaitskill Mound,** an Adena burial mound dating to between 800 B.C. and A.D. 700.

Although they're not of the same magnitude, this area boasts two other cultural artifacts, instances of a nearly extinct type of American entertainment: the drive-in theater. The **Sky-Vue Drive-In** (606-744-6663) is situated about halfway between Lexington and Winchester near the intersection of Highways 60 and 1678, and the **Judy Drive-In** (606-498-1960) is north of Mount Sterling in Judy on Highway 11. Both are open from Memorial Day to Labor Day with feature films beginning nightly at sundown. Call for admission prices and other information.

In downtown Mount Sterling there is another artifact from the 1950s. **Berryman's Tasty Treat,** since 1951 on East Main Street, is a full-fledged vintage carryout dairy freeze famous for its chili hotdogs. Berryman's is open 8:30 A.M. to 11:00 P.M. Monday through Saturday and 9:00 A.M. to 11:00 P.M. Sunday. It closes for the winter in mid-November. Its annual reopening in early March is a sign to area residents that spring has arrived. For information call (606) 498-6830.

For more area information, stop by the Mount Sterling Chamber of Commerce, 51 North Maysville Street, in the old **Bell House** building, circa 1815, previously a hat shop and county jail. Ask about October Court Days, a big trading festival reminiscent of earlier times when each county held court once a month in a central location so the more remote farmers didn't have to come to town more often. During this three-day extravaganza, approximately 100,000 people crowd into the town of 5,400. Do arrive early and wear your walking shoes, because the one thing you probably won't find is a parking place anywhere near downtown. Just uphill at the corner of Broadway and High Street is the **Ascension Episcopal Church,** a beautiful little church with walnut paneling, exquisite carved wood, exposed beams, and stained-glass windows thought to be the first to cross the mountains (by oxcart!). The doors are open during the day so visitors can drool at the 1877 gem.

> ## TRUE BLUE
>
> Nearly 1,000 people attended the funeral of famous racehorse Man O' War in 1947. He was the first horse to lie in state. In 1977 his grave and monument were moved to the Kentucky Horse Park.

Mount Sterling has a darling downtown area, and its Main Cross Historic District (Main and Maysville Streets in downtown) has been beautifully restored. You can shop for country furniture and other collectibles at **Monarch Mill Antiques** (606-498-3744), located in what was once a feed mill at 101 South Maysville Street. A great place to have lunch is **Simply Delicious** (606-497-9265) which lives up to its name with homemade soups, sandwiches, salads; yummy chess, butterscotch, and chocolate pies; as well as muffins, cookies, and cappuccino. It could also be called Simply Beautiful, with its airy atmosphere, open ceilings, honey-hued wood floors, and stenciled walls.

Just up the street at 321 Maysville Street is the **Trimble House Bed and Breakfast,** owned by Jim and June Hyska. The plantation-style house (circa 1872) is graced with antiques, a swimming pool, and a Jacuzzi. A delicious Southern breakfast is always served. Call (606) 498–6561 for reservations. If you're a history buff, make arrangements to tour **Morgan Station,** the site of the last Indian raid in Kentucky. Daniel Boone's cousin, Ralph Morgan, built the big stone house east of Mount Sterling at 3751 Harpers Ridge Road. The owner, Danny Montgomery, is often willing to show visitors around. Call first at (606) 498–2011.

Mount Sterling boasts a fine woodworker, **Paul Williams,** whose special interest is making stringed instruments—dulcimers, Celtic harps, arch-top jazz guitars, acoustic guitars, vertical and lap harps, and mandolins—out of native Kentucky hardwoods. Although Martin and Gibson brands have made mahogany and rosewood the standard guitar woods, maple, walnut, and ash can also sound and look beautiful. He welcomes visitors to his workshop, which is behind his house at 209 Rogers Avenue. Please call him ahead at (606) 498–7175.

Employing the same careful craftsmanship, and the same material as Williams, but with an entirely different result, Jim Chambers is turning his **Bluegrass Bird House Company** into a nationally known source for ornamental birdhouses. Jim is interested in the artistic aspect of the houses, but birds love them, too. His work ranges from exquisite little tree ornament houses at $11 to completely custom-made bird abodes with antiqued copper roofs at close to $200. Chambers' workshop is at 313 East Main Street. Please call ahead at (606) 498–1048.

Mount Sterling is sweet tooth heaven. Make a molasses run (but not as slowly as molasses itself runs) to **Townsend's Sorghum Mill,** 11620 Main Street (also Highway 460), in Jeffersonville, south of Mount Sterling. Go any time of year because they always have pure sorghum syrup (and occasionally maple syrup) on hand, but from the end of August through November you can watch them process the cane. The Townsend family has been raising cane for 150 years. Although they use tractors to do the real work, at festivals they bring out the mule team to turn the old-fashioned cane break. Call Judy and Danny Townsend at (606) 498–4142, or plan to come by after 4:00 P.M.

The ultimate dessert is chocolate, real food for real people. Walk into ❖ **Ruth Hunt Candies** and faint. The aroma of liquid chocolate, sweet cream, and roasting nuts will do in even the strong of heart. Everything is handmade and very fresh. Just like in the old days, you can ask the clerk for a quarter pound of pulled cream candy, a half pound of caramel and bittersweet chocolate balls, and a handful of hot cinnamon suckers, and they'll reach into the big, colorful bins for the goods.

This operation is small and friendly enough that Larry Kezele, the owner, may have time to show you the whole production process. Ruth Tharpe Hunt started the business in 1921 after her bridge buddies encouraged her to go public with her candy making. The Blue Monday Sweet Bar, a dark chocolate with pulled cream in the center, which is perhaps the most famous of their products, was named by a traveling minister who was eating Sunday dinner at the Hunts' and claimed that he needed candy to get through those blue Mondays. Look for Larry and his staff dressed like Blue Mondays in parades. The company, located at 426 West Main Street, is open Monday through Saturday, from 9:00 A.M. to 5:30 P.M., and Sunday from 1:00 to 5:00 P.M. Call (606) 498–0676 if you need more information.

## MORE GOOD LODGING

**MOUNT STERLING**

**Days Inn,** I–64 exit 110; (606) 498–4680 or (800) 325–2525. About $60 per night.

**BEREA**

**The Doctor's Inn,** 617 Chestnut Street; (606) 986–3042. Luxurious B&B accommodations in an elegant Colonial-style mansion. About $120 per night.

**WINCHESTER**

**Holiday Inn Winchester,** Mount Sterling Road at I–64 exit 96A; (606) 744–9111 or (800) HOLIDAY. About $60 per night.

## MORE FUN PLACES TO EAT

**BEREA**

**Hometown Cafeteria,** I–75 exit 76; (606) 986–7086. Legendary for its home cooking—enjoy *real* mashed potatoes and straight-from-the-oven pie.

**Jazzman Café,** 3 North Main Street; (606) 744–6425. Sidewalk barbecue and other delicious soul food.

MOUNT STERLING
**Marikka's Restaurant und Bier Stube,** Main and Maysville
Streets; (606) 498–0052. Hearty German fare and a good selec-
tion of imported beers. Open for dinner Monday through
Saturday.

# CITY LIGHTS

"When I start working, I might as well climb into the wood—that's
how intimate it gets," says woodworker **Connie Carlton** of
Lawrenceburg. Connie looks for the perfect tree in the woods, cuts
it before the sap runs, splits long sections of the trunk lengthwise
with a sledge and froe, and shapes the wood on a vise-bench of
ancient design called a "shaving horse" amid a tiny sea of curled
wood shavings. (The place smells like heaven.) The results are long,
smooth, shapely pitchforks, rakes, barrel staves, woodworking tools,
and the like. He also makes sorghum molasses and cuts hair. If you
want to buy fine wooden tools or get a haircut by a man with a
steady hand, from Highway 127 take Highway 62 west about 2
miles and turn left on Rice Road. His is the first house on the left.
Call ahead at (502) 839–6478.

More than 95 percent of the bourbon whiskey made in America is
made in Kentucky, and most of it comes from this area. ❖ **Wild
Turkey Distilleries** (of Boulevard Distillers and Importers, Inc.) is
just the place to get a fascinating bourbon education. From
Lawrenceburg, take Highway 62 east of town until it splits with Highway 1510. Bear right, go downhill, and watch for the Visitors Information Center on the right. (Note the high train trestle spanning the
Kentucky River. Young's High Bridge is a single-span, deck-over cantilever 281 feet high and 1,659 feet long, the last of its kind.)

The Wild Turkey Distillery has been operating continuously since
the mid-1860s, except during Prohibition, when nearly all distilleries were shut down. During World War II this facility made only
surgical alcohol. Federal law states that for whiskey to be called

straight bourbon, it must be manufactured in the United States, of at least 51 percent corn, and stored at 125 proof or less for at least two years in new, charred, white oak barrels. Char caramelizes the wood, which gives the bourbon its rich color and flavor. The corn is ground, cooked, and cooled. The distillers add rye for starch, then barley malt, which converts the starch to sugar (unlike moonshiners who simply dump cane sugar in the corn mash). Yeast is added, and when the fermented mash is steamed from below, whiskey vapor rises to the top where it is condensed into liquid form. The whiskey is distilled again, put in barrels, and aged from four to twelve years. It's tasted at every stage, and meticulous production records are kept for every batch. Free tours are available Monday through Friday at 9:00 and 10:30 A.M., and at 12:30 and 2:30 P.M. The distillery runs 24-hour days every day except Sunday, when liquor is not made anywhere in the United States. Call (502) 839-4544.

From Lawrenceburg take Highway 127 north into Frankfort, the state capital. On Second Street look for an ornate Queen Anne–style house with gingerbread trim, the official **Frankfort Visitor Center** (502-875-TOUR). Because the city's layout is confusing, a map is good headache prevention.

Directly across Capitol Avenue from the visitors center is **Rebecca-Ruth Candy, Inc.,** at 112 East Second Street. Chocolate and candy addicts will love the tour of one of Kentucky's oldest houses of sweet repute. In 1919, Rebecca Gooch and Ruth (Hanly) Booe quit teaching and went into business making candy. Ruth's son, John Booe, is the president of the company, and his son, Charles (who claims to eat a pound of candy a day), intends to uphold the tradition.

Tour the production area to see pipes running full of liquid Dutch chocolate and churning vats of sugar and thick cream. Edna Robbins, expert confectioner of more than sixty years, makes some candies completely by hand on the original 1919 marble slab. Rebecca-Ruth sells literally hundreds of varieties including delicate mints, crunchy chocolate turtles, fudge galore, and variations on the delicious theme of the bourbon ball. The salesroom is tantalizing. Hours are Monday through Saturday 8:00 A.M. to 5:30 P.M.

Tours are given Monday through Thursday from January through October. Call (502) 223-7475 or (800) 444-3766 for tour schedule or free catalog.

Go down St. Clair Mall and over the singing bridge, a blue bridge with a steel grid roadway that welcomes cars to Frankfort with a high-pitched hum. Look for the **Rick's White Light Diner,** 114 Bridge Street (502-227-4889), an irresistible little hamburger joint that's been doing regular business since 1927. The signs painted on the wall by the door read COURTEOUS SERVICE and, my favorite, LADIES INVITED. Hours are 7:00 A.M. to 2:00 P.M. on weekdays and 8:00 A.M. to 2:00 P.M. Saturday. Sit on one of the spinning stools at the counter and try one of chef Rick Paul's unusual burgers, such as the garlic burger or the super hot Cajun cheeseburger. Finish the feast with a strong espresso and perhaps a good-natured argument with Chef Paul, whose strength of opinion is rivaled only by the strength of his spices.

♦ **Luscher's Farm Relics of Yesterday: Museum of the American Farmer** is an unusual museum with the commendable mission of preserving the history of American agriculture by displaying a slew of old equipment (that works!). From town, take Highway 127 north to its junction with Highway 898 (or Manley-Leestown Road); turn left and look for the sign.

On display are rows and rows of Luscher family pieces and other collected items that were used in Kentucky from 1840 to the present—Model T trucks, steel-wheeled tractors, wooden plows, a steam engine, horse-drawn mowing machines, plus hundreds of smaller tools, including wrenches, yokes, ice picks, saws, sickles, churns, and washing machines, and on and on. The tool with the best story is a 1922 limestone pulverizer. In the words of the late Albert Luscher, "When it was first used the neighbors remarked about those crazy Luschers, picking up rocks on their fields, grinding them up into dust and putting them back on the fields. Pretty soon, though, everybody was liming their fields." From Memorial Day to Labor Day, hours are 10:00 A.M. to 4:00 P.M. Monday through Saturday and 1:00 to 4:00 P.M. Sunday. Call (502) 875-2755.

Through each of their varied projects, Sherri and Marc Evans of ♦ **Shooting Star Nursery** are accomplishing the goals of educating people about preserving the world's biodiversity and of promoting renaturalization in Kentucky and elsewhere. The nursery itself supplies more than 3,000 species of nursery-propagated (from seeds, cuttings, and divisions) native plants for gardening, landscaping, and restoring damaged lands such as strip mines and tired farmland. Sherri and Marc spend lots of energy doing consultation for those involved in ecological restoration. Ask about their "septic wetland" design, which is basically a 7-by-20-foot pit filled with 18 inches of gravel, water, and water-loving wild plants. The "brown" wastewater from a house goes in one end, and clean, safe water comes out the other after the plants do the filtering work with their roots. This system can even be made to work on a bed of rock. Visit the nursery to shop for container and bare-root plants and seeds.

**TRUE BLUE**

Kentucky towns bear an international array of names. Kentucky has a Moscow, Athens, Cairo, Dublin, London, Manila, Paris, and Warsaw.

From Frankfort, take Highway 127 north out of town to the Frankfort/Owenton exit and turn left; go 10 miles, just past the road's intersection with Highway 2919, to Bates Road. Shooting Star is half a mile in on the left. Nursery hours are Thursday, Friday, and Sunday 1:00 to 5:00 P.M. and Saturday 9:00 A.M. to 5:00 P.M. from April through June; Saturdays only July through October. Otherwise, appointments to visit are welcome. Call (502) 223–1679 or 223–2906 or write them at 444 Bates Road, Frankfort 40601, to receive a catalog or information about upcoming "Ecological Restoration and Stewardship" workshops.

About 8 miles north of Frankfort is **Canoe Kentucky** (7265 Peaks Mill Road; 502-227-4492 or 800-K-CANOE-1), home base to Ed Councill, canoeist and Elkhorn Creek conservation activist extraordinaire. Canoe Kentucky offers a variety of excursions on a dozen Kentucky waterways, but it is the one in his own backyard, Elkhorn Creek, that is most dear to his heart. Take an excursion and you'll soon understand why. This long and winding waterway— more than 100 miles through parts of six counties—played an important role in the settlement of the Bluegrass area. Poet Walt

Whitman, whose soldier brother was encamped in Kentucky in 1863, wrote of "the vale of the Elkhorn." Whether your interest is historic sites, fishing (some sections are great for catching bass), picnicking, or just a quiet-at-your-own-pace getaway, Councill can suggest a good paddle route. Canoe Kentucky even offers moonlight excursions for groups. ("We found that these weren't as much fun when it was a group of people who didn't know each other," Councill explained.) If you want to learn all about the Elkhorn, its history, its wildlife, and the need to protect it in light of rapidly encroaching development, or if you want to try a more unusual aspect of canoeing such as winter canoeing, Ed Councill's the one to go up (or down) the creek with. Prices vary depending upon length and type of excursion. An unguided 6-mile (2½-hour) excursion costs $26 per person; two people to a canoe. A guide on the trip would cost $50 more per group.

From Frankfort go west on I–64 or Highway 60 to Shelbyville. In 1825 Julia Tevis founded ◆ **Science Hill,** a girls' school, at 525 Washington Street in downtown Shelbyville because she believed young women needed an education in math and science, not just needlepoint and etiquette. During its 114-year operation, Science Hill was known as one of the best preparatory schools in the country. Etiquette, however, never lost its essential place. A former student remembers this story about Miss Julia Poynter, the last principal of the school. The mother of a "town boy" had a party in her home. One of the students thanked the hostess by saying, "I enjoyed myself thoroughly." Miss Julia reprimanded the girl, saying, "You do not go to a party to enjoy yourself, you go to enjoy others. Tell your hostess that you enjoyed her party."

Today the fully restored Science Hill complex houses six boutiques, the Wakefield-Scearce Galleries, and a restaurant, the **Georgia Room** of Science Hill Inn. In keeping with the nineteenth-century atmosphere, the restaurant serves fine American food with a heavy Kentucky accent. Lunch is served daily, except Monday, from 11:30 A.M. to 2:30 P.M.; dinner is served Friday and Saturday from 5:30 to 8:30 P.M. Call (502) 633–2825. **Wakefield-Scearce Galleries** (502–633–4382) are chock-full of elegant English (plus a touch of Oriental, American, and European) furniture, silver, china, rugs, paintings, and other decorative objects. Much of the furniture is antique, and the reproductions are beautifully made. The quality is high, as are the prices. Whether or not you can afford the decor, these museumlike galleries provide room after room of visual and tactile delight.

A few blocks west of Science Hill, at 707 Washington Street, follow the bagpipe music to Nicol Wendy Fay and Sally Nicol's store, **The Scotland Yard,** Kentucky's only all-Scottish extravaganza. In the center room is a chart listing family names and their respective tartan plaids. If your last name is Douglas or Stewart or (Lord help you) Colquhoun or Farquharson, you will be able to find ties, skirts, and scarves in all possible weave variations on your tartan. All 490 tartans are represented in addition to family crests and clan car badges, kilt outfits, bagpipe supplies, maps, jewelry, music, and a room full of very British foods. Hours are 10:00 A.M. to 5:00 P.M. Monday through Saturday. Call (502) 633-0116 or (800) 636-0116.

Across the street, at 702 Washington Street, is a gastronomically tempting little place called **Spices and More.** Herbs, coffees, teas, special pastas, locally made salad dressings, dried fruit, and more are within reach. Owners Bill and Anne Matz also offer cooking demonstrations every Saturday from noon to 4:00 P.M. Call (502) 633-8084 for more information.

In the early 1800s, when Highway 60 was called "the Lexington and Louisville Turnpike," the **Old Stone Inn,** circa 1805, was well known as a hospitable stagecoach inn and tavern. New proprietors have restored the inn as a restaurant, gift shop, and bed and breakfast. Humor writer Bonnie McCafferty commented that "the combination of decor restraint/decor run amok struck me as what a bordello would look like if it were operated by Southern Baptists." The food is rich and pure Southern, so come hungry when the old dinner bell rings for lunch, served from 11:00 A.M. to 3:00 P.M., and for dinner, from 5:30 to 8:00 P.M. nightly. Four rooms on the second floor are used for lodgings at the rate of $85 per night, which includes a full breakfast. Call (502) 722-8882. Old Stone Inn is in Simpsonville, 8 miles west of Shelbyville on Highway 60.

Follow Highway 60 (or, if you're in a hurry, take I-64 West) to Louisville, largest city in the state and home of the world-famous

**Kentucky Derby.** The greatest two minutes in sports are also part of the greatest twenty-four hours in fashion. For a week before the Derby, everyone and everything is dressed to the nines—houses are repainted, yards are relandscaped, and bodies are clothed in the latest styles, no matter the cost or the weather. For Kentuckians, the Derby marks the beginning of early summer and, therefore, the first day that it's acceptable for women to shed their dark winter garb and wear white again. Fashion sometimes follows need and sometimes it leads. Several years ago we had a bitter cold, rainy Derby Day, but the dresses were already purchased, and hats were garnished. Women simply wore thermal underwear under sleeveless gowns and men, for once, were happy to keep on their coats and ties.

The Kentucky Derby is run the first Saturday in May at the Churchill Downs Race Track on Central Avenue (502-636-4400). The gates open at 8:00 A.M., and you can join the party on the Infield or wander the Clubhouse Grounds for $30—standing room only or bring-your-own chair or blanket. Racing begins at 11:30 A.M., but the Run for the Roses isn't until 5:30 P.M. (There's not a rosebush on the grounds, by the way.) Dress however you want and keep your eyes peeled for celebrities. Churchill Downs also hosts Thoroughbred racing during a Spring Meet, which runs from the end of April to the beginning of July, and a Fall Meet, from late October through late November.

If you're planning to be seen at the Derby and want to be on the cutting edge of fashion, you might want to check out the annual pre-Derby fashion show held in mid-April at the **Kentucky Derby Museum** on the grounds of Churchill Downs. Celebs and local media personalities model the latest in hats and clothes, setting a precedent for the masses. Any time of year the Kentucky Derby Museum is an interesting stop. Naturally, the exhibits feature the Derby's history, but there are others concerning the whole Thoroughbred industry. Hours are 9:00 A.M. to 5:00 P.M. daily. Also on site is the Finish Line Gift Shop and The Derby Café. Call (502) 637-1111.

Far from the madding crowd, but not far from Churchhill Downs, are several peaceful sites. The most surprising is just inside the I-264 loop between Poplar Level Road and Newburg Road; the

**Beargrass Creek State Nature Preserve,** (502-458-1328). This forty-one-acre wood has a remarkably diverse community of flora and fauna and, since it's smack-dab in the middle of the city, is constantly in use for environmental education. So if you placed all your bets badly at the track, here's a balm. This lovely spot is open daily from sunrise to sunset.

The park is named after Beargrass Creek, which empties into the Ohio River just above the famous Falls of the Ohio, a rocky series of rapids over a 3-mile descent, which stopped early travelers on their way south. Beargrass Creek proved to be a place to rest and to develop a strategy for getting around the falls. In 1778 George Rogers Clark set up a military and civilian camp nearby, on Corn Island. Floods on the island caused the settlers to move to the mainland (somewhere between what are now Twelfth and Rowan Streets), where they started building the city of Louisville. Since the installation of the Portland Canal and the McAlpine Dam (easily seen from town near the Northwestern Parkway and Twenty-seventh Street), the **Falls of the Ohio** is an exposed coral reef, a fossil bed over 350 million years in age. To get a good look at the fossils, cross the river into Clarksville, Indiana, park at Riverside Park, and walk near where the Fourteenth Street railroad bridge and five dam gates meet the shore.

Next to Beargrass Creek Park is the **Louisville Zoological Garden** (100 Trevilian Way; 502-459-2181), home to more than 900 animals. The zoo has an exhibit of birds of prey and a HerpAquarium, which features a simulated rain forest. It is open daily and the admission fee, for any age, is $5.50.

From the zoo, take Newburg Road to Eastern Parkway and go west to Third Street; turn right and you're on the University of Louisville campus. The ◆ **J. B. Speed Art Museum** at 2035 South Third Street (502-636-2893) is an outstanding museum not to be missed at any cost. The permanent collection includes works from all periods, including some distinguished medieval, Renaissance, and Dutch masterpieces, and a broad representation of contemporary art. The museum also maintains a stimulating schedule of traveling exhibitions. Hours are 10:00 A.M. to 4:00 P.M. Tuesday through Saturday and 1:00 to 5:00 P.M. Sunday. During the summer, more culture is in store at the corner of Fourth and Magnolia Streets in Central Park. The **Kentucky Shakespeare Festival** performs free, high-quality, live Shakespeare productions from mid-June to early August. Curtain time is 8:00 P.M.

Indoor theater is always happening in this town. Check the *Louisville Courier Journal* for performances by the myriad little theaters and check the schedule at **Actors Theatre,** 316 West Main Street. In addition to producing a surprising variety of plays all year (except during July and August), Actors has become nationally known for the Humana Festival of New American Plays. Shows in the festival are booked early, so get the schedule and make reservations by calling (502) 584–1205 or (800) 428–5849. There's a restaurant downstairs at Actors Theatre.

Main Street is art street in Louisville. The glass structure with the big whimsical sculpture is the **Kentucky Center for the Arts** at 609 West Main Street. The center hosts a little of everything, including the Louisville Opera, ballet, orchestra, theater for all ages, and a series of national and regional performers. Call (502) 584–7777. A few doors down, the **Kentucky Art and Craft Gallery** (502–589–0102) features the work of some of the state's finest craftspeople. Nearby is the **Zephyr Gallery,** 812 West Main Street (502–585–5646), an art cooperative that never fails to hang imaginative shows.

The next stop is for kids. The **Louisville Science Center,** 727 West Main Street, is a big, colorful, hands-on place orchestrated for discovery. The selling point for adults is the IMAX theater, a four-story screen surrounded by speakers; the experience blows your confidence in logic to pieces. "It's just a movie," you tell yourself as you clutch your sweetheart's arm to keep from falling. Call the museum at (502) 561–6100 for show times and admission charges.

You certainly don't need us to point out that there's a 120-foot baseball bat at Main and Eighth Streets, but the bat, beacon for the **Louisville Slugger Museum** (502–588–7228), is just too much fun to leave out. Youngsters, and baseball fans of all ages, will love the museum and plant tour, too. There's a full-size dugout, a replica of Orioles Park, a replica of a northern white ash forest, and many exhibits tracing the history of the game and its most famous brand of bat. Despite being called the Louisville Slugger, for twenty-two years the bats were actually made across the Ohio River in southern Indiana. In 1996, the manufacturing plant returned to Louisville in a big way. The museum is open 9:00 A.M. to 5:00 P.M. Monday through Friday. Admission is $4.00.

Since there are so many restaurants of every kind in town, let's just consider breakfast and dessert. If having breakfast at **Lynn's Paradise Café** (984 Barret Avenue; 502-583-3447) doesn't get your day off to a smiling start, you might as well just give it up and head back to bed. Owner Lynn Winter's taste in decor is certainly eye-opening—there's an 8-foot red coffeepot out front and all manner of knickknacks inside—but there's nothing silly about her efforts in the kitchen. This place serves great breakfast burritos, chunky French toast topped with fruit and whipped cream, fabulous cheese home-fries, and all sorts of other inventive and filling approaches to "home cooking." Lynn's is open 8:00 A.M. to 2:00 P.M. Tuesday through Saturday. For you oversleepers, she also serves dinner starting at 5:00 P.M. Thursday, Friday, and Saturday.

The prize for the most unusual business combination that serves dessert is the **Quonset Hut Concrete Statuary Garden and Ice Cream at the Overlook.** You can eat ice cream or frozen yogurt while you shop for concrete birdbaths, statues, pots, urns, or garden fountains, all at reasonable prices. Recently the Quonset Hut folks have also started making and selling high-quality hammocks that you can try out. Or you can simply gaze down from the top of Phoenix Hill onto the Louisville skyline. This is a good place for a first date. Take Broadway east to Baxter Avenue and turn left (north) to Hull Street; turn left (west) to the top of the overlook and you're there. Hours are 4:00 to 10:00 P.M. Monday through Friday, 9:00 A.M. to 10:00 P.M. Saturday, and 1:00 to 10:00 P.M. Sunday. Call (502) 584-0814.

**Kizito Cookies** (502-456-2891) wins a prize for the most unusual method of dessert distribution. Elizabeth Kizito started her business by carrying baskets of scrumptious chocolate cookies through the downtown streets *on her head* during lunch hours. She is from Uganda, where it's commonplace for folks to keep their hands free by means of this balancing act, but in Louisville, she's become famous for it. These days she has a retail store at 1398 Bardstown Road, where you can buy coffee, cookies, and muffins while looking over a colorful selection of African earrings or small carvings from Kenya and Uganda. Hours are 7:00 A.M. to 6:00 P.M. Tuesday through Friday and 9:00 A.M. to 6:00 P.M. Saturday.

More wonderful African-oriented skills are featured at ◆ **Kente International** (1954 Bonnycastle Avenue; 502–459–4595), a gallery/store that carries a line of imported goods from South America, Pakistan, India, and Africa. You'll fall in love with the colorful clothing and tapestries and the striking jewelry and sculpture. The owner, Musa Uthman, is a percussionist extraordinaire and, not surprisingly, sells handmade drums from Africa and India, plus a few made in the United States by Native Americans. The most popular is the beautiful Djamba drum from Senegal; it's hand-carved from a local hardwood, and it has a goatskin head that is tuned with ropes. Musa teaches basic techniques and rhythms during drum workshops, which he gives by appointment on Sundays and just after hours. The store is open from 10:00 A.M. to 6:00 P.M. Monday through Saturday.

There are two well-established traditional potteries in Louisville, both of which are worth a visit. **Louisville Stoneware** (731 Brent Street; 502–582–1900), famous for dinnerware, is really a pottery industry, but the process is almost the same as you would find in the small studio of an individual potter. Tours are available twice a day and there are pieces for sale in a retail showroom. Open 8:00 A.M. to 5:00 P.M. Monday through Saturday. **Hadley Pottery,** in Butchertown on 1570 Story Avenue, was started by Mary Hadley in 1940. Her original style has been maintained, and although the pieces are no longer hand-thrown, they are all hand-painted. Come at 2:00 P.M. weekdays for a guided tour. Hours are 8:30 A.M. to 5:00 P.M. Monday through Friday and 9:00 A.M. to 1:00 P.M. Saturday. Call (502) 584-2171.

If you're looking for antique pottery and almost anything else imaginable, pay a visit to ◆ **Joe Ley Antiques** at 615 East Market Street. Joe Ley's place is two acres under one roof full—and I mean full—of antique treasures. For architects and home restoration folks, this is an endless toy shop. Stained glass, chandeliers, mantels, carousel horses, stuffed moose, fine silver—you name it, it's here. Hours are Tuesday through Saturday from 8:30 A.M. to 5:00 P.M. Call (502) 583-4014.

Don't quit with Joe Ley's. Head on down to **Architectural Salvage** at 614–618 East Broadway for more of the same. This place is crammed full of mantels, hardware, stained glass, real doors, wrought iron, and on and on. Call (502) 589-0670 if you care to ask specifics. I recommend the browsing method myself.

A little-known cultural reference library of sorts is found in the halls of **Tattoo Charlie's,** a dermagraphic extravaganza. Tattoo art has come a long way since bones and charcoal or needles in a cork. For the uninitiated, you can watch consenting clients being decorated by a certified tattoo technician wielding an electric needle that looks and sounds like a dentist's drill. Prices range from $25 for a single music note, for example, to more than $3,000 for a series of full-color illustrations. Even if you aren't personally interested in a tattoo, check out the tattoo design gallery. Owner and tattoo master Charlie Wheeler has lined the walls with possible patterns. Then there are hundreds of photographs and slides of customers displaying actual tattoos, no matter where they are. Charlie has a motorcycle seat in his booth where you can relax and watch the show or, perhaps, try out your new tattoo in the correct posture. Tattoo Charlie's is located at 1845 Berry Boulevard, on the south side of town; the easiest way to get there is to take Highway 31 south and turn east on Seventh Street Road, then veer onto Berry Boulevard. No appointment necessary. Call (502) 366-9635 for hours.

If you want to get away from the rush of the city, escape to **Cherokee Park,** off Eastern Parkway east of downtown, for great bicycling, jogging, and picnicking. (You can rent bikes at **Highland Cycle** nearby at 1737 Bardstown Road; 502–458–7832). Or take Third Street south to **Iroquois Park** and admire a nearly 200-year-old forest or rent a horse from **Iroquois Riding Stables** (502–363–9159) and take a trail ride. Louisville has some of the most beautiful public parks found anywhere, thanks to foresight on the part of city leaders. In 1891 Louisville hired Frederick Law Olmstead to design and construct the city's park system. Olmstead is known as the father of landscape architecture; his other credits include New York's Central Park, Biltmore Gardens, and the 1893 Chicago World's Fair. When Olmstead retired in 1895, his stepson, John C. Olmsted, completed the Louisville plan. In all, the Olmsteads created sixteen Louisville parks between 1891 and 1935. Although a 1974 tornado took its toll, citizens rallied in the late 1980s to conserve and, where necessary, restore the parks' beauty.

## MORE GOOD LODGING

LOUISVILLE

**Camberley Brown Hotel,** Fourth Street and Broadway; (502) 583-1234 or (800) 555-8000. A 1920s landmark with an excellent restaurant. $99 up.

**Galt House,** Fourth Avenue at River Road; (502) 589-5200. Overlooking the Ohio River. About $115.

**Old Louisville Inn,** 1359 South Third Street; (502) 635-1574. An elegant eleven-room Victorian guest house; great breakfast popovers. About $95.

**Seelbach Hotel,** 500 South Fourth Avenue; (502) 585-3200 or (800) 333-3399. A luxurious Beaux Arts showplace in the heart of downtown. About $150.

## MORE FUN PLACES TO EAT

LOUISVILLE

**Café Metro,** 1700 Bardstown Road; (502) 458-4830. Casual chic with great desserts.

**Lilly's,** 1147 Bardstown Road; (502) 451-0447. Creative cooking by nationally recognized owner and chef Kathy Cary.

**Mazzoni's Oyster Café,** 2804 Taylorsville Road; (502) 451-4436. Originator of the rolled oyster in 1884.

**Mike Linnig's,** 9308 Cane Run Road; (502) 937-9888. A local fried-fish institution, with outdoor dining. Very casual.

**Vincenzo's,** 150 South Fifth Street; (502) 580-1350. Fine Italian cuisine, for a special dinner out.

# ABBEYS AND ART

What was once an abused tract of tired farmland is now ◆ **Bernheim Forest Arboretum and Nature Center,** a 10,000-acre native forest protected since 1928. Available in this legacy of the "Knobs" are hiking, picnicking, limited fishing, unlimited daydreaming, and a self-education in the nature center's museum or in the arboretum, where an enormous variety of ornamental plants are grown in meticulously labeled, manicured beds. I used to skip high school in the spring to make an annual pilgrimage here armed with my bicycle and a sketch pad. The forest is open from March 15 to November 15 from 9:00 A.M. to 6:00 P.M. Call (502) 543-2451 for information. Bernheim Forest is right next to the intersection of I-65 (exit 112) and Highway 245.

While traveling, Mark Twain was asked by the luggage inspector if he had anything besides clothing in his suitcase. Twain said no, but I guess he looked suspicious because the man opened his case anyhow and found a fifth of bourbon whiskey. "I thought you had only clothes!" the man roared. "Ahh," Twain answered, "but that's my nightcap." Twain's drink of choice had to be bourbon, and it had to be from the limestone hills of Kentucky, which provide the water that gives Jim Beam and other regional bourbons a distinctive flavor that makes them the best in the world. For a crash course in whiskey mash, take a free tour of the **Jim Beam American Outpost and Museum** (502-543-9877) on Highway 245, a mile east of Bernheim Forest. Hours are 9:00 A.M. to 4:30 P.M. Monday through Saturday and 1:00 to 4:00 P.M. Sunday.

If you're going toward Bardstown from the west on Highway 245, not stopping at **Rooster Run General Store** (502-348-8753) is like being in Memphis and skipping Graceland. The store, formerly called Evans Beverage Depot, was the only place in Nelson County in the late sixties that sold alcohol. One day a man had too many drinks, and his wife showed up with fire in her eyes, stood in the door, and snarled his name. When the drunk man sped to her side, someone remarked, "Well, would you look at that old rooster run." Such is the history of town names in our state. I still wonder whether the name had anything to do with the fact that the next town over is called Hen Peck. Whatever the truth may be, Joe Evans put the place on the map by selling over a million Rooster Run caps to truck drivers and celebrities alike.

Bardstown is dense with well-advertised historically significant treasures, such as **My Old Kentucky Home State Park** and house of John Rowan. Rowan invited his cousin from Pittsburgh, Stephen Foster, to visit in 1852, and shortly afterward, Foster wrote the tune that is now our official state song. The mansion and gardens are open year-round. From June 9 to September 2, the famous musical, *The Stephen Foster Story,* is performed outdoors. You can't miss the signs. Call 800-323-7803 for more information.

Most people do know about **Wickland,** finest example of Georgian architecture in the country and "the only home in America where three governors have lived," but there's a story about this place that opens the mind to a new way to trace history. Charles Wickliffe, a rags-to-riches figure, built the place in 1815 for his bride, Margaret Crepps. Charles was a Kentucky governor, and his son, Robert, became Louisiana's last pre–Civil War governor. Their daughter, Julia Tevis, married William Beckham, and they lived in Wickland with their ten children, one of whom, John Crepps Wickliffe Beckham, also became governor of Kentucky. That makes three governors in the family. The Beckhams were second-generation nouveaux riches with Deep South connections and a penchant for lavish Southern-style living, which included owning slaves. When the Civil War broke out, they were harassed, so the family fled from Wickland to Canada.

As is true for many women during many eras, Julia left her record of the times in the form of a quilt. Her stunning, full-sized Baby Blocks quilt is made entirely of silk and velvet pieces from family ball dresses and gowns. Not designed for wear-and-tear, the quilt showed that even after the "recent unpleasantness," Julia had a place in her life for nonfunctional beauty, but also that ball dresses weren't needed any more—posh days were over. Wickland's fourteen rooms are fully furnished with exquisite antiques. The museum offers guided tours year-round but hours may vary. Admission is $3.50. Go about 1 mile east of Court Square on Highway 62. For more information, write Wickland, P.O. Box 314, Bardstown 40004, or call (502) 348–5428 and talk to resident curator Sara Trigg.

Another old Southern-style mansion that bore big-time political figures into the world is **The Mansion,** 1003 North Third Street, an eight-room bed and breakfast. Built in 1851 by Lt. Governor William E. Johnson, the house marks the site where the Confederate flag was first raised in the state of Kentucky. Daily tours are conducted at 1:00 and 5:00 P.M. by reservation. Call Mr. or Mrs. Joseph Dennis Downs for lodging reservations at (502) 348–2586.

**Amber LeAnn Bed and Breakfast** is a nicely restored, pink two-story Victorian house, located at 209 East Stephen Foster Avenue, that visitors can use for fancy, downtown lodging or simply for a historic tour. The 1820 building's most obvious claims to fame are the wooden mantels in every room that were carved by Alexander Moore, the artisan who did the original finish carpentry at My Old Kentucky Home. For a tour or reservations call (502) 349–0014 or (888) 828–3330.

Two on-the-beaten-path restaurants in town are **Old Talbott Tavern,** the oldest western stagecoach stop in America, circa 1779, which also has bed and breakfast lodging in the old inn (502–348–3494), and **My Old Kentucky Dinner Train** (502–348–7500), where you dine in vintage 1940s dining cars pulled by old diesel-electric engines on a two-hour ride to Limestone Springs and back. Both have their merits, but *the* local place to eat is the **Hurst Restaurant** (502–348–8929), a small downtown diner facing Courthouse Square. The soups are homemade and the local talk is always juicy.

While you're downtown in Courthouse Square, pay your respects to John Fitch, the unhappy inventor of the steamboat in 1791. Then listen to the earth rumble when Robert Fulton turns over in his grave—wherever he's buried, may he rest in some peace. John Fitch was not born in Bardstown, but he died here after a lifetime of work on steam navigation and a lifetime of struggle with inventor James Rumsey, who, like Fulton, claimed to have been the first to apply it successfully. After failing to get sponsors, analogous to today's lusted-after research grants, Fitch came to Nelson County, built steamboat models, and tested them in local streams. **John Fitch's grave** in the square is marked by a small steamboat replica.

At the corner of Highway 62 West, also called Stephen Foster Avenue, and Fifth Street is the **Saint Joseph Proto-Cathedral.** The cathedral, circa 1823, is the oldest west of the Alleghenies and contains a collection of paintings given by the French King Louis Philippe, Francis I, King of the Two Sicilies, and Pope Leo XII. Here's what impresses me: Six solid tree trunks, lathed and plastered, were transformed into the building's huge Corinthian columns. St. Joseph's is open every day until 5:00 P.M. Admission is free, but donations are encouraged. Call (502) 348–3126.

Behind the cathedral is **Spalding Hall,** circa 1826, a large brick building that was originally part of Saint Joseph College, Seminary, and later Prep School. Two adjoining museums housed here are the **Bardstown Historical Museum** and the **Oscar Getz Museum of Whiskey History,** both free. Displays range from items like Jenny Lind's cape and Jesse James's hat to an original 1854 E. G. Booz bottle, which inspired the word *booze,* and a Carrie Nation exhibit. Hours from May through October are 9:00 A.M. to 5:00 P.M. Monday to Saturday and 1:00 to 5:00 P.M. Sunday. From November through April the museums open at 10:00 A.M. and close at 4:00 P.M., except on Sunday, when they are open from 1:00 to 4:00 P.M.

Think about the basis of homesteading—self-sufficiency. Now apply the concept to the visual arts and you will begin to appreciate Jim and Jeannette Cantrell. The **Bardstown Art Gallery,** downstairs in Spalding Hall, is a fine-art gallery, a framing shop, pottery and painting studios, a hand-set printing press operation, an office, a home, and a small book sales business, which boasts one of the country's most comprehensive collections of Thomas Merton's writings. That both Cantrells have a love of high quality is apparent in everything from Jim's treatment of light and reflections in his oils to Jeannette's hand-set letterpress gallery announcements. Jeannette curates group and solo shows in addition to displaying Jim's originals in oil, watercolor, pen and ink, and anything else that catches his eclectic eye. Beware: You'll be tempted to take something home.

It was by accident that Jeannette became a Merton expert. One of the monks at the nearby abbey asked if she wouldn't mind selling a few of Merton's books to tourists. She started with a few copies of *Seven Storey Mountain,* and now she carries a respectable line of Merton's out-of-print writings, valuable limited editions, related scholarly works, and cassettes of Merton himself reading from his works or just talking about such subjects as Rilke's poetry, silence, art, and beauty. Hours at the Bardstown Art Gallery are officially BY CHANCE or BY APPOINTMENT, but someone is usually there from 10:00 A.M. to 5:00 P.M. Monday through Saturday and from 1:00 to 5:00 P.M. Sunday. Contact the Cantrells by writing to P.O. Box 417, Bardstown 40004 or calling (502) 348–6488.

To visit Thomas Merton's residence, the ◆ **Abbey of Gethsemani,** oldest Cistercian monastery in the United States, follow Highway 31E south from Bardstown, veer left at Culvertown onto Highway 247, and watch for TRAPPISTS signs.

From the heart of Italy around A.D. 500, Saint Benedict developed a set of rules to help monks in a spiritually based community follow the example of Christ as closely as possible. These Trappist monks take vows to renounce the capacity to acquire and possess goods, to obey the house rules and the abbot's advice, and to remain celibate. Silence is encouraged but not required. "Enclosure," I've been told, "is enforced not so much to keep lay people out as to keep the monks in." But these monks do indulge in some wandering. Thomas Merton, quintessential ascetic aesthete monk from this abbey, was known to go "out" to lecture, to meet with other spiritual people, and occasionally to hear jazz. While visiting the abbey, I met a monk who travels to Owensboro for the barbecue festival. And the organist and composer Father Chrysogonus is a musical genius who often travels to Europe for research. No matter what else you think, their life choice is radical.

Economic survival is perhaps the greatest difference between early and modern cloisters. The seventy-six resident monks make and sell fruitcakes and three kinds of Port Salut Trappist cheese, a pungent, creamy, French-style aged cheese. Everyone takes part in all aspects of the work, from making cheese to doing dishes to answering the phone or laying sewer pipes. The slogan *Ora et Labora* means "prayer and work," but they don't have "all necessary things" on their 2,000-acre farm. They use hired help to raise the beef cattle and to do some construction and maintenance. Health care, for example, is sought in the secular world, including modern services such as weight loss centers.

**Abbey of Gethsmani**

Laypeople are welcome to join in parts of life at the abbey. Mass is always open, if you can make it at 6:15 A.M. on weekdays (the monks will have been awake for three hours by then), and there are a variety of other prayer services and vespers throughout the day. Sunday mass is at 10:30 A.M. in the main chapel, a long, narrow, modern building where the choir's chant reverberates as if produced in outer space. Gethsemani has a retreat house with thirty rooms that can be reserved for personal or group retreats. Women are welcome only during the first and third full weeks of each month, and men can make retreats during the second and fourth weeks. Call far in advance at (502) 549-3117. For more information or to order cheese, write Abbey of Gethsemani, Trappist 40051.

If you drive south from Bardstown on Highway 31E, you will arrive in the tiny town of New Haven. Downtown on Main Street the old train depot now houses the ✦**Kentucky Railway Museum,** where you can hop a train to Boston—that's *Bawston,* Kentucky—11 miles away on the old Louisville & Nashville Railroad's former Lebanon Branch. Members of the museum completely restored an L&N steam locomotive (No. 152) and the streamlined No. 32 of the former Monon, made in the late 1940s. When these babies pump by, you feel your heart making reply. From April through November, trips run between 10:00 A.M. and 4:00 P.M. on weekends, when the museum and gift shop are also open. In the summer it's open daily, except Monday. For exact fares, times, and dates contact the Kentucky Railway Museum, P.O. Box 240, New Haven 40051-0240, or call (502) 549-5470 or (800) 272-0152.

To visit one of the state's most famous and picturesque whiskey distilleries, take Highway 52 east from New Haven, or Highway 49 south from Bardstown, to Loretto; then take Highway 52 east until you see the sign on the left for **Maker's Mark Distillery.** Like the process, the facility is old. In 1953 Bill Samuels, Sr., bought the shabby country distillery where folks were accustomed to filling their own jugs straight from casks of whiskey in the Quart House. Now Maker's Mark is known around the world for its supersmooth bourbon (nicknamed "Kentucky champagne"). The distillery is open year-round, except on Saturdays in January and February. Free forty-minute tours are given between 10:30 A.M. and 3:30 P.M. Monday through Saturday and from 1:30 to 3:30 P.M. on Sunday. For more information, call (502) 865-2881.

In Loretto, take Highway 49 north, then veer right at a fork in the road onto Highway 152. You'll soon see the sign for **Loretto Motherhouse.** The Sisters of Loretto, founded in central Kentucky in 1812, was one of the first American religious communities of women. They moved here in 1824 from Little Loretto at nearby St. Charles. Near the entrance of the grounds is the restored cabin, circa 1808, of Father Charles Nerinckx, founder of the order. Going toward the cemetery you'll see one of the country's first outdoor Stations of the Seven Dolors, installed in 1911. On the east side of the drive, you'll see **Knobs Haven Retreat,** a center at which folks can reserve space for taking a serious, personal retreat. For rates and further information, contact Elaine Prevallet, S.L., Director, Knobs Haven, Nerinx 40049, or call (502) 865-2621.

## END OF THE ROAD

I have driven KY 1262, a winding country road off U.S. 460 between Georgetown and Frankfort, many times, but never with as much apprehension as on this dreary March morning in 1997. Normally this would be a pleasant drive, to one of my favorite Kentucky landmarks—the Switzer Covered Bridge. Each of Kentucky's remaining covered bridges is special. After all, including Switzer, there are only thirteen left in a state where there once were more than 400—but even within this exclusive group, Switzer stands out. An 1855 beauty with sawtooth entrance and small windows overlooking Elkhorn Creek, it had been beautifully restored in 1990, the centerpiece of a delightful little country park, the perfect place to fish or picnic on a sunny afternoon.

And now it might be gone.

Just a few days before, the worst flooding in decades had hit Central Kentucky. Among the devastation: Switzer was swept right off its foundation. My heart sank as I saw it crumpled against the bank, somewhat intact, but folded in upon itself. Others, who like me, didn't want to believe it without seeing it, roamed the banks. "My dad was born on that hill over there. We've always loved this bridge," one woman noted. "My church does its baptisms in the creek here. It just won't be the same without the bridge," said another.

There is a glimmer of hope. A lot of folks around here love Switzer Bridge, and almost immediately there was talk of lifting it and rebuilding it. It will take money, some say several hundred thousand dollars, and skills that may be even more precious: The last of the old-time bridge-builders, Louis Stockton Bower, died in 1995. So I can't really tell you how this story ends. I hope that next time you're in Central Kentucky, you'll drive up to Switzer to find out.

Next to the main church and convent, circa 1860–63, you'll notice a group of abstract sculptures in various media. This is the work of Jeanne Dueber, S.L., nun and artist in residence at Loretto. Her studio is in ◆ **Rhodes Hall Art Gallery**, at the north end of the driveway. Her work is amazing in its variety and feeling, and her exploration of form is almost religious. Large refined abstract sculptures in wood, resin, metal, and paper fill the big rooms. A large willow, struck by lightning, has been transformed into a powerful piece called "Tempest," in which Dueber strategically added heads and arms of a man and a woman in such a way that they seem to be sliding away from each other while reaching toward each other. Many pieces are playful, like a series on Pelé, the soccer star, or an academic charcoal drawing of a heavy, drooping nude woman entitled "Homage To Gravity." Pieces about Prometheus, ecstasy, companionship, and yoga positions accompany overtly religious work such as crucifixes for churches. If she's working in the first-floor studio and isn't too busy, tell her what you think. You can visit the gallery daily from 9:00 A.M. to 5:00 P.M. To buy a piece, just put your money in the slotted box by the stairs—a self-service fine-art gallery! Contact Jeanne Dueber, Rhodes Hall, Nerinx 40040, or call (502) 865–5811.

For local lodging head south on Highway 49 into Lebanon and check into the **Myrtledene Bed and Breakfast** at 370 North Spalding Avenue. The house is an 1833 formal brick affair with a colonial columned portico. Famous Confederate raider General John Hunt Morgan used Myrtledene for headquarters in 1862, and a year later, when he returned with the intention of destroying Lebanon, it was from here that he waved the white flag of truce. During his stay, Morgan rode his horse into the front door of Myrtledene and up the front steps; the hoofprints survived well into this century. A room with full breakfast costs $65 a night. Call (502) 692–2223 or (800) 391–1721 for reservations.

Since Lebanon is out of the way, you might be happy to know that the little town boasts a classy eating establishment at 157 West Main Street called **Henning's Restaurant** (502–692–6843). In addition to occupying a handsomely restored building in the historic district, the restaurant offers homemade soups, entrees, breads, and desserts, recommended by the locals.

Although there were once more than 400 covered bridges in Kentucky, there are now only thirteen. The **Mount Zion Bridge,** in the northwest corner of Washington County, is the only remaining example of two-span Burr Arch construction, and the longest in the state. It was almost lost recently before the county restabilized the piers and may yet be moved to a more accessible location. For now, the easiest way to see it is to get off the Blue Grass Parkway at exit 34 and go south on Highway 55; at Mooresville take Highway 458 north and

**Rhodes Hall Art Gallery**

## LLAMALLAND

Most people think of horses when they think of the Bluegrass, but at **Seldon Scene Farm,** 1710 Watts Ferry Road in Woodford County (606–873–1622), animal lovers Lindy and Paul Huber offer close encounters with other kinds of fascinating beasts. Their "Llama Trek," is a guided picnic hike along scenic trails and meadows overlooking the Kentucky River in the scenic Palisades area. You don't ride the llamas. Instead, you lead, and your friendly llama carries lunch fixings and other gear. A typical four-hour trek includes a 2- to 3-mile hike, a gourmet lunch grilled in the open air (steak, or chicken, or even emu, if you're daring enough), and a tour of the farm, home to about 20 llamas, 30 alpacas, a yak, miniature donkeys, goats, and reindeer. A trek costs $40 per adult, $10 for children under 12; the trek is not advised for children younger than 6 because of the distance covered. Families with younger children would probably enjoy the hourlong animal tour, $5 per person. Call in advance to schedule either.

watch for the bridge on the left spanning the Beech Fork Creek. The bridge is closed to traffic, but you can walk through it.

Get back to Highway 55 and go north less than a mile; turn south on Highway 529 and bear left at the next T in the road. From the Bluegrass Parkway, take exit 42 onto Route 555 and turn left; go about 15 miles to the first light and turn right onto Highway 150. Watch for the sign advertising **Glenmar Plantation Bed and Breakfast.** This museumlike, 1785 vintage brick country home, possibly the oldest brick home in Kentucky, is about as cozy a mansion as one could hope for. There are twenty rooms, six bathrooms, and eight fireplaces (Tolstoy would be right at home). In the plantation tradition, Glenmar is a working, 300-acre farm, sporting llamas, buffalo, and other exotic animals and a large pumpkin patch. Guests can look forward to a hearty country breakfast served by candlelight in the morning. In the summer or whenever the inn is full, the host, Kenny Mandell, brings in live entertainment for guests, everything from musicians to dancers to magicians. Write: 2444 Valley Hill Road, Springfield 40069 or call (606) 284-7791 or (800) 828-3330.

Like nearby Hodgenville (covered in the South Central Kentucky chapter), central Washington County is a repository of sites and stories connected to Abraham Lincoln. Abe's parents, Thomas Lincoln and Nancy Hanks, were from this area, and several of their family buildings are restored or replicated. For details, go by the **Lincoln Homestead State Park** at the intersection of Highways 438 and 528, just 5 miles north of Springfield off Highway 150. An eighteen-hole golf course has been built on old Mordecai Lincoln's land, and I'll bet he's rolling over violently in his grave. The park also has several log structures, such as the original Berry Home where Nancy Hanks lived when she and Thomas were courting. The park is open May to September from 8:00 A.M. to 6:00 P.M. and on weekends in October. Ask at the park for a map of the "Lincoln Heritage Trail." For more information, call (606) 336-7461.

In downtown Springfield, notice the **Washington County Courthouse** on Main Street (606-336-3471). Built in 1816, it is the oldest courthouse still in use in Kentucky. Records in the files, including the marriage certificate of Abraham Lincoln's parents, date back to 1792. If court isn't in session, look at copies of this and other documents hanging on the walls. Open 8:30 A.M. to 4:30 P.M. Monday through Friday and 9:00 A.M. to noon Saturday.

**Susie's Restaurant** (606-336-7975), near the courthouse, is the quintessential small-town cafe, with tables full of hot "country cooking" and the air filled with the latest local news. It's open 5:00 A.M. to 2:00 P.M. daily.

The **Maple Hill Manor Bed and Breakfast** and gift shop is 2¹/2 miles out of town to the east on Highway 150 (Perryville Road). The house is a striking antebellum Greek Revival mansion, circa 1851. Bob and Kay Carroll have kept this place as fancy as it ought to be and added more than the usual trappings for guests, like a Jacuzzi in the honeymoon room and grills on the patio. Call (606) 336-3075 for reservations.

# MORE GOOD LODGING

**BARDSTOWN**
**Beautiful Dreamer Bed & Breakfast,** 440 East Stephen Foster

Avenue; (502) 348-4004 or (800) 811-8312. A new home built in classic Federal style, across from My Old Kentucky Home. $79 to $99 per night.

**Hampton Inn Bardstown,** 985 Chambers Boulevard; (502) 349-0100 or (800) HAMPTON. Newer motel with pool. About $65 per night.

**Jailer's Inn,** 111 West Stephen Foster Avenue; (502) 348-5551 or (800) 948-5551. Renovated historic jail, with elegant Jacuzzi suites and one lightheartedly decorated "cell room." $65 to $95 per night.

### NEW HAVEN

**Sherwood Inn,** 138 South Main Street; (502) 549-3386. Bed and breakfast in a restored railroad hotel next to the Kentucky Railway Museum. About $50 per night.

## MORE FUN PLACES TO EAT

### BARDSTOWN

**Bardstonian Restaurant,** 521 North Third Street; (502) 349-1404. An inventive approach to traditional regional cooking. Homemade soups and bread. Lunch and dinner. Closed Monday.

**Dagwood's,** 204 North Third Street; (502) 348-4029. A varied menu for lunch and dinner in a casual setting.

**Kurtz Restaurant,** 418 East Stephen Foster Avenue; (502) 348-8964. Always a soup/sandwich/pie special for lunch; country and regional cooking for dinner.

### NEW HAVEN

**Sherwood Inn,** 138 South Main Street; (502) 549-3386. Dinner served Wednesday through Saturday.

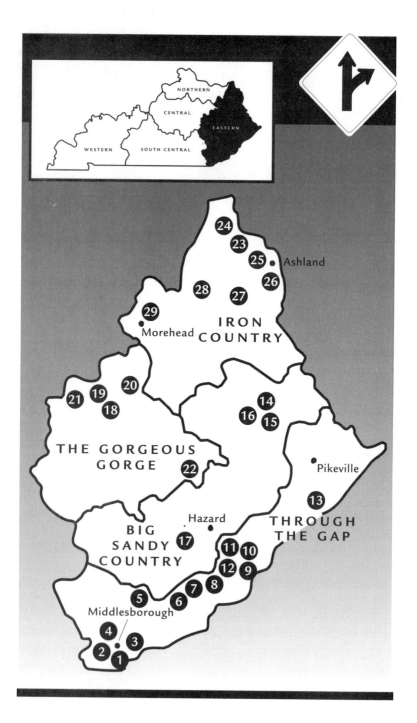

# EASTERN KENTUCKY

1. Cumberland Gap National Historic Park
2. Ridge Runner Bed and Breakfast
3. Lockheed P-38F Lightning restoration
4. Hemlock Garden Trail
5. Red Bird Mission Crafts
6. The Little Shepherd Trail
7. Pine Mountain Settlement School
8. Kingdom Come State Park
9. Bad Branch Nature Preserve
10. Appalshop
11. C. B. Caudill Store
12. Lilley Cornett Woods
13. Breaks Interstate Park
14. Butcher Hollow
15. Jenny Wiley State Resort Park
16. Mountain Arts Center
17. Frontier Nursing Service
18. Natural Bridge State Resort Park
19. Kentucky Reptile Zoo
20. Swamp Valley Store and Museum
21. Furnace Mountain, Inc.
22. Robinson Forest
23. Jesse Stuart State Nature Preserve
24. Bennett's Mill Bridge
25. Kentucky Highlands Museum
26. Paramount Arts Center
27. Mount Savage Furnace
28. Carter Caves State Resort Park
29. Kentucky Folk Art Center

# EASTERN KENTUCKY

Most of North America is inhabited by a wild soup of dissenters' descendants, but what makes eastern Kentucky different is the mountains.

The Appalachian Mountains are a long, beautiful line of steep, nearly impregnable rock that has always tended to keep outsiders out and insiders in. Although the Appalachian culture initially strikes outsiders as foreign, visiting can have the strong allure of a homecoming, in part because your roots may be in European cultures that are better preserved here than anywhere else in the big melting pot. The isolation has also caused east Kentuckians to live close to the land, close to one another, and to survive self-sufficiently. As you meet people, listen to the language of this region, the beautiful phrases loaded with humor, knowledge of quirky human nature, and sensitivity to the cycles of the natural world.

There are opportunities in this region to expose yourself to very fine traditional craftsmanship by meeting individual artists or craftspeople and by visiting craft cooperatives where knowledge and tools are being shared with those who want to take the baton. Music and dance, for which mountaineers have always been admired, have developed in fascinating ways and play an important role in life in this region. Festivals and community dances, which are always open to visitors, are good events to attend if you want to get an authentic taste of the music here. In addition to music, the mountains themselves can soothe the soul.

I have a wonderful recent memory of traveling through the mountains at the end of a long, hot day and stopping on a bridge where a "passel" of people had gathered. Below, by the side of a wide brook, a small revival was in progress. Babies were being passed from lap to lap and people of all ages were sitting in folding chairs by the little stage, clapping and singing. A sweet hymn in an irresistible minor key rising just above the constant tumble of the water calmed me and opened my eyes to the changing mountains, rosy in the last light of the setting sun. Even in the heat of summer, a mist gathers in the folds and hollows of the land and baptizes everyone equally, even passersby.

# THROUGH THE GAP

Dr. Thomas Walker was hired by Virginia's Loyal Land Company to go west in search of fertile settling land. In 1750 when Walker found the only natural route west, a divide he named Cumberland Gap, he built a small cabin to claim the territory, mapped the route, and went home. You can visit a replica of Walker's crude cabin at the **Dr. Thomas Walker State Shrine** on Highway 459 off Highway 25E just southeast of Barbourville (606-546-4400). Though they missed reaching the Bluegrass region by just a few days of traveling, they did succeed in blazing a trail through the mountains for more than 300,000 pioneers to roll toward a new life in the West.

## TRUE BLUE

Between 1750 and 1783, some 12,000 settlers had entered Kentucky through the Cumberland Gap.

The 20,000 acres of ◆ **Cumberland Gap National Historic Park,** off Highway 25E south of Middlesborough, include the 800-foot natural break in the Cumberland Mountains through which Native Americans and, later, Daniel Boone and other settlers entered Kentucky. Go to Pinnacle Overlook and you can see three states, as well as the twin tunnels that go 4,600 feet through the mountain to connect Kentucky and Tennessee. Seventeen years in the making, the tunnels finally opened in 1996, replacing a stretch of Highway 25E so treacherous that it was known as "Massacre Mountain."

More than 50 miles of trails wind through the park, but one of the most interesting is the Ridge Trail on Brush Mountain, which leads to the **Hensley Settlement,** a restored cluster of farms and houses inhabited from 1903 until 1951. To drive, take the Brownies Creek Road from Cubbage, or take a shuttle from the visitors' center in Middlesborough. For all park information, stop by the center during business hours or call (606) 248-2817.

Well-researched historic tours by private guides Tom and Barbara Shattuck of the **Wilderness Road Tours** are available daily. Make reservations by writing them at 224 Greenwood Road, Middlesborough 40965, or calling (606) 248-2626. The 2½-hour Cumberland Gap Area tour, which is given from an air-conditioned van, can begin from a number of regular starting points in the area or from wherever you're staying locally. The guides have distilled the area's dramatic history down into memorable narratives, while the countryside speaks eloquently for itself as you watch it flow by your window.

Middlesborough is just north of the gap, outside the national park, in a circular basin that was probably formed between 30 million and 300 million years ago by a large meteor that disintegrated or was blown back into space upon impact. Another possibility is that the cusp was formed by the collapse of an underground cavern, since no meteor fragments have been found. Coal, on the other hand, is everywhere and at the heart of the recent history of the area. The Bell County Chamber of Commerce on North Twentieth Street is housed in a building faced with forty tons of bituminous coal. Next door is **The Coal House Museum,** a little open-air collection of mining artifacts—old mine train cars, headlamps, drill bits, and photos. Ask about the **Cumberland Mountain Fall Festival,** which is held annually in Middlesborough during late October as a celebration of the area's English heritage. The event that will knock your socks off is the Official Kentucky State Banjo Playing Championship. Call (606) 248-1075.

Follow North Twentieth Street to the top of the hill, turn left on Edgewood, right onto Arthur Heights, and left when the road comes to the edge of the cliff. The second house on the left is the ◆ **Ridge Runner Bed and Breakfast,** a twenty-room grand Victorian home built in the early 1890s especially for the secretary-treasurer of the American Association, the English company that developed the town. The street, too, is named after Alexander Arthur, Middlesborough's founder. The Ridge Runner has four rooms available for between $55 and $65 per night. A tornado that narrowly missed the house in the late 1980s managed to clear the trees from the front hillside, leaving an open view of the town below. Irma Gall and Sue Richards, the two women who own and run the place are involved in a fascinating community center/clinic/mission in Stinking Creek, Knox County. Ask them about the history of the center and their continuing work there—great stories. Call (606) 248-4299 for reservations.

**Miracle Mountain Crafts** is an education and a delight. Go north of Middlesborough about 5 miles on Highway 25E; just north of a bridge and just south of the road's junction with Highway 188 is a small house on the right sitting by itself. James Miracle (pronounced MY-ra-cle) is in his wood shop all day, every day but Sunday. He loves his work and he'll take time to talk. Since 1967 when the Smithsonian discovered the handy Miracle family, James has been busy making expressive wooden animals, chairs, dulcimers, and myriad toys, the most popular of which is the "limberjack," a jointed

**TRUE BLUE**

Kentucky has more waterways than any state except Alaska.

puppet that dances when you bounce it on a thin board tucked under your leg. Split oak for chair bottoms, yellow poplar for small animals—all come from his farm. When an out-of-state customer called to order the biggest dough bowl James could make, he cranked out a massive 28-by-43-by-10-inch yellow poplar bowl, big enough to satisfy even amazon bakers. To place an order write James Miracle, Route 2, Box 151, Middlesborough 40965. To visit, call (606) 248-2971 or just surprise him.

With genius and fine craftsmanship in mind, stop by the Bell County Airport, located just 2 blocks off Cumberland Avenue on the west side of Middlesborough, where Bob Cardin and his crew of mechanics are doing a full ◆ **Lockheed P-38F Lightning restoration.** This World War II fighter plane was the fourth in a formation of six Lightnings that made forced landings on a remote glacier in Greenland on July 15, 1942, because they ran out of fuel. For fifty years the planes were buried deeper and deeper under glacial snow and ice until Pat Epps, the owner of Epps Aviation at Atlanta's DeKalb-Peachtree Airport; Richard Taylor, an Atlanta architect; and a group of technical specialists formed the Greenland Expedition Society in order to find and retrieve a plane. The story of the expedition is amazing. Over a three-year period, the crew located the planes, then dug through 268 feet of glacier with a huge hole-melting device designed just for this project, then carefully removed the plane, part by part, and flew it to a hangar in Middlesborough. Financially supported by a Middlesborough businessman (and now, about fifty corporate sponsors), the restoration has been ongoing since October 1992. After it is completed—in late 1998 or early 1999, Cardin expects—the plan is to fly the original mission route to England. Visitors are welcome to watch the work in progress weekdays from 8:00 A.M. to 5:00 P.M. Admission is free. When the plane is done, there still will be only six P-38Fs flying in the world.

Between Middlesborough and Pineville are the **Kentucky Ridge State Forest** and the **Pine Mountain State Resort Park,** both of which have entrances off Highway 25E. Follow signs to the Herndon J. Evans Lodge at the top of the mountain, where you can get trail maps and park information, or call (606) 337–3066. At the park's nature center, notice what looks like a petrified tree trunk by the entrance. The trunk was found at a strip mine in the northwest Bell County. The tree, which may be 300 million years old, grew in a swampy area and was buried in flood sediments, which caused it to rot. Over the course of a few million years, sand percolated through the cavity and hardened, making a fossilized sandstone cast of the tree.

One of the most special trails in the whole state park system is the ◆ **Hemlock Garden Trail** through a 782-acre area protected by the Nature Preserves system. The Hemlock Garden is a ravine featuring massive hemlocks, tulip poplars, beech trees, and a beautiful mountain brook. On the southwestern boundary of the park, it can be reached on the Laurel Cove Trail or the Rock Hotel Trail. Linger as long as you are able. After all, how often are you in the presence of living beings more than 200 years old?

During the last weekend in May, the **Mountain Laurel Festival** is held to celebrate the blooming of the much-loved mountain flower. The whole event is held in the Laurel Cove Amphitheater, a beautiful natural stage that seats more than 3,000 people, and culminates in the crowning of a Mountain Laurel Queen. **The Great American Dulcimer Festival** is also held outdoors during the third or fourth weekend of September. This is a wonderful, small festival during which dulcimer makers sell, demonstrate, and teach in booths during the day. At night spectators wrap up in quilts under the stars and watch some of the best performers play on a stage behind a reflective pond. Styles range from traditional to classical, pop, big band, and country rock, all played on lap or hammered dulcimers.

From within Pine Mountain State Park, go west on Highway 190 toward Frakes. Along the way, in Chenoa, stop by **Kathy's Needle and Thread** to see traditional quilting in action. The large quilting frames hang from the ceiling in the old way and are lowered to chair height for work. Most work is commissioned, but there are always finished pieces for sale. If you have a quilt top tucked away in the attic and would like to sleep under it, contact Kathy Jones at (606) 337-6753. Hours are Monday through Friday from 9:00 A.M. to 5:00 P.M. Write Kathy's Needle and Thread, Route 2, Box 115, Pineville 40977.

Just west of Chenoa in Frakes is the **Henderson Settlement,** a United Methodist ministry started in 1925 as a school and community outreach center. Now Henderson Settlement is a multipurpose community service facility and the only Methodist mission in the country with an agricultural development program—1,300 acres of land, livestock, orchards, gardens, and a big community greenhouse. The old high school houses a library, offices, and a weaving room where people can learn and pursue the craft. Weavings and other locally made crafts are sold in **Log House Craft Shop** (606-337-5823). Visitors are welcome to tour the place or to come for an extended stay for a retreat or work camp. Call ahead for reservations at (606) 337-3613.

## TRUE BLUE

Among the country music stars from eastern Kentucky are Billy Ray Cyrus from Greenup County; the Judds from Ashland; Tom T. Hall from Carter County; Keith Whitley from Elliot County; Lorretta Lynn and Crystal Gayle from Johnson County; and Dwight Yoakum from Floyd County.

The Red Bird Mission in Beverly is another similar United Methodist mission complex with a school, hospital, community outreach program, work camps, and a craft shop. From Pineville, follow Highway 66 north for 26 miles. From the Daniel Boone Parkway, take exit 34 and go south on Highway 66 into town. Directly across the street from the mission hospital is ◆ **Red Bird Mission Crafts,** in operation since 1921. The area craftspeople represented there are especially skilled at making hickory bark furniture, exquisite willow baskets, and hand-woven rugs. Hours are 10:00 A.M. to 4:00 P.M. Monday through Saturday. You can reach the craft shop at (606) 598-2709.

Head northeast on Highway 119 to Harlan, a little mountain town populated primarily by people of Welsh descent. Natives say that because the Welsh have always been fantastic vocalists, it's no surprise that Harlan's fame is musical. **The Harlan Boys' Choir,** an all-male, award-winning choir, received national acclaim after performing at the inauguration of President George Bush. What most people don't know is that the choir was an offshoot of a 1945 girls' group called The Harlan Musettes, now under the direction of Marilyn Schraeder (606-573-3577). David Davies (606-573-3559) directs the boys, who range from third grade through high school. The repertoire is classical and the sound exquisite. Stop by the school to catch a rehearsal or call one of the directors for the performance schedule.

Another Harlan original is the **Poke Sallet Festival,** held during the last week in June. The festival affords you plenty of opportunities to eat poke sallet, barbecued chicken, corn pone, and buttermilk—a mountain meal if ever there was one. Poke sallet is a cold salad of very young poke plant leaves (which are bitter and mildly poisonous when the plant is several months older); the leaves are cooked way down, like turnip greens, and have a flavor similar to asparagus. They're said to have healing powers. Call (606) 573-4717 for more information on the festival.

Head north of Harlan on Highway 421, straight up the mountain. At the summit of Pine Mountain you'll see a sign for ◆ **The Little Shepherd Trail,** a 38-mile graveled trail that runs along the ridge of the 2,800-foot Black Mountain all the way to Whitesburg. Midway is the Kingdom Come State Park, near Cumberland. It's recommended that you use a four-wheel-drive vehicle, walk, take horses, or ride mountain bikes on the trail.

On the other side of Pine Mountain, make a hard right onto Highway 221, go east "a far piece" (in this case, about 10 miles) and turn onto Highway 510, then immediately into the driveway of the ◆ **Pine Mountain Settlement School** (606-558-3571). The history of the place begins with an early settler named William Creech, who recognized the need for a school based on what he knew of a settlement school in Hindman. That school was founded by Katherine Pettit, who, in turn, based her ideas on Jane Addams's work in urban settings. From 1913 until 1972 the Pine Mountain Settlement School was a remarkably wholesome and successful school, community center, and medical facility.

After the regular school closed in 1972, the folks at Pine Mountain decided to flow with the real needs of the community, and it became an environmental education center. Good timing—eastern Kentucky was and is suffering massive environmental exploitation in a nation tending toward overconsumption, waste of resources, overpopulation, and a general lack of concern for and understanding of the fragile, crucial cycles of the natural world. More than 2,000 students a year come for hands-on, outdoor learning. A long waiting list indicates that there is greater need than this one small institution can fill. Write for more information: Pine Mountain Settlement School, Pine Mountain 40810. Visitors are welcome to tour the fascinating campus daily from 8:00 A.M. to 8:00 P.M.

The next major town to the east is Cumberland. Downtown on West Main Street, across from the Public Library, is the **Poor Fork Arts and Craft Guild,** a shop for more than seventy-five local members who make various craft items—everything from quilts to dulcimers to wooden trains. A trend throughout this region is to make things out of coal. A painter may put a bright barnyard scene on the face of a big chunk of coal, and a carver may make small sculptures of miners from the dark, black, familiar material. Hours are 10:00 A.M. to 5:00 P.M. Monday through Saturday. Call (606) 589-2496.

Directly above Cumberland is the ♦ **Kingdom Come State Park** (606-589-2479). Here is another access point to the Little Shepherd Trail. The trail and the park are named after John Fox, Jr.'s famous novel about Appalachian life, *The Little Shepherd of Kingdom Come.* In 1903 it was the first American novel to sell over one million copies. This park is known for its incredible vistas and rich mountain woodlands. Two of the most spectacular sites are the Log Rock, a natural rock arch that looks like a log, and Raven Rock, a huge hunk of stone that thrusts some 290 feet into the air and has at its base a capacious sand cave, which is used for performances. Stop by the visitors center for trail maps.

Still heading east along the gap line, Highway 119 leads to Letcher County. As you wind along the Cumberland River bottom for about 15 miles, watch for Highway 806, which leads to a little community called Eolia. Nestled between Pine and Black Mountains, the two highest in Kentucky, Eolia gets its name from the Indian word meaning "valley of the winds." About 2 miles from Highway 119 on 806, look for the **Valley of the Winds Art Gallery** (606-633-8652), the studio and sales gallery of a family of artists, Jeff and Sharman Chapman-Crane and their young son Evan. Sharman constructs wall pieces using natural and recycled materials; she uses images of endangered animals in her work and often writes accompanying poems. Jeff does sensitive, realistic portraits of local Appalachian people and places. A spare portrait of an old man smoking in his chair has the powerful ability to take one's mind into a home and a world, almost to the point of making the viewer feel as if he or she is intruding. Original works as well as prints of simple, expressive line drawings that make great note cards, are for sale. Visitors are welcome; the gallery is open by chance on most weekdays and many weekends.

Get back on Highway 119 and head east 1 mile to Highway 932 on the right (east) side of the road. Turn and go 1.7 miles to the entrance of the ❖ **Bad Branch Nature Preserve** (502-573-2886) on the left. This place is so special that I barely have the nerve to include it here, but if you visit, you must promise to treat it with great care, to soak it into your soul, and to support nature preserves here and everywhere in any way that you are able. This gorge, which is rimmed by hundred-foot cliffs, is home to a very unique ecosystem of rare plant species and breathtaking wildflowers. The trail leads you through a hemlock and rhododendron kingdom along some of the only clean, pure water you're going to see. At the end is a spectacular, 60-foot waterfall arching over the edge of a sandstone cliff. Open sunrise to sunset daily.

Get back on Highway 119 again and head over Pine Mountain into **Whitesburg.** Be sure to stop at one of the high lookout points, where you can get a more abstract sense of the texture and shape of the land. You'll also get a very nonabstract sense of the meaning of "mountaintop removal," a method of strip mining coal by taking off whatever is above it, usually the entire top of a mountain. With this panorama before you, pay mental tribute to one of Letcher County's great native sons, the late Harry M. Caudill: writer, teacher, lawyer, politician, and outspoken activist in Appalachian social and economic issues. His historical writings, including *Night Comes to the Cumberlands* and *Theirs Be the Power,* are disturbing and powerful books about the troubled power relations in these mountains. In his storyteller (preserver) mode, Caudill has written a number of honest, intimate portraits of his people in books such as *The Mountain the Miner and the Lord.*

In downtown Whitesburg, next to the North Fork of the Kentucky River, is the ❖**Appalshop** building, which is open to visitors. Appalshop is a community-oriented, not-for-profit arts and education center working to preserve traditional culture and history and to encourage conscientious involvement in contemporary arts and social issues. Appalshop is best known for making powerful documentaries about folk-culture figures and about social activism in

> ## TRUE BLUE
> Kentucky's highest point is Black Mountain, off Highway 160 near Benham: 4,145 feet.

Appalachia. While visiting, you can ask to watch almost any of their videos—for example, "On Our Own Land," about the history and demise of the broad form deed in Kentucky, or "Chairmaker," about the life and work of Dewey Thompson, a furniture maker from Sugarloaf Hollow. The Headwaters Television series is a weekly broadcast of these documentaries on public television.

June Appal Recordings, Appalshop's own record label, also has made a massive cultural contribution by recording Appalachian musicians and storytellers, famous and obscure, ranging from contemporary folk-dulcimer artists, such as John McCutcheon, and traditional mountain banjo players, such as Morgan Sexton (who won a National Heritage Award from the National Endowment for the Arts in 1990), to mountain storytellers, including Ray Hicks. Appalshop's Roadside Theatre is a small theater and storytelling troupe that delights and instructs folks all over the region. Appalshop also runs a community radio station, WMMT 88.7 FM, to which you are hereby commanded to tune in while in the area. Like the river,

Appalshop's efforts flow out into the whole Kentucky-Virginia area, giving us all an education and a renewed sense of pride and hope. For literature and catalogs, write: Appalshop, 306 Madison Street, Whitesburg 41858, or call (606) 633-0108.

Have a meal downtown at the **Courthouse Café** (606-633-5859), a charming little restaurant that serves healthy, delicious lunches and dinners made from scratch—baked turkey breast sandwiches, large salads, and ever-changing special meals. Josephine Richardson, one of the owners, acts as dealer for a number of local artists and craftspeople. The quilts, wood carvings, paintings, and photographs she has on display in the restaurant are for sale. Hours are 10:30 A.M. to 8:30 P.M. Monday through Friday. Read through a copy of the local paper, *The Mountain Eagle*. There's a very democratic section, usually on page B4, called "Speak Your Piece," for which you anonymously call an answering machine and the editor prints, verbatim, what you say. The "pieces" range from heated discussions about the latest war in the Persian Gulf or elsewhere to layoffs at the coal mines to "I hate my boyfriend's guts and I hope he knows it."

One of the woodcarvers who is represented at the Courthouse Café and on many a desk at Appalshop is **James Bloomer.** From downtown take Highway 931 south through Whitco and turn right (west) on Highway 588. You'll see his little red shop in front of his white frame house in a very deep curve in the road. Most of his work is in buckeye, a wood that is almost white at the carving stage but gets lovely gray streaks as it ages and dries. He carves all sorts of animals, but highly detailed decoys are his forte. You should call ahead at (606) 633-4279.

On the west side of the county in a community called Blackey is an area museum disguised as a general store, the ◆ **C. B. Caudill Store** (606-633-7738). From Whitesburg, take Highway 15 north, then turn on Highway 7 south toward Isom. The store is just past Blackey on the right. There are usually a few fellows chatting on the big front porch. The store, which opened in 1933, is now owned by Joe Begley, an upbeat, dedicated activist who has used his store to unite diverse groups over issues such as the 77th Strip Mining Bill and the area health clinic. "Everyone should be a politician," he says. "Even Christ was a protester, and a strong one at that." But the walls of the store tell some of their own stories. Joe has intentionally collected mining artifacts, everything from hats, boots, lights, and tools to scrip, old mine company currency useful only within the mining camps. His unintentional collections are amusing—scan the shelves for things like fifty-year-old tubes of hair-restoration creme.

Ask Joe Begley or the folks at Appalshop about the **Carcassonne Dance.** Once or twice a month at the Carcassonne community center, people get together for a big square dance, the traditional kind with a caller and usually a live "house" band. Mountain squares and contra lines are so unique that even if you're an experienced country dancer, this will be a challenge. Just listen and have fun. From C. B. Caudill Store, stay on Highway 7 for a few hundred yards and turn right on the first road on the right, Elk Creek Road. Follow the pavement to the very top of the mountain.

Back on Highway 7, go west past Blackey and the Caudill Store, turn south on Highway 1103, and follow the signs to the ◈ **Lilley Cornett Woods.** Because this is one of the only old-growth forests in the state, it is of great value to ecological researchers and to beauty addicts alike. The wise and eccentric Lilley Cornett purchased this land just after World War I and did not allow any live timber, except for blighted chestnuts, to be cut. His children continued the tradition and finally, in 1969, the state purchased the

**TRUE BLUE**

Some of the trees in Lilley Cornett Woods pre-date the arrival of the Pilgrims in America in 1620.

land and continues to preserve it. Time is the key. Old-growth forests are characterized by a large number of trees that are more than 200 years old, many of which are of great commercial value.

In order to protect the forest, visitors are not allowed to hike without a guide. The guides, however, are real treats, and they will take you out whenever you arrive. You'll learn more in an hour hiking with these folks than you could in a year reading dendrology books. Come between 9:00 A.M. and 5:00 P.M. From May 15 to August 15 the woods are open daily, and in April, May, September, and October, they are open only on weekends. Contact: Superintendent, Lilley Cornett Woods, HC 63, Box 2710, Skyline 41851, or call (606) 633-5828.

On the east end of Letcher County, very near the Virginia border on Highway 119 North, is a town called Jenkins, originally a mining camp built by Consolidation Coal Company—note the rows of identical houses. On the east side of town, watch on the left for **Whitaker Music Store,** an old, rundown music store with a surprising collection of old albums, sheet music, books, and a few instruments. The rock 'n' roll albums are funny, but there are some valuable items in Ervin Whitaker's country music collection. The store is open from 9:00 A.M. to 5:00 P.M., Monday through Saturday.

Leaving Jenkins to the east on Highway 119, you'll soon be entering Pike County, the largest county in the state. South of Pikeville, in the center of the county on Highway 1789, is **Fishtrap Lake,** a large lake known for its largemouth bass, bluegill, and crappie. Directly south of Fishtrap Lake on the state border with Virginia is the ◆ **Breaks Interstate Park,** where the Russell Fork River, a tributary of the Big Sandy, has done its darndest to imitate the Grand Canyon. For more than 5 miles, the river canyon has high jagged walls, some exceeding 1,600 feet in height. Unlike the Grand Canyon, this gorge is lush and tree covered. It is believed to have been formed primarily during the late Paleozoic era, some 250 million years ago. The park has four fantastic overlooks, one of which is at the Rhododendron Lodge and Restaurant. Contact: Breaks Interstate Park, P. O. Box 100, Breaks, VA 24607, or call (540) 865-4413.

Pike County is known nationally as the locale of the infamous Hatfield-McCoy feud, a violent interfamily vendetta that began during the Civil War and was sustained almost until the turn of the century. Buried in Pikeville in the **Dils Cemetery** are several major figures in the feud on the McCoy side. This cemetery also was the first in eastern Kentucky to be racially integrated. In 1996, a Pikeville College professor began an inventory of the African American graves; since then, markers have been placed on many that had no headstones. The City of Pikeville has leased the cemetery from Dils family descendants, and it is open year-round during daylight hours. Take the Bypass Road to the east side of town; the cemetery is just north of the Bypass's split with Highway 1460 on the east side of the road. For more information, contact the Pikeville

Tourism Commission at (606) 432-5063.

Much is made of the **Pikeville Cut-Thru,** a massive rerouting of highways, railroads, and rivers on the west side of town. After fourteen years of labor, millions of dollars, and a whole lot of blasted and hauled rock and dirt, the cut-through was completed in 1987. You have to see it to believe it. For the best view, take the Bypass Road to the northwest side of town, turn uphill on Oak Lane, and curve around to Cedar Drive. For more information on this huge project, stop by the Pikeville Tourism Office at 101 Huffman Avenue between 8:30 A.M. and 4:30 P.M. Monday through Friday or call (606) 432-5063.

# MORE GOOD LODGING
## MIDDLESBOROUGH
**Best Western Inn,** 1623 East Cumberland; (606) 248-5630. $44 and up.

## PIKEVILLE
**Daniel Boone Motor Inn,** Highway 23 North; (606) 432-0365. $40 and up.

**Days Inn,** Highway 23 South; (606) 432-0314. $49 and up.

## BENHAM
**School House Inn,** 100 Central Avenue; (606) 848-3000. Country inn in restored school building. $60 to $85.

# MORE FUN PLACES TO EAT
## MIDDLESBOROUGH
**J. Milton's Steakhouse,** Highway 25 East; (606) 248-0458. Steaks, chicken, and seafood.

## PIKEVILLE
**Pine Mountain State Resort Park,** Highway 25 East; (606) 337-3066. Varied menu including traditional Kentucky dishes.

## CUMBERLAND GAP, TN
**Ye Olde Tea and Coffee Shop,** 529 Colwyn Street; (423) 869-4844. Mountain view.

# BIG SANDY COUNTRY

A few miles west of Paintsville off Highway 40, you can visit **Mountain HomePlace** (606-297-1850) and get a sense of what farm life in the mountains was like in the mid-1800s. Set up as a living history farm, the complex includes a home, crib barns, horse-powered gristmill, chicken house, blacksmith shop, and small school. As you walk through, you'll see people going about the activities of daily life, from tending the garden to preparing and eating their daily supper. Mountain HomePlace is open Wednesday through Saturday from 9:00 A.M. to 5:00 P.M. and Sunday from 1:00 to 5:00 P.M. Admission is $5.00 for adults, $3.00 for children.

Johnson County's history involves some outstanding women. Country music stars Crystal Gayle and Loretta Lynn are both Johnson County natives. Loretta Lynn was born and raised in a beautiful setting in ◆ **Butcher Hollow,** near Van Lear. From Paintsville, take Highway 23 south to Highway 302; turn east and follow the signs to the board-and-batten cabin where she lived. The place was rebuilt for the filming of the 1980 movie *Coal Miner's Daughter,* a biography of the singer's difficult but triumphant life. Remnants of an orchard make the place feel authentic. Stop by Webb's Grocery (606-789-3397), owned by Loretta Lynn's brother Herman Webb if you want to take a tour. They're given year-round, most every day.

In Van Lear's tiny downtown in the former Consolidated Coal Company office building is the **Van Lear Historical Society Museum.** If you haven't yet seen a real-life mining camp, check out the model of a typical company town in the museum. Hours are 9:00 A.M. to 3:00 P.M. Monday through Saturday from March through November. Admission is free.

Another legendary woman is Jenny Wiley, an early settler of the Big Sandy area who survived a remarkably tragic capture by Shawnee Indians and subsequently escaped. She died at seventy-one and is buried in a cemetery 5 miles south of Paintsville on Highway 23 near the site of **Harmon Station,** the first white settlement in eastern Kentucky. Mathias Harmon was one of the hunter–Indian fighters now known as "Long Hunters" because of the length of their sojourns in the wilderness. In 1750 he and his companions built a fortlike log hunting lodge on this site; in the late 1780s they built a more permanent blockhouse.

The trail that Wiley and the Indians followed was once well worn and cleared, but it had disappeared into the undergrowth until recently. The 180-mile **Jenny Wiley Trail** has been restored and is now marked for hikers. You can access the trail from Greenbo Lake, Carter Caves, and Jenny Wiley state parks. If you want to hike the whole thing, you can start in South Portsmouth (Greenup County) and travel south. The best way to see eastern Kentucky is on foot, and this trail roughly traces the Pottsville escarpment and runs the gamut of sites; you see lush gorges, open farmland, strip mines, mountain towns, and miles and miles of woods. For more information on the Jenny Wiley Trail, contact the ◆ **Jenny Wiley State Resort Park** (800-325-0142 or 606-886-2711) between Paintsville and Prestonsburg on Highway 3, just east of Highway 23/460 on **Dewey Lake,** a clear lake famous for its white bass run (April only).

The **Jenny Wiley Summer Music Theatre** presents one very colorful, musical version of the legendary Jenny Wiley story in addition to three Broadway musicals, which have included *Hello, Dolly* and *The Sound of Music.* You can take in a different performance every night for four nights in a row. The outdoor performances are at the Jenny Wiley State Resort Park in an amphitheater open from late June through mid-August, Tuesday through Sunday, with curtain time at 8:00 P.M. *The Jenny Wiley Story* is performed free on Wednesday and Sunday morning at the park's campgrounds. Call (606) 886-9274 for more information.

Prestonsburg is also home to the ◆ **Mountain Arts Center,** a beautiful 47,000-square-foot entertainment complex that opened in late 1996. This center, with recording studio, classrooms, and a 1,000-seat performance hall, began as the dream of a retired music teacher, Billie Jean Osborne. Osborne, who is from Betsy Layne (country singer Dwight Yoakam grew up a few houses away), envisioned a theater where eastern Kentucky audiences could enjoy top entertainment. Refusing to take no for an answer, she spurred a coalition of state and local officials to make her theater a reality. The center features top entertainers in all genres—from country and gospel to classical music—along with regular performances by the

Kentucky Opry, Osborne's own country music showcase. Performance times vary; call 1-888-MACARTS for ticket information.

The Mountain Arts Center is on a section of Highway 23 that has been designated **Kentucky's Country Music Highway.** Along a stretch running from Ashland to Letcher County, through seven counties, signs honor a dozen country and bluegrass music stars who came from the region, from Billy Ray Cyrus (Greenup County) and The Judds (Boyd County) to Patty Loveless (Pike County).

The David community, which is about 6 miles southwest of Prestonsburg on Highway 404, has two surprises in store for you. One is a small crafts shop called the **David Appalachian Crafts,** which features quality traditional mountain crafts like split oak baskets, wood carvings, and quilts. Hours are 9:00 A.M. to 4:00 P.M. Monday through Friday. Tuesdays and Thursdays between 10:00 A.M. and 3:30 P.M. are prime times to visit because that's when most of the craftspeople work at the shop. Write them at: P. O. Box 2, Highway 404, David 41616, or call (606) 886-2377. Also in town is the David School, a nonsectarian, not-for-profit, wonderful school committed to educating local high school dropouts from low-income families. In 1972 Dan Greene founded the school in an old mining camp with hopes of helping kids who were functionally illiterate. Now, more than 95 percent of the David School students have finished their high school education, and there's always a waiting list. Other schools around the state and nation are looking to Greene's program as a model. If you are inspired, stop by.

Due south of the David School is a longer-lived educational institution built upon similar hopes, **Alice Lloyd College** (606-368-2101). Take Highway 7 south, then Highway 899 southwest into Pippa Passes, in Knott County. The school's founder, Alice Lloyd, was a Radcliffe graduate who contracted spinal meningitis at the age of forty and moved with her mother to the mountains of Kentucky to die in an abandoned missionary house. Despite her illness she typed letters with her left hand to businesspeople and friends in Boston, asking for help in establishing a school. It was opened in 1917 on the hillsides of Caney Creek Valley, where it stands today.

Alice Lloyd, who lived until 1962, gave her students a free education, but there was one string attached—she requested that after graduation, the students return to eastern Kentucky to work and live. Almost 4,000 graduates have become teachers in the region and more than 1,000 have become mountain doctors and other professionals. Visitors are welcome to tour the beautiful campus all year.

Just a few miles away on Highway 550, slightly south of Highway 80, is Hindman and, strung along Troublesome Creek, the **Hindman Settlement School** (606-785-5475), yet another educational facility that long has been a social and cultural gold mine. The school was founded in 1902 on the folk school plan and operated successfully for many years, but like other settlement schools, it closed and has had to serve the community in new ways. Today it hosts some of the best workshops in the state on traditional dance and mountain crafts and culture. Visitors can tour the campus free, Monday through Friday between 8:00 A.M. and 5:00 P.M. You'll see a film about Jean Ritchie, the nationally acclaimed folk musician and composer from the nearby town of Viper.

Take Highway 160 north out of Hindman and proceed a few more miles through the junction of Highways 1087 and 160. Just past the sign that says AT THE END YOU MEET GOD, turn right (east) up a steep, blacktopped driveway to **Quicksand Craft Center** (606-785-5230). These folks are widely renowned for their fine weaving. When the Shaker Village at Pleasant Hill in Mercer County was being restored, these weavers were commissioned to make complex reproduction rugs, runners, and coverlets for the museum. If you're in the market for a high-quality handmade rug, pay a visit Monday through Friday between 8:00 A.M. and 4:30 P.M.

You're in store for more regional crafts and an architectural museum of sorts at the **Pioneer Village,** due south of Hindman. Take Highway 160 south to Carr Fork Lake, then take Highway 15 south just a little farther into Red Fox and watch the east side of the road for the long driveway to the village. This group of cabins was moved to this location in Rainbow Hollow when the Carr Fork Dam was built. Some of the log structures date as far back as the 1780s. Presently the cabins are standing, but the logs are not chinked (filled in between with mud, rock, straw, etc.). The craft shop, which pays for the cabins' maintenance, features all local handmade crafts by more than 200 craftspeople and sold on consignment. Ask to see the cornhusk dolls made by folk singer Jean Ritchie's sisters, Kitty, Mallie, and Jewel. Hours are Monday through Saturday from 10:00 A.M. to 6:00 P.M. and Sunday from 1:00 to 6:00 P.M. Call (606) 642-3650.

Nearby Hazard is a booming little riverside town at the end of the Daniel Boone Parkway. Because it sits on and near some of the widest, richest seams of coal in the area, coal is at the heart of almost everything here, a fact made loud and clear during the third weekend of September when Hazard hosts the **Black Gold Festival.** In town, spend a little time at the **Bobby Davis Museum** (234 Walnut Street; 606-439-4325) next door to the visitors' information center (606-439-2659). This free museum is a visual history book of the area from the nineteenth century through World War II. Hours are 8:30 A.M. to 4:30 P.M. Monday through Friday.

Let me be devious and point out a more modern artifact of history. Go north of town on Highway 15 and turn onto Dawahare Drive and into the Holiday Inn parking lot. The ground under the west wing of the building is sinking, so the building is collapsing as if it had been in an earthquake. It wasn't. The east part of the inn is built on natural, solid rock while the west disaster was built on "fill," rock and dirt added to fill the area—a process some engineers believe can be done on reclaimed mine sites.

An architectural treat is in store just north of Hazard in Buckhorn on Highway 28, which is off Highway 15 North. **The Log Cathedral,** now functioning as the Buckhorn Lake Area Church, is an unusually large and beautiful log structure built in 1907 as part of the Witherspoon College campus. Harvey S. Murdoch of the Society of Soul Winners helped found a Christian elementary and high school and called it a college in order to give the students extra status. The massive logs are white oak, cut from the surrounding woods. Inside, the space is lovely and impressive. The gem in the crown of the cathedral is a Hook and Hasting pipe organ, which has been restored and sounds great. Sun streaming through the old amber glass windows bathes the oak sanctuary (and you) in a warm and beautiful golden glow. To experience it, stop by the parsonage next door. If the pastor's not home, try the little store across the road, where caretakers also have a key. You're also invited to come for services, Sunday at 11:00 A.M.

Like the mountain schools in the area, ◆ **Frontier Nursing Service** in Hyden (Highway 421; 606-672-2317) is an institution committed to promoting health and growth, but in this case their main concern is with the physical body. Mary Breckinridge started Frontier Nursing as a school in 1925. Her original students and the generations of nurses to follow have made strong impressions on the minds of everyone who has encountered them riding on horseback to remote hollers and mountain towns to deliver babies and administer health care. Folks at Frontier Nursing have revised their charter and are also involved in child care, general education, and regional economics. The grounds are lovely, and the history of the service is inspirational. Make sure to go in the tiny chapel, which has a fifteenth-century Flemish stained-glass window, and to see the Wendover Big House, a log home built in 1925 for the founder. Four rooms for rent in the house are the only lodging in the county. The rates of $25 to $35 per night include breakfast.

If I were giving an award for the best town name in the state, the prize would have to go to Leslie County's Hell Fer Certain, a little, not-even-on-the-map community north of Hyden just off Highway 257. Runners-up in the area would include Devil's Jump Branch, Confluence, Cutshin, Thousandsticks, Yeaddis, Smilax, Yerkes, and Krypton.

# MORE GOOD LODGING

**BUCKHORN**
**Buckhorn Lake State Resort Park,** Highway 1833; (606) 398-7510. $54 and up.

**HAZARD**
**Days Inn,** 359 Morton Boulevard; (606) 436-4777. $54 and up.

**PRESTONSBURG**
**Holiday Inn,** Highway 23 South; (606) 886-0001. $66 and up.
**Super 8,** 550 Highway 23; (606) 886-3355. $49 and up.

# MORE FUN PLACES TO EAT

HAZARD

**Blake's Road House,** 173 Village Lane; (606) 436–4409. Steaks, chicken, and seafood.

**Frances' Diner,** 449 Chester Street; (606) 439–9085. Home cooking.

**North Fork Grill**, 470 Main Street; (606) 436–0769. Daily specials.

BUCKHORN
**Buckhorn Lake State Resort Park,** Highway 1833; (606) 398–7510.

PRESTONSBURG
**Jenny Wiley State Resort Park,** 39 Jenny Wiley Road; (606) 886–2711.

# THE GORGEOUS GORGE

The Red River Gorge in the Daniel Boone National Forest is one of the most beautiful and best-loved wilderness areas in Kentucky. Actually the area was quite obscure until its existence was threatened in the late 1960s by a proposed 5,000-acre impoundment on the Red River's North Fork. Intense controversy raged until 1975, when the plan was nixed. All the publicity caused the park to be badly overused by visitors who weren't ecologically sensitive. Today the park has been reorganized; large areas are strictly protected, and visitor education is an important part of forest management.

The gorge was formed by erosion and weathering, in much the same way that the Grand Canyon was carved out by the Colorado River. The North Fork of the Red River cut through the area more than 340 million years ago and left behind some fantastic geologic phenomena in limestone, conglomerate sandstone, and siltstone, all of which are tucked under a layer of shale. The most outstanding of these phenomena are the eighty natural rock arches, a number surpassed in the United States only by Arches National Park in Utah.

The Daniel Boone National Forest is 60 miles east of Lexington on the Bert T. Combs Mountain Parkway. A good place to begin exploring the Red River Gorge, at the northern end of the forest, is ❖ **Natural Bridge State Resort Park** (606–663–2214), a full-fledged state park with a big lodge, cottages, camping, a pool, recre-

**Natural Stone Bridge**

ation areas, and a variety of hiking trails leading to a spectacular natural stone bridge. This park is not very isolated, but it can serve as a point of reference for outings to more remote places. From I-64, take the Bert T. Combs Mountain Parkway southeast, get off at the Slade Interchange onto Highway 11, and follow signs to the park.

On the way in or out, you should have a meal at **Miguel's Pizza** (606-663-9530), a little building with a beautifully carved wooden front door on the left near the park entrance. Miguel Ventura's parents, who live next door, grow an enormous and wonderful garden. Order a veggie pizza and you'll be likely to find it laced with whatever's in season—heavenly. If you're a climber, take note that this is the only store in the area that sells a good variety of climbing supplies. Miguel's is open most weekends (except during the winter) and whenever people are out and about.

Just on the west side of Miguel's I am sure you will notice the ✦ **Kentucky Reptile Zoo** (606–663–0907). After all, how many places do you pass that look like a faux Swiss chalet with a painting of a man astride an alligator on it? Despite its oddball facade (it's a converted restaurant building), the Kentucky Reptile Zoo is actually a very well run and educational reptile center. And its founder, Jim Harrison (the man depicted astride the alligator), is well respected in venom research circles. He is a leading supplier of snake venom for medical research and also is helping a university in Brazil breed rattlesnakes whose venom may be used to help hold human skin together after surgery. In addition to seeing several dozen kinds of snakes (including pythons and black mambas) and three alligators, your visit will include an informational demonstration by Harrison or a staff member, and possibly a demonstration of venom extraction. From Memorial Day through Labor Day the zoo is open daily from 11:00 A.M. to 7:00 P.M. In September, October, and March through May, it's open only on weekends. Closed December through February. Admission is $3.50.

There is a designated driving loop through the area beginning in Nada, a mile and a half west of the Slade Interchange on Highway 15. Take Highway 77 north through the **Nada Tunnel,** a 10-foot-wide, 13-foot-tall, 800-foot-long tunnel cut by hand in 1877 to give small-gauge trains access to the big timber in the area. Stay on Highway 77 and it will run into Highway 715, which runs parallel to the river. At Pine Ridge, Highway 715 connects with Highway 15 again, which leads back to Natural Bridge. Ask for a map in the lodge at Natural Bridge.

Big timber is the subject of a small museum in the recently restored **Gladie Creek Cabin,** which you'll pass on this loop drive. This was the 1884 cabin of John Ledford, who bought and logged more than 4,000 acres here. The U.S. Forest Service recently rebuilt the cabin and filled it with historic objects that refer to the early years of the logging industry in eastern Kentucky, including log branding irons, tools, models of old equipment, and photographs.

**Gladie Creek Historical Site** also serves as the visitors center for the north end of the Daniel Boone National Forest. This is another good place to get trail maps, weather reports, and general advice about hiking or anything else concerning the National Forest. Hours are 8:00 A.M. to 4:30 P.M. Monday through Friday, and vary on weekends. Call the Stanton Ranger District (606-663-2852) for information. Aside from the driving loop, another way to reach Gladie Creek is from the north. Take Highway 77 south to Highway 715; go east for about 11 miles and watch the right side of the road.

The absolute best way to be in the Red River Gorge is to be hiking, crawling if you must, for driving does not do the woods justice. You must sweat, propel yourself by your own energy, drink when you're thirsty, eat when you're hungry (or can't wait any longer for the granola bar), feel the leaves brush against your legs, feel the sunshine on your shoulders when you come to an opening in the forest canopy, hear and see the animals, and so taste the life of the mountains. More than 165 miles of foot trails in the Daniel Boone Forest offer ample opportunity to be here the right way. Get maps from the Hemlock Lodge at Natural Bridge or at Gladie or anywhere you see a ranger. Hike as many trails as you're able.

## TRUE BLUE

Middlesborough is home of the oldest municipal golf course in the nation.

The **Sheltowee Trace** (Trail #100) is the only backpacking trail that traverses the entire length of the Daniel Boone National Forest. It goes 257 miles through nine counties, beginning in Rowan County in the north and ending in Tennessee, where it connects with the John Muir Trail (named for the father of the Sierra Club), which connects to the great Appalachian Trail. If you're planning a backpacking trip, check with a ranger. The Sheltowee Trace is marked with a white diamond or turtle-shaped blaze. The world *Sheltowee* is Shawnee for "Big Turtle," Daniel Boone's Indian name when he was captured and adopted by Shawnee Chief Blackfish.

The **Pioneer Weapons Hunting Area** is a 7,480-acre area in the National Forest, north of the gorge, which is designated for hunting deer, turkey, grouse, and squirrel, but you must use only primitive weapons—black powder muzzle loaders, bows and arrows, blow guns, spears, rubber bands, whatever. Before you hunt, be sure to call the forest supervisor (606–784–6428) so that you understand the regulations.

From Frenchburg, which is in the heart of the National Forest near the Pioneer Weapons Hunting Area, take Highway 36 north, then Highway 1274 east for 2.2 miles to the first paved road on the right (south), marked only by a small brown sign denoting **Spratt Stoneworks.** Turn and bear left onto a gravel road, then left again until you find yourself at a third fork in the road. Go to the brick house on the hill and ask for Verne Spratt, the old man who owns the land where there are a number of curious and very well-preserved stoneworks and earthen constructions. The Kentucky Heritage Council gave Spratt a grant to preserve the site and to develop a trail.

The large stone effigy or geometrical construction is thought to be a serpent mound, but this has not been proven archaeologically. It's a strange series of stone walls completely blanketed in moss. To the southeast is a group of about two dozen small stone mounds, some linear, some round or ovate. Because the land surrounding these constructions is not arable, it's unlikely that these were built by white farmers. They are probably prehistoric; a number of stone mounds found in this region have been dated to the Middle and Late Woodland periods. Spratt is likely to tell you stories about how John Swift's hidden silver mines are nearby. He can point out eighteenth-century graffiti on the rocks and will read to you from Swift's diary, which names rock formations that seem to correspond with some on his farm. To visit the site, you must call Spratt ahead at (606) 768–6619, preferably in the evening. This is guaranteed to be a strange adventure, something that will pique your curiosity forever.

In downtown Frenchburg at the intersection of Highways 460 and 36 is the **Corner Restaurant** (606–768–2844), a big social spot and the place to get down-home cooking. Stop in for coffee if nothing else because the dining area is decorated with parts of old stills, farm machinery, hand-painted porcelain cafeteria-style plates, and more. If you've got the traveling blues, these friendly folks will lift your spirits.

If you turn toward the north from the Corner Restaurant on

## STRANGE AS IT SOUNDS

Eastern Kentuckians have their own way of saying things, and as you travel this part of the state you'll not only notice a distinctive accent, but you'll also encounter some fascinating local expressions. For example, man or woman, don't be surprised if you're called "honey" by total strangers of both sexes. A ghost is a "haint"; "loaded for bear" means angry or looking for a fight; and a "passel" is one way to indicate a large quantity. If someone tells you to "quit lollygaggin' around," it means to stop delaying or taking so long; and there are a passel of other local expressions. One day a friend from Hazard and I were having lunch at a local restaurant when an acquaintance of hers came in. In the course of conversation, I mentioned that I wasn't from the area. "Oh, honey, I knew that," he said. "You talk way too plain to be from around here."

Highway 36, take the first street to the right, follow it to the end, and you'll see a trail going up the hillside. This trail leads to **Donathan Rock**, a great huge rock teetering near the edge of a cliff from which you get a perfect aerial view of Frenchburg below. Park in town and walk over. Traveling a mile farther north on Highway 36 brings you to the **Roe Wells School.** Watch carefully for it on the left—the sign is small. The schoolhouse is a typical one-room country school and quaint as can be. Look in the windows; the old desks and books, chalkboard, and even a few messages from the teacher remain. It would make a perfect movie set. If you want to go inside, make an appointment by calling (606) 768-3323.

Leaving Frenchburg in the southeasterly direction, there are several surprises in store for you. Take Highway 460 east for 7.5 miles and look on the right side of the road for **Barton's Foods, Manufacturer of Relish, Sorghum, and Jellies.** Charlotte Roe is glad to show visitors around the operation. Your nose will tell you what's cooking at the moment. One day it's a hot chowchow relish; the next, it's cinnamon and pear preserves (which tastes like apple pie); and the next it's old mill molasses, Delano Roe's magnum opus. Barton's is best known for Moonshine Jelly that contains just 10 percent Georgia Moon. Many of their delectables are available for sale. Hours are 8:00 A.M. to 4:30 P.M. Monday through Friday. Call (606) 768-3750.

One half-mile east of Barton's is another surprise and treat, the ◆ **Swamp Valley Store and Museum** (606-768-3250). The humor around here runs thick, but it's all deeply rooted in the history of the area. Clayton Wells, the jovial owner, was a pack rat from his youth, and now it has paid off. He kept every little thing of his and his family's and other folks' too. In the past twenty years or so, Clayton has restored and moved a whole slew of historic buildings onto the property near his country store. He filled each one with appropriate artifacts, and voila! A museum. What makes the place outstanding (and funny) are his accompanying stories: "My people always told about..."

The main museum house, for example, was the home of John Poplin, Clayton's great-great-grandfather, a slave driver who brought slaves from Sand Gap, Virginia, to Lexington, Kentucky. Other buildings include an old metal silo called "Photo Silo," which could be a twist on the little drive-in photo developing units that sit in mall parking lots, but it's not. Inside are school photos of every child in Menifee County for fifty years. Clayton and his friends also record music here and sell square dance tapes for $10. They're pretty good. Other buildings included the E-Z Rest Casket Shop, which is full of authentic, family tools for blacksmithing, shoe repair, stone masonry, and casket making; the Doctors Museum, which is chock-full of the tools and oddities that local country docs used to carry; and the Cheese Shop, supplied with everything necessary to make cheese, except milk. There's more, but you have to visit Swamp Valley to appreciate it. It's worth the drive. Even folksy National Public Radio personality Garrison Keillor stopped by once to do a little historical research. Keillor wanted to verify the record-breaking length of marriage of Lynn Boyd Wells and Alydia Rupe Wells, Clayton's oldest uncle and aunt. They were married something like eighty-two years! Amen.

The old **Botts School** building stands about 200 yards away from Swamp Valley. Although it's now a community building, you can still feel its age; it was a one-room schoolhouse since before the time Menifee County was a county. If it catches your fancy and you want to see inside, ask Clayton Wells of Swamp Valley Store or stop by the Botts General Store that's directly across the street. Either way, you'll get some stories.

One of the most special surprises in this immediate area is ◆**Furnace Mountain, Inc.,** a spiritual community founded in 1986 by Zen Master Seung Sahn. The community owns 500 acres of beautiful woodland near Clay City in Powell County, where visitors are welcome to hike or join in daily meditation practices. The main function of Furnace Mountain is to host a variety of retreats, primarily traditional three- to ninety-day Zen Buddhist retreats. Retreats are also conducted in other disciplines such as twelve step programs, Christian meditation, and clinical pastoral education.

*Kwan Se Um San Ji Sah,* which means "Perceive World Sound High Ground Temple," is indeed a place that sits beautifully on high ground and affects the way one perceives the world due to its exquisite blend of eastern Kentucky craftsmanship with Far Eastern aesthetics. This timberframe temple has the classic tapering vertical lines and uplifting roofline of Oriental architecture and the materials of the mountains—recycled Douglas fir siding, a cherrywood floor, and deep sky-blue

## TRUE BLUE

Kentucky's Red River Gorge area has the largest concentration of rock shelters and arches east of the Rockies.

ceramic roof tiles. For more information, please write c/o the Abbess, P. O. Box 545, Clay City 40312.

Furnace Mountain offers sustenance for the soul, but if it's real food you're hungering for, head into Clay City and have a meal at **Clay City Restaurant** (4493 Main Street; 606-663-4517). For breakfast there's country ham, home fries, fried apples, biscuits, and gravy. The lunch and dinner menu features home cooking specialties such as pork tenderloin, country-fried steak smothered in gravy, fried chicken, vegetables, and all kinds of pie. And if you're looking for philosophy, just eavesdrop on the regulars sitting at the special table with the sign over it that says TABLE OF KNOWLEDGE. The restaurant is open daily from 6:00 A.M. to 9:00 P.M.

You are still in beautiful country when you travel to the south side of the Red River Gorge. From Natural Bridge, head south on

Highway 11 through Zachariah and Zoe (my name town and the site of my worst bicycle wreck) to **Beattyville,** a friendly little mountain town with the best-named restaurant in the world, **The Purple Cow,** on Main Street. Eat any meal there any day of the week, just for the fun of it. The weekend after the third Monday in October, Beattyville is host to the world's only **Woolly Worm Festival,** devoted to the humblest of all meteorologists. Call (606) 464-2888 for festival information. The town's two most important claims to fame, however, are, first, that it is the place where all three forks—North, Middle, and South—converge to form the Kentucky River, and second, that Beattyville has been the lifelong home of Nevyle Shackelford, Kentucky's (and my) most loved syndicated nature and mountain culture columnist. One of my earliest childhood memories involves seeing apples and pears growing on the same tree at Uncle Nevyle's house.

From Beattyville take Highway 11 south and turn east on Highway 30 to Booneville, home of **Morris Fork Crafts** (606-398-2194). The shop offers traditional mountain items including quilts, baskets, toys, and wooden items. Hours are usually Monday through Friday from 9:00 A.M. to 3:00 P.M. Continue on Highway 30 east and you'll come to Jackson. This town was originally known as Breathitt, but in 1845 it was renamed to honor President Andrew Jackson, who died that year. The **Breathitt County Museum** (336 Broadway; 606-666-4159) on Broadway has exhibits on logging and coal mining along with Civil War artifacts. It's open Monday through Friday from 9:00 A.M. to 4:00 P.M.

About 9 miles south of Jackson on Highway 15 you'll come to a community called Lost Creek. While there, grab a bite to eat at **Pogo's Patio Restaurant** (606-666-4369), open seven days a week except during church because the cook's a preacher.

Scuba divers, take note of the **Scuba Center,** next door to Pogo's. The owner, Raymond Hudson, rents and sells equipment and gives diving lessons seasonally in the swimming pool at his store. The local businessmen who told me about Hudson's store said, "We may be 500 miles from the ocean, but we've got a scuba center to beat all." The center is open by appointment only. For information, call (606) 666-4354.

From Highway 15 south, veer off to the southeast on Highway 476 to ◆ **Robinson Forest,** a large research and educational forest owned and managed by the University of Kentucky. Visitors can take a self-guided hike along a nature trail and see a wide variety of flora and fauna typical of this area. A climb up the Camp Robinson Lookout Tower is worth the effort. To get to the tower, take Highway 426 way into the forest and turn left on Clemons Road to the tower trail. Call (606) 666-5034 for more information.

## MORE GOOD LODGING

ROGERS

**Cliffview Resort,** near Natural Bridge; (606) 668-6550. Furnished cabins, hiking trails, lake. $125 and up.

JACKSON

**Jackson Inn,** Highway 15; (606) 666-7551. $44 and up.

BEATTYVILLE

**Travelwise Motor Inn,** Highway 11; (606) 464-2225. $40 and up.

## MORE FUN PLACES TO EAT

BEATTYVILLE

**Purple Cow,** Main Street; (606) 464-9222.

SLADE

**Rose's Restaurant,** 1289 Natural Bridge Road; (606) 663-0588. Pinto beans and cornbread, sandwiches, and a daily special.

**Natural Bridge State Resort Park,** Highway 11 near Slade; (606) 663-2214.

CLAY CITY

**Wagon Wheel Restaurant,** 20 Black Creek Road; (606) 663-0658. Great buffet with skillet-fried chicken and real mashed potatoes.

# IRON COUNTRY

*If these United States can be called a body,*
*Kentucky can be called its heart.*

These words are from the first stanza of "Kentucky Is My Land," a poem by the late poet laureate of Kentucky, Jesse Stuart, a wholesome, hopeful writer whose work was deeply rooted in his eastern Kentucky homeland. Because W-Hollow was Stuart's home and source of inspiration, more than 700 acres have been made into a pastoral museum and maintained as Stuart knew it—cattle graze in some pastures and young forests are being allowed to grow to maturity. The ◆ **Jesse Stuart State Nature Preserve** lies between Highways 1 and 2 just west of Greenup, off Highway 23. Visitors can walk the hills and fields Stuart walked and visit Op's Cabin, the old white clapboard house where he did some of his writing. For those who know his work, the fictional Laurel Ridge is Seaton Ridge. His home borders the preserve but is private property. The Kentucky State Nature Preserves Commission (502-564-2886) maintains the nature preserve and the Jesse Stuart Foundation, a nonprofit organization devoted to preserving and sharing Stuart's work. To order books, write the foundation at P.O. Box 391, Ashland 41114, or call (606) 329-5232.

Continue south on Highway 1 to **Greenbo Lake State Resort Park,** where the lodge is named after Jesse Stuart. The last weekend in September the park hosts a Jesse Stuart Weekend during which speakers lecture on the life and works of Stuart, a guided tour of W-Hollow is given by family members, films are shown, and exhibits are open (606-473-7324). Otherwise, the lake is marvelous for fishing, the dining room is popular, and camping is available.

Nine miles south of the park, at the intersection of Highways 1 and 3111, is the **Oldtown Covered Bridge,** spanning the Little Sandy River near the site of a Shawnee village. The 194-foot-long, two-span, Burr-type bridge was built in 1880 and has not been restored. ◆ **Bennett's Mill Bridge** is 1 foot longer, twenty-five years older, and has one less span than the Oldtown Bridge, and it's functional. It was built in 1855 for access to Bennett's Grist

## THERE'S A MORAL TO THIS STORY

Eastern Kentucky communities have festivals celebrating all kinds of foods, from Gingerbread Days in Hindman in September to the Kentucky Apple Festival in Paintsville in early October. There's even a Poke Sallet Festival, honoring a local green, in Harlan in June. But the most exotic eastern Kentucky food festival has to be the Mountain Mushroom Festival in Irvine in late April. Up to 20,000 people show up in this town of 2,800 with mushrooms on the mind—grilled, fried, baked, and en casserole mushrooms, that is. For many years, folks in Estill County have gone to the woods to hunt for the morels, or wild mushrooms, that pop up in poplar thickets and apple orchards in the spring. Locally, these delicacies are called landfish for their somewhat fishy taste. The annual festival includes a hunt to see who can find the biggest morel, a mushroom cook-off, and even a "Fungus Run." Call the Estill County Chamber of Commerce at (606) 723-2554 for the current year's festival dates. *If you're planning to do any mushroom gathering on your own, make sure you know what the edible variety looks like. (Check out the poster hanging in the Irvine City Council chambers.) You don't want to take home a poisonous variety.*

Mill on Tygart Creek. What is amazing is that the original frame and footings are intact. This bridge is on Highway 7, just west of the Greenup County Locks and Dam. (Warning: Grays Branch Road, the direct route from the dam, is a rough, dirt logging road.)

Follow the Ohio River south on Highway 23 into **Ashland,** the largest city in Kentucky east of Lexington and headquarters for Ashland Oil and Armco Steel (not to mention that it's the hometown of country music stars Naomi and Wynonna Judd). Downtown you'll notice a surprising number of large, ornate houses built by early industrialists during the last half of the nineteenth century. My favorite is at 1600 Central Avenue. The highest peaks of the roof sport two cast-iron dragons, reminiscent of French *faitages* or the figures on ancient Macedonian tombs, meant to ward off evil spirits. It was originally built at the corner of Winchester Avenue and Seventeenth Street but was hauled intact to the present site some twenty years later by a team of mules! The dragons did their job.

Another awesome building is the Mayo Manor, circa 1917, at the corner of Bath and Sixteenth Streets, which now houses the ◆ **Kentucky Highlands Museum.** Even without the museum items, the mansion would be worth touring. Make sure to climb the grand staircase to the third floor, where there is a large panel of handsome stained glass in the ceiling. The museum is organized by subject and period, and exhibits range from Adena, Fort Ancient, and Hopewell Indian cultures to rail, steam, and industrial histories, the evolution of radio, a World War II room, an impressive antique clothing collection, and a special exhibit on the third floor that usually is worth a visit in itself. Hours are 10:00 A.M. to 4:00 P.M. Tuesday through Saturday. Admission is charged. Call (606) 329-8888 for special programs and more information.

Not far from the museum in downtown Ashland is **Central Park,** a forty-seven-acre area set aside when Ashland was laid out in the 1850s. It contains a number of ancient Indian mounds that have been restored to their original proportions. They were found to contain human bones and pottery and other artifacts that correspond with the Adena period (800 B.C. to A.D. 800).

For more contemporary local human artifacts, try the **Ashland Area Art Gallery** (1516 Winchester Avenue; 606-329-1826). The gallery changes exhibits monthly and features regional artists. Hours are 10:00 A.M. to 4:00 P.M. Monday through Saturday.

Architecture buffs, brace yourselves. The ◆ **Paramount Arts Center** (1300 Winchester Avenue; 606-324-3175), is out of this world. Art deco has never been better, and the people of Ashland cared enough to give this place an enormous face-lift (but what a face!). If you're in town on a night when a cultural event is scheduled, go, no matter what's playing. They book everything from Marcel Marceau to the Sistine Chapel Choir to Ray Charles. Or you can just tour the building between 9:00 A.M. and 4:00 P.M. Monday through Friday.

In the early 1920s Paramount-Famous Lasky Corporation

planned to build a chain of "talking picture" theaters like the Paramount across the nation to showcase Paramount Studios films. After a few theaters were built, the Depression hit and truncated the plan. In 1931 this joint was built for $400,000. The ceiling is painted with the famous art deco pseudo-Moravian sunburst surrounded by leaping gazelles. On the red walls are murals of sixteenth-century theatrical figures. The seats are done in plush red velvet. Ornamental pewter and brass are everywhere, even in the bathrooms. Opulent is the word.

About ten miles from Ashland on Highway 23N is Russell, home to numerous antiques shops and restaurants. Not to be missed, however, is **Rail City Hardware** (606-836-3121)—part general hardware store, part railroad museum. Owners Sharon and Bill Lanham collect miniature trains as a hobby and have two tracks set up right in the store. Over the years, other people in the area have brought in items from the C&O railroad, which ran through the town. So in addition to the usual hardware goods for sale, at Rail City you also can see a fascinating collection of (not-for-sale) railroad lanterns, oil cans, even pot-bellied stoves. The store is right in the center of town on Highway 244, and it is open Monday through Saturday from 9:00 A.M. to 5:00 P.M.

More opulence is in store for you at **Irish Acres Antiques,** a seemingly endless gallery filled with very fine American, European, and Asian antiques of all periods. The furniture will leave you wide-eyed, but don't fail to notice the significant details—glassware, silver, Oriental rugs, and ceramics. To get there, take I-64 west, get off at the Cannonsburg exit, turn right, and follow signs for 12 miles to Irish Acres. Hours are 10:00 A.M. to 5:00 P.M. Tuesday through Saturday. Call (606) 928-8502. This is a sister store to the Irish Acres Antiques in Nonesuch, owned by the same family and run with the same pizzazz.

Two pig-iron furnace ruins near Ashland are accessible to the public. One is the **Clinton Furnace,** built by the Poage brothers in 1833. Take Highway 60 south, turn left (east) on Highway 538 and left again on Shopes Creek Road to the furnace ruins. The other, **Princess Furnace,** was put into operation in 1864. From town, take Highway 60 south, then Highway 5 north; watch for a rough stone structure near the road.

# BREATHITT COUNTY'S ICE MAN

Paul Griffith, a retired highway department maintenance analyst, has created his own winter wonderland in his yard on Highway 30, near Shoulderblade, about 8 miles west of Jackson. When the first real cold spell hits, Griffith goes into action. He turns on an elaborate system of hoses that spray water from five ponds over trees and other frames. The results are strange and glistening cascading ice formations that draw the delighted attention of passing motorists and school bus passengers. Griffith says he just enjoys looking at his icy creations. "They're beautiful," he explains. "It just relaxes me to sit and look out the window at them." But he doesn't get so relaxed that he isn't planning ahead: He's still trying to figure out a way to add color to his creations (adding food color to the water didn't work; he thinks that tinted spotlights might).

Both furnaces were part of a much larger community of pig-iron operations. Because the sites are usually in bad condition and none of them are part of guided tours, let me explain how they worked. It was a clumsy process, but these furnaces produced tons and tons of rough pig iron that was refined into steel, wrought iron, and ingot iron. The Civil War was fought with bullets and cannonballs from these humble industries. The earliest furnaces of the late eighteenth century produced approximately three tons of iron from nine tons of ore—today's steel furnaces need only about half an hour to produce the same amount of steel the old furnaces could produce in a year.

Enormous stones were quarried from the nearby mountains and used to build the furnaces by the sides of hills. A bridge was built to the top of the chimney, where they dumped the "charge," which consisted of iron ore, also mined locally; limestone, which acts as a fluxing agent; and charcoal, for heat. The charcoal, in turn, was made by burning prime hardwood down to lumps of black, porous carbon. When all this was dumped into the top of the furnace, pig iron and slag came out the bottom and cooled in ditches. When you visit these old furnaces, climb inside, if possible, and look up the stack; often they taper

**Mount Savage Furnace**

beautifully to a small round opening at the top. In my opinion, the art of stonemasonry of this quality is dead. It's important to know what's possible.

The furnace tour continues west of Ashland in Carter County. Just 2 miles north of Grayson is a little community called **Pactolus** on Highway 1 (or 7), birthplace of Leonard Sly, better known as Roy Rogers. Pactolus also has a rundown furnace right by the road. This one was a blast furnace that used hydropower from the Little Sandy River. If your interest is piqued, continue north on Highway 7 to the ruins of **Iron Hill Furnace,** once the largest charcoal-powered blast furnace in the region. Stay on Highway 7 until it merges with Highway 2, then continue to Highway 1773, turn left (west) and go 4 miles to **Boone Furnace** on Grassy Creek. This blast furnace, built by Sebastian Eifort, started producing iron in 1857.

South of Grayson is the ◆ **Mount Savage Furnace,** one of the best preserved and most beautifully made furnaces in the state. If you only want to see one furnace, this is the judge's choice. Take Highway 7 south of Grayson and turn east on Highway 773. The furnace is on the left, about 1¹/₂ miles east of Hitchins. The gorgeous stonework was done in 1848 by a Prussian mason named John Fauson.

Carter County is the only county in Kentucky with two state parks. From Mount Savage Furnace, continue south on Highway 7 to **Grayson Lake State Park,** which boasts one of the clearest, most serene lakes (1,500 acres) in the state. Camping, boating, fishing, swimming, and picnicking are what the park has to offer—all the ingredients necessary for a relaxing, all-American vacation. Call (606) 474-9727 for more information.

The other park is ❖ **Carter Caves State Resort Park,** one of the most magnificent in this whole region of the United States. From Grayson, take I-64 or Highway 60 west, then go north on Highway 182. In addition to a lodge, camping facilities, a pool, canoe trips, and hiking trails, there are twenty navigated caves, three of which are lighted for tours. Many of the caves are wild and can be seen only if you're excited by the idea of real spelunking. One of the best times to try your hand (and elbows and knees) at caving is during the park's annual Crawlathon in early February, when the best guided tours are given.

Two of the park's most significant parts are **Bat Cave** and **Cascade Caverns,** both of which are State Nature Preserves. Bat Cave is part-time home to one of the nation's largest wintering populations of the Indiana bat, a federally endangered species. The bats hang in tight clusters in cracks and on the ceiling. There are no winter tours of this cave because it is important *not* to disturb these creatures during the winter; they have stored just enough fat to keep them alive during hibernation, and flying would use up their reserves. Cascade Caverns is not contiguous with the rest of the park. Take Highway 182 south, turn west onto Highway 209, and follow signs. Above ground on the north slopes by the caverns are some rare plants that are usually found much farther north, and there are a number of mountain maple trees, a shrublike tree found here along the stream that flows out of the cave toward Tygarts Creek, where, by the way, the hemlock forest will take your breath away. Call for information about any facets of Carter Caves State

Resort Park at (606) 286-4411 or (800) 325-0059.

While driving from Carter Caves to Cascade Caverns, watch for the **Northeastern Kentucky Museum** and gift shop. From late April through October, 9:00 A.M. to 5:00 P.M., seven days a week, you can take a visual crash course in regional history beginning with ancient Indian artifacts through pioneer times, the Civil War, World War II, and into the present. If you're visiting in the winter and want to tour this informative amateur museum, make an appointment with Jim Plummer at (606) 286-6012.

**Morehead** is a typical university town except that it's plopped right down in the hills of eastern Kentucky. A friend of mine chose to go to Morehead State because he loves to rock climb and sail, two sports one can't pursue in one's free time at most Kentucky colleges. Sailing and all other forms of boating and water play are available at **Cave Run Lake,** an 8,270-acre lake fed by the Licking River. If you're interested in learning about how such massive bodies of water are formed and maintained, arrange a tour of the Corps of Engineers dam and towers. If you want a less technical view, just dive in. Fishing may be the most popular thing to do at Cave Run. In fact, it's becoming known as the "muskie capital of the world." For information on fishing, camping, or anything concerning the lake, call the Morehead Tourist Commission at (606) 784-6221.

At ◆ **The Kentucky Folk Art Center** (606-783-2204) in Morehead, you'll find a surprising, delightful, thought-provoking, and ultimately impressive collection of carvings, paintings, assemblages, walking sticks, painted furniture, gourd creatures, and other works by folk artists from across Kentucky. The collection began in one room of the Morehead State University art department and was later moved to a small house on campus. Now an independent and fully accredited, nationally recognized museum, it is housed in a renovated historic building at 102 West First Street near the Highway 60 Bypass. By some definitions, folk art comprises objects that are part of everyday life and that somehow reflect the beliefs, social structure, and experiences of the people in a given region; formal training is usually not received outside the culture from which it springs. You'll understand better when you see the collection. You'll also find yourself thinking deeply and laughing your head off—great responses to art of any kind. There's also a museum store, and ask to see the "Folkmobile." This van was decorated by area artists and museum volunteers for use in the museum's Folk-to-Folk educational outreach program; you couldn't help but be intrigued if you saw this doodad-laden, wildly painted assemblage-on-wheels pull into your school's parking lot. The Kentucky Folk Art Center is open Monday through Saturday from 8:30 A.M. to 4:30 P.M.

While in Morehead, stop by the **Dixie Grill** (172 East Main Street; 606-784-9051) for beans and cornbread. Folks will know you're from out-of-town if you don't eat it properly: The cornbread should be crumbled into the bowl and eaten right along with the beans.

Down at the bottom tip of Cave Run Lake, where the Licking River begins to look like a river again, is the town of West Liberty, the Morgan County Seat. Come to town the last weekend in September for the **Morgan County Sorghum Festival.** In the evenings, people around here put on their dancing shoes. During the day someone always sets up a mule-drawn sugar cane mill at the Old Mill Park on the banks of the Licking River so you can see how sorghum molasses is made the old-fashioned way. Call (606) 743-2300 for more information. If you can't make it during the festival, you can get some good sorghum at **Wyck Smith's farm** (606-725-4660) on Highway 772. You can see his cane mill from the road. The sorghum is boiled down in September, and it is usually sold out by December.

# MORE GOOD LODGING

### ASHLAND
**Ashland Plaza Hotel,** 15th and Winchester Streets; (606) 329-0055. $80 and up.

### MOREHEAD
**Holiday Inn,** I-64 at Highway 32; (606) 784-7591. $55 and up.

### BLAINE
**Gambill Mansion,** Highways 201 and 32; (606) 652-3120. Room and suites in a 1923 home with spacious front porch. $50 and up.

CATLETTSBURG

**Levi Hampton House,** 2206 Walnut; (606) 739–8118 or 888–538–4426. Four rooms in a renovated 1847 Colonial Revival mansion. $70 and up.

# MORE FUN PLACES TO EAT

ASHLAND

**C. R. Thomas Old Place,** 1612 Greenup Avenue; (606) 325–8500. Gourmet burgers.

**Damon's,** 500 Winchester Avenue; (606) 325–8929. Ribs.

RUSSELL

**Fletcher House Café,** 342 Belfonte Street; (606) 836–0955. Sandwiches, barbecue, steaks, and seafood.

GREENUP

**Greenbo Lake State Resort Park,** Highway; (606) 473–7324. Variety of sandwiches, entrees, and regional specialties such as country ham and fried catfish.

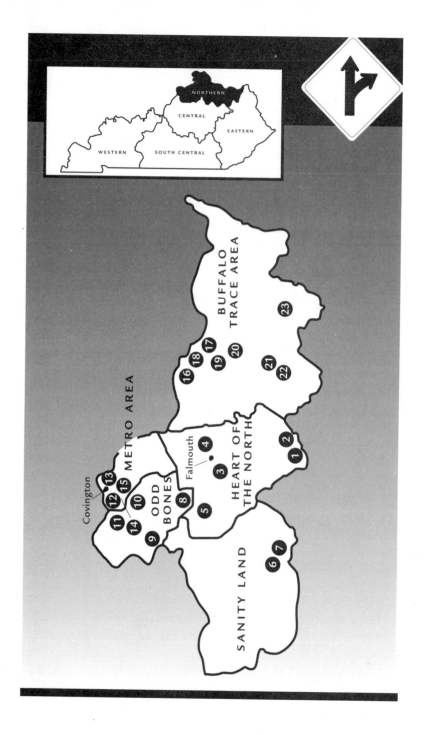

# NORTHERN KENTUCKY

1. The Seldon-Renaker Inn
2. Wyle Wynde Nursery and Iris Garden
3. Sugar Bush Farm
4. Kincaid Regional Theatre
5. The Quilt Box
6. Jubilee Candle Shop
7. Larkspur Press
8. Curtis Gates Lloyd Wildlife Reserve
9. Big Bone Lick State Park
10. Tewes Poultry Farm
11. Anderson Ferry
12. Cathedral Basilica of the Assumption
13. Mimosa Mansion Museum
14. Sandford House Bed and Breakfast
15. The Village Puppet Theatre
16. The Beehive Tavern
17. National Underground Railroad Museum
18. Joseph Byrd Brannen & Co., Antique Furniture Reproductions
19. Washington
20. Brodrick's Tavern Food & Spirits
21. Mays Lick
22. Blue Licks Battlefield State Park
23. Goddard (White) Covered Bridge

# NORTHERN KENTUCKY

Like some of its most fascinating inhabitants, northern Kentucky is a bit eccentric. Places to explore range from exquisite Gothic cathedrals and puppet theaters in dense urban areas to anachronistic service stations and prehistoric museums in sparsely populated rural regions. Mark Twain once said that when the world came to an end, he wanted to be in Kentucky because it's always a good twenty years behind. Such misconceptions! Innovation has always been at the heart of this area's delightful idiosyncrasies. Northern Kentucky boasts architecturally significant bridges, downhill snow skiing, and refreshingly creative farms that specialize in everything from irises and turkeys to maple syrup. Historic buildings and fine craftspeople round out the picture, making this relatively small area one of the most diverse in the state.

## HEART OF THE NORTH

Cynthiana, a small town on Highway 27 about 30 miles north of Lexington, offers classy overnight lodging at ◆**The Seldon-Renaker Inn,** 24 South Walnut Street. Go downtown, turn right on Pleasant Street, then right again onto Walnut Street, and watch for the sign on the right. The inn is a graceful Victorian house, built as a residence by Seldon Renaker in 1885 and later used as a boardinghouse, dress shop, tearoom, and doctor's office. Rooms are $50 to $65 per night. In the morning coffee and doughnuts or coffee cake are available in the first-floor communal parlor. For reservations call (606) 234-3752.

◆**Wyle Wynde Nursery and Iris Garden** is a painter's paradise and a gardener's endless shopping spree. In mid-May the rows and rows of bearded iris on the nursery's hillside explode into mind-boggling color variations, and a sweet, subtle, cantaloupe-like aroma fills the air. The scene may cause you to have a wreck when you crest the hill about 6 miles east of Cynthiana on Highway 62. You may also be fortunate enough to veer into the driveway, hike up your pants, grab your wallet, and take a leisurely walk around six acres of beds filled to capacity with iris and other ornamental plants.

Owner-gardeners Norvel and Rita Glascock do their own

hybridizing. The result is a shocking variety of plants, such as the large Starburst iris in lush autumn colors or Caesar's Brother, a tall, elegant plant with small, blackish-purple blooms. Come by for freshly dug iris and daylilies. The nursery is open from late April through September daylight to dark daily. Call (606) 234–3879 for more information.

The most delectable maple syrup south of the Mason-Dixon line comes from the steep woods of ◆ **Sugar Bush Farm,** where the two best kinds of maple, sugar maple *(Acer saccarum)* and black maple *(Acer nigrum)*, grow abundantly. Robert Aulick and Paul Haubner have rigged a spider's weblike plastic tubing system that links three groups of 200 tapped trees and runs the sap downhill to the bottomland near Fork Lick Creek and into old milk tanks. In late winter and early spring, the sap is hauled twice a day to a tobacco barn and pumped into overhead tanks that feed into the wood-fired evaporator. The sap is boiled at about 220 degrees Fahrenheit, and liquid gold flows into the small finishing tanks where it is admired by the alchemists before they strain and can it for the world's pleasure. Even the state health inspectors like to examine the product. It takes thirty-five to forty-five gallons of sap to make one gallon of syrup. Eat it over fresh yogurt or hot pancakes and you will be eating like a god.

You can find the Sugar Bush Farm folks every year at several regional festivals, including Pendleton County's Wool Festival (606–654–3378), held off Highway 159 next to Kincaid Lake State Park during the first weekend of October. You are also welcome to go directly to the farm to meet these delightful folks in their own setting. To get there from Highway 25, which runs parallel to I–75, go to Williamstown and take Highway 22 east out of town about 5 miles. Turn south on Highway 1054 for about 3 miles and look for a green sign on the right side of the road. Take Jenkins Road all the way to the end. Come in February to see syrup-making in action. Depending upon the size of the harvest, there may or may not be any left at other times of the year. It's best to call ahead (606–654–3433) if you want to come visit.

In Williamstown, there are several antiques shops to explore. For refreshment, stop at the **Lucas-Moore Drug Store** (112 North

Main Street, 606-824-3349), where there's a small but authentic soda fountain. The drug store has been in business over 100 years, and the fountain has been there for perhaps 50, but the original equipment looks and works as good as new. You can get a reasonably priced sandwich, a soft drink, or a yummy milk shake whipped up in a Hamilton Beach blender and poured from a stainless steel container.

If you really want to get away from it all, spend the night at **Mullins Log Cabin** in Cordova, south of Williamstown via Highway 36. There's no phone, no television, no electricity, not even running water (the old-fashioned privy is out back, about 150 feet from the house). The cabin has become popular for "pioneer weddings," in which some couples even don period clothing and arrive in horse-drawn carriages. Contact owner Judy Mullins at (606) 824-4306 for information about visiting or staying overnight.

**Thaxton's South Fork Canoe Trails, Inc.** offers canoe trips on the Main Licking River, the South Fork, and the Middle Fork from April through October. Seeing the countryside by its natural roadways can connect one to the land in a way that driving a car cannot; no road noise, no cursing at your fellow human beings for passing on a hill, nothing between your skin and the living world. Located in Butler just 9 miles north of Falmouth, the Main Licking Outpost is near a bridge on Highway 27 a few hundred yards south of its intersection with Route 177. Call (606) 472-2000 for more information.

In the 200-year-old town of Falmouth, the most notable well-preserved historic building is a handsome two-story log cabin, circa 1790, called the **Alvin Mountjoy House** (203 Chapel Street, which runs parallel to Main Street downtown; 606-654-3165). In addition to the traditional walls of huge poplar logs, pine floors, and big fireplaces built of stone from the nearby Licking River, it is one of the few existing eighteenth-century cabins with basements. The present-day owners, Carol and Nancy Houchen, are glad to show the house. Stop by their store, called Houchens, which is just two doors away. Their daughter, who lives in the Mountjoy cabin, is also willing to let you in, when she is home.

The ❖ **Kincaid Regional Theatre** is a small, professional summer theater that features new shows every season. From mid-June through the end of July, you can see Broadway musicals in Falmouth Auditorium. In downtown Falmouth, go east on Shelby Street, south on Chapel Street, and look for signs. Curtain time is 8:15 P.M. Thursday through Saturday and 2:30 P.M. Sunday. Dinner packages are available. For reservations or a performance schedule, write KRT, Route 5, Box 225, Falmouth 41040, or call (606) 654-6911 or 654-2636.

Every quilter I know harbors a special kind of gratitude for ◆ **The Quilt Box,** one of the largest and most comprehensive quilt shops in the state. When I first laid eyes on Charlotte Willis's marvelous quilt, "Kentucky Pride," my initial question was, "Where did she find such gorgeous materials?" This shop has them: Natalie Lahner and her daughter Darcy Koenig have made it their mission to carry every quilt-related item imaginable, including more than 2,000 bolts of 100 percent cotton fabric in colors and patterns that will make you drool, along with patterns, notions, books, and finished quilts. They make custom quilts based on wallpaper or upholstery samples or unusual designs.

The store is in a restored 150-year-old log structure, which is tastefully married to the Lahners' residence, a reproduction seventeenth-century house. (An addition was completed in 1997.) Kids love seeing the rabbits, chickens, sheep, ducks, miniature horses, or whatever current farm residents are on the loose. The shop hours are from 9:30 A.M. to 5:00 P.M. Monday through Saturday. From I-75, take the Dry Ridge Owenton (exit 159) and go west on Highway 22. Turn right on Highway 467 or Warsaw Road, go exactly 2.4 miles, and look for the Walnut Springs Farm mailbox and the sign for THE QUILT BOX. Follow the gravel road 0.4 miles to the second house on the road. Call (606) 824-4007.

The **Country Grill** at 21 Taft Highway in Dry Ridge serves consistently good-'n'-good-for-you meals made from fresh ingredients. Hours are 9:00 A.M. to 9:00 P.M. Monday through Thursday, 9:00 A.M. to 10:00 P.M. Friday, 8:00 A.M. to 10:00 P.M. Saturday, and 8:00 A.M. to 9:00 P.M. Sunday. Their phone number is (606) 824-6000. It's a good sign when the parking lot is always full.

# MORE GOOD LODGING

WILLIAMSTOWN

**Days Inn,** I–75 exit 154; (606) 824–5025. $45 and up.

**Red Carpet Inn,** 401 South Main Street; (606) 824–4305. $55 and up.

DRY RIDGE

**Super 8,** I–75 exit 159; (606) 824–3700. $45 and up.

# MORE FUN PLACES TO EAT

WILLIAMSTOWN

**Alice's Restaurant,** 115 North Main Street; (606) 824–7633. Home cooking.

CRITTENDEN

**B & E Log Cabin Restaurant,** I–75 exit 166; (606) 428–2907. Home cooking and homemade desserts.

DRY RIDGE

**Little Shrimp Restaurant,** 20 Broadway; (606) 824–5000. Sandwiches and ice cream.

# SANITY LAND

A few miles south of Owenton on Highway 127 sits a pink frame house in a yard full of angular alligators and stylized wide-eyed beasts. This is not a cubist zoo, but **Siegel Pottery.** Although Greg Siegel has a reputation for producing clay reptiles and collectible marbles, he also makes a variety of functional pots, but not without some humor. For example, a big, sturdy dinner plate glazed with a long pink spiral surrounded by blue comma-shaped dots is called "Boys and Girl." All the pieces are made of stoneware clay and high-fired to about 2,400 degrees Fahrenheit. Many of the sculptural pieces are decorated with local clays and fired in a wood-burning kiln, which produces a rich, earthy effect. The Siegels work at home, so hours are by chance. Rebekka Siegel is nationally known for her exquisite modern quilts. If you have a serious love for this art, ask to see a few of her favorites, or whatever is in progress. She also teaches seminars in quilt technique and design. You can reach the Siegels at (502) 484–2970.

About 10 miles south of Owenton on Highway 127, the little town of Monterey has a few pleasant surprises. One is the ✦ **Jubilee Candle Shop** (502–484–0179). The owner, Paula Nye, has dominated the handmade candle scene in Kentucky since the mid-1970s. Her daughter, Sara Ellis, and several apprentices are continuing the tradition. The Jubilee style is distinctive—bold colors and all imaginable shapes. Call for directions to the studio, and see how art candles are made. Monterey has several other craft studios that feature locally made works. Ask anywhere about arts events, such as literary readings, concerts, and dances held every so often at the Monterey Volunteer Fire Department.

Also in Monterey is ♦ **Larkspur Press,** sponsor of many of the aforementioned literary readings and a fine, fine little press that is Gray Zeitz's pride and joy. Larkspur books, primarily small chapbooks or broadsides by Kentucky writers, are of high quality in form and in content. All productions are done in letterpress from type set by hand and printed on paper that makes you want to touch and linger. Visitors are welcome, but call ahead, because the press may be moving and Zeitz keeps odd hours. Write to Larkspur Press at 340 Sawdridge Creek West, Monterey 40359 or call (502) 484-5390.

To get to Port Royal from Monterey, take Highway 355 north. From the Frankfort area, go north on Highway 421 a little way, then veer onto Highway 193 and go "a right smart piece." When asking directions in Kentucky, you need to understand how far "a piece" is.

## TRUE BLUE

The Franklin Sousley Monument in Flemingsburg honors one of the World War II veterans who raised the American flag at Iwo Jima.

Unfortunately, I can't give you an absolute definition. "Just a little piece" can mean a couple of miles or a few hundred yards, depending on the look in a person's eyes and the tone of the voice. If you don't imply, by your demeanor, that you will believe the directions, the direction-giver may as well lie . . . and might. A body can travel "a little piece" without completely running dry on patience. Private polling tells me "a little piece" is equivalent to "two whoops and a holler." "A far piece" is as far as language permits us to discuss distance and is, in fact, unattainable. "A right smart piece" is pretty far, but you can get there. And, finally, you must be warned about "no piece at all" or it will fool you all your life, because it sounds like you're already there, but it's farther than that. Allen M. Trout defined it this way: "Say you take a chew of tobacco when you start.

When you have walked far enough to have chewed and spit all the flavor out, you have come no piece at all." Those who abstain from tobacco use will surely be lost.

There is nothing to see in Port Royal but the land and the people who live by the land. That's all there is to see in many other areas of the state, but I'd like for those who are familiar with writer, teacher, and farmer **Wendell Berry** to take a good look at northern Henry County where he makes his home. The Kentucky River forms the eastern border of the county. Here the river basin is wide, the flat bottomland soil rich, the steep hills wooded and deserted. This varied terrain insists that it be farmed in various ways. Except in the wide river bottomland, the arable areas are limited to small, odd-shaped patches, which Wendell Berry chooses to farm with a team of draft horses.

One of the truths Berry repeats is that finicky areas like these are not unique to Henry County. The idiosyncrasies of all lands must be intimately and humbly understood before we can live on them as responsible stewards, he contends. We talk of preserving the wilderness, but we don't preserve the farmland from which we feed ourselves. Farmers are, after all, people who use nature directly, not only for themselves, but also for consumers, by proxy. Wherever you live and travel, look at the land and think about the mystery of your dependency on nature and about how you can respond responsibly. Don't try this alone—talk to people and read Wendell Berry's work.

From Port Royal, follow Highway 389 north into Carroll County, through the town of English, where there are ramps onto I-71, and into Carrollton.

Downtown Carrollton boasts two unusual places of lodging. The **P. T. Baker Bed and Breakfast House** at 406 Highland Avenue is cozy and serves breakfast at the hour of your choosing. For reservations, call (502) 732-4210 on weekends; on weekdays call (606) 525-7088. The **Carrollton Inn** at 218 Main Street is a restored 1812 Colonial inn with ten rooms and a full dining room and lounge. The phone number is (502) 732-6905.

Just upriver a few miles is **Warsaw,** a peaceful one-traffic-light river town in the smallest county in Kentucky. The Gallatin County

Historical Society has restored and furnished an 1843 Gothic Revival–style home. Follow 1-75 to I-71 west and take the Warsaw exit. In town, turn right by the courthouse (the second-oldest continuously operating courthouse in the state, circa 1837) at the only stoplight and look behind the funeral home for the **Hawkins-Kirby House.** For a tour, call a local historian; try Sue M. Bogardus at (606) 567-4591.

## MORE GOOD LODGING

**CARROLLTON**

**Days Inn,** I-71 at Highway 227; (502) 732-9301. $55 and up.

**General Butler State Resort Park,** Highway 227 North; (502) 732-4384. $65 and up.

**Holiday Inn Express,** I-71 at Highway 227; (502) 732-6661. $59 and up.

**GHENT**

**Ghent House,** 411 Main Street; (502) 347-5807. Bed and break fast in antebellum home overlooking the Ohio River.

## MORE FUN PLACES TO EAT

**CARROLLTON**

**Aunt Gabby's,** 1968 Highway 227; (502) 732-9028. Family-style.

**Admirals Supper Club,** 121 Fifth Street; (502) 732-9907. Varied dinner, alcohol served.

**General Butler State Resort Park,** Highway 227 North; (502) 732-4384. Varied menu with buffet.

**Welch's Riverside Restaurant,** 505 Main Street; (502) 732-9118. For breakfast and lunch.

## ODD BONES

Eccentricity saves lives. (How's that for a bumper sticker?) The little-known ◆ **Curtis Gates Lloyd Wildlife Reserve** (606-428-3193) would not exist if the eccentric Mr. Lloyd had not written a twenty-four-page will that thoroughly outlined the future management plan for his 365-acre farm down to every detail. Before he died in

1923, Lloyd erected an enormous granite monument to himself in the woods. One side reads: "Curtis G. Lloyd Born 1859—Died 60 or more years afterwards. The exact number of years, months and days that he lived nobody knows and nobody cares." The other side says: "Curtis G. Lloyd Monument erected in 1922 by himself for himself during his life to gratify his own vanity. What Fools These Mortals Be!" A fool? Not quite. His preserve boasts one of the shamefully few stands of virgin timber in Kentucky. A forest teeming with wildlife and wilderness left to its own beautiful accord—a black walnut, 36 inches in diameter, towers over acres and acres of huge red oaks and poplars. (Please be careful during deer hunting season!) To think that I-75 is within earshot. . . . From Crittenden, follow Highway 25 south a few miles and look for the sign.

◆ **Big Bone Lick State Park** is probably the only prehistoric graveyard you'll ever lay eyes on. From Florence, take Highway 127 south (through Sugartit) and turn west on Highway 338 (Beaver Road) at Beaverlick to the town of Big Bone, then follow signs to the park. Probably during the end of the Ice Age (more than 10,000 years ago), many of the largest mammals on the continent that came to this area to lick the rich veins of salt and sulphur died, leaving their bones scattered around the massive mineral deposit. Some of the bones have been identified as belonging to the huge ground sloths, tapirs, musk oxen, giant bison, and deerlike animals called cervalces, all now extinct. No one knows exactly what the cause of the worldwide destruction of these species was. Some say that glacier expansion drove animals south and created an overly dense population that eventually starved. Others blame an epidemic, unscrupulous primitive hunters, or the hand of a god.

The salt lick also was used by Native Americans and, after 1729, by pioneers who boiled down the brines to make highly valued salt. Legend has it that early Virginian settlers, who were fascinated with the massive bones, used mastodon ribs for tent poles and vertebrae for stools. Even Thomas Jefferson was intrigued. He reportedly had more than 300 specimens kept in the White House for research, but a servant pounded them into fertilizer. Not all the bones are lost, however; Big Bone Lick State Park's museum houses an incredible collection of vertebrate fossils from the area. Hours vary throughout the year. Call (606) 384–3522 for information.

Are you ready for a lesson in botany? Directly across the road from the state park is **Big Bone Gardens,** a six-acre pleasure garden and sales nursery owned by Mark Lawhorn and Mary Ellen Pesek. There are two big "twin" ponds, a bog area, two little ponds full of decorative aquatic plants that are for sale, and a super-duper campy concrete garden sculpture collection (baby deer and hoboes). Plant prices range from $1.00 to $50.00, and the varieties range from common native waterside grasses to Asian lotus plants. The gardens are open on weekends from early spring through July and by appointment otherwise. Park at the Methodist church across the street (but not during Sunday services, please). For an appointment, call (606) 384–1949.

## TRUE BLUE

People from across the nation send or bring their Christmas cards to the little town of Bethlehem, in Henry County, for a special Christmas postmark.

Although thousands of people on I-75 see the sign on the side of the barn daily, ✦ **Tewes Poultry Farm** is off the beaten path in spirit. The Tewes family (pronounced TOO-wis) raises and processes more than 3,000 turkeys annually, and more than 600 chickens every two weeks in addition to keeping some Leghorn hens for eggs. Poultry isn't everything, however. Mary Tewes, the head of the 100-acre farm and omnipresent matron, is the proud mother of eighteen, grandmother of seventy-eight, and great-grandmother of an ever-growing number. After almost half a century on the place, she still makes meals on a big wood cookstove, works alongside the younger generations sorting and washing eggs, tends to customers, and does the hundreds of tasks that are necessary on a "small" farm.

Way before the Interstate existed, the Teweses made final payments on their land by selling Easter chicks dipped in pastel-colored food dyes. Today I-75 cuts through the front pasture, a lumberyard sits adjacent to the house, and planes rush overhead to the Greater Cincinnati International Airport. Easter chicks would barely pay the feed bills and aren't considered ethical anymore. Despite the changes, the Teweses carry on a diverse, wholesome operation. Stop to get fresh fryers, big-breasted roasters, turkeys, bacon, eggs, and a vitamin-like dose of friendliness. The birds are dressed on Thursdays or Fridays. Tewes Poultry Farm is just north of Florence. From I-75, take the Buttermilk Pike exit and go into Crescent Springs. Turn left on Anderson Road and look for the farm about a mile on the left. They're always home and you're always welcome, but call ahead anyway at (606) 341-8844.

Said to be "the world's smallest house of worship," the **Monte Casino Chapel** (606-344-3309) measures just 6 by 9 feet—no better place for an intimate conversation with God. Just close the door and let fly. The chapel was built in 1810 in a vineyard on a hill just outside of Covington by Benedictine monks. In the late 1960s the chapel was moved to its present site on the campus of Thomas More College. From I-75, take I-275 east and exit on Turkeyfoot Road. Monte Casino Chapel is next to a large pond on the left side of the road.

If you take the Buttermilk Pike exit and cross to the east side of the Interstate, you won't miss the **Oldenberg Brewery and American Museum of Brewing History** complex (606-341-7223). As you tour this operating brewery, you'll also see what is billed as the largest collection of beer and brewing memorabilia ever assembled. (There are nearly 1 million items on display, so who's to argue?) Beer can collectors, this is the place for you! Tours of the museum and the brewery are given daily from 10:00 A.M. to 5:00 P.M. A tour and taste costs $5.00.

Head toward the river, get on Highway 8, follow it west into Constance, and look for the ◆ **Anderson Ferry** (606-485-9210), a two-boat operation in business since 1817. Today this is the quickest crossing from Cincinnati, via Ohio's Highway 50, to the airport on I-275, especially when the bridges nearer town are choked by rush hour. Paul Anderson's two ferries, Boone 7 and Boone 8 or Little Boone, haul passengers on demand year-round. On the Kentucky landing an old character named Arnold hangs out and "treats" customers to an endless pseudohistory of the boats and his life. From November through April, hours are 6:00 A.M. to 8:00 P.M., and from May through October, from 6:00 A.M. to 9:30 P.M. On Sunday they start running at 7:00 A.M. The ferry runs about every fifteen minutes. Cars are charged $2.75.

# MORE GOOD LODGING

BURLINGTON

**Burlington's Willis Graves House,** 5825 Jefferson Street; (606) 344-0665. Antebellum house decorated with antiques. $75 and up.

**First Farm Inn,** 2510 Stevens Road; (606) 586-0199. Bed and breakfast in an 1870s home on a working horse farm. $75 and up.

FLORENCE

**Best Western Inn,** 7821 Commerce Drive; (606) 525-0090. $54 and up.

**Wildwood Inn Fundome and Spas,** 7809 Highway 42; (606) 371-6300. $75 and up.

FORT MITCHELL

**Drawbridge Estate,** I-75 at Buttermilk Pike; (606) 341-2800. Adjacent to Oldenberg Brewery. $70 and up.

# MORE FUN PLACES TO EAT

FLORENCE

**Burbank's Real Bar-B-Q,** 7908 Delta Avenue; (606) 371-7373.

FORT THOMAS

**El Midway Café,** 1017 South Fort Thomas Avenue; (606) 781-7666. Great fajitas and other mesquite fare in a restored 1890s saloon.

FORT MITCHELL

**Indigo Bar and Grill,** 2053 Dixie Highway; (606) 331-4339. Salads, pastas, and gourmet pizza.

CLARYVILLE

**Ingram's,** Highway 27 and Lickert Road; (606) 635-0022. Country diner with great pies.

## METRO AREA

If Covington's century-old ◆ **Cathedral Basilica of the Assumption** at the corner of Twelfth and Madison Streets (606–431–2060) were in a major coastal city or in Europe, people would rave about it. As it is, this remarkable work of French Gothic architecture is little known to the world. The building is closely modeled after Paris's Notre Dame and the Abbey Church of Saint Denis, complete with flying buttresses and fantastic gargoyles perched high on the facade. Glass is everywhere. Eighty-two windows, including two enormous rose windows, glow endlessly with the changing sun. Measuring 24 feet by 67 feet, the hand-blown, stained-glass window in the transept is said to be the largest in the world. The rich color, variety of shapes, and expressive details can leave you staggering and dizzy in the huge chamber. In one chapel are several paintings by Frank Duveneck, a Covington native who became an internationally known portrait and genre painter and sculptor. My favorite is the austere center panel of the Eucharist triptych of Mary Magdalene at the foot of the cross. To the visual strength of the space, add the music of three massive pipe organs, and you will be transported. (The basic building was constructed, beginning in 1894, for the price of $150,000, the cost of many of today's middle-American homes.)

The altar in the Blessed Sacrament Chapel reads "Behold the Bread of Angels Becomes the Food of Wayfarers," so the faith-inspired beauty of this temple of worship is available to us worldly wanderers. The basilica is open daily from 10:00 A.M. to 4:00 P.M., when greeters are present to answer your questions.

Adjacent to the basilica is the former chancery and the recently opened **Cathedral Museum,** where the cathedral treasures are on display. Gold and silver vessels for worship are decorated with cloisonné enamel and semiprecious stones. The choice of the first Catholic missionary to Kentucky, Father Brodin is included in the collection. Museum and gift shop are open when the cathedral is, except on Monday.

**Mutter Gottes Kirch** (West Sixth and Montgomery Streets; 606–291–2288) is another of Covington's fabulous churches that is open to visitors. Started in 1870, Mutter Gottes Kirch (translated,

Mother of God Church) was built in Italian (rather than French) Renaissance basilica design. Clock-bearing twin spires over the front facade seem to be held in place by the large apse dome. Inside, the lower panels of the magnificent stained-glass windows depict Old Testament promises while the upper panels depict the corresponding fulfillments. Other inspirational art includes sculpture, some by Covington artist Ferdinand Muer, Stations of the Cross, an 1876 Koehnken and Grimm pipe organ, beautiful floor tile, and large frescoes and murals by Johann Schmitt, who was once Frank Duveneck's teacher and whose work is in the Vatican.

### TRUE BLUE

Main Street in Cynthiana, Kentucky, has more cast-iron-front buildings than Chicago.

Go through Covington's Riverside Drive–Licking River Historic District on the east side of town by "the Point" where the Licking River empties into the mighty Ohio. Follow Second Street east until it becomes Shelby Street and wraps around to become Riverside Drive. On the strip of land between the street and the river is the **George Rogers Clark Park,** so named because Clark supposedly stopped at the site to gather forces on his way to Ohio to fight Shawnees. In the park are a few new pieces of sculpture by George Danhires. The most fun is a bronze likeness of James Bradley, an African-born slave who worked his way to freedom, crossed the Ohio River, attended seminary in Cincinnati in 1834, and went down in history as the only former slave to participate in the famous, fiery Lane Seminary debates on abolition. Bradley is depicted as reading thoughtfully on a park bench facing the river. The piece is so realistic that passersby stop talking so as not to disturb the man.

Across the street the Natchez-like houses seem self-conscious, built to be worthy of facing the river. ◆ **Mimosa Mansion Museum,** at 412 East Second Street, is the only building open to the public in the area. Built in 1853–1855 by Thomas Porter, Mimosa Mansion is said to be the largest single-family home in all of northern Kentucky. Touring the mansion you experience the original gas lighting system and the first electric system with its carbon filament light bulbs, high-style Belter furniture, double parlor, and two turn-of-the-century player grand pianos that actually

**Cathedral Basilica of the Assumption**

play classical music. From January through November hours are 1:00 to 6:00 P.M. Saturday and Sunday. During December, special Christmas tours are given on weekends from 1:00 to 8:00 P.M. or by appointment. Admission is $4.00. Call (606) 261–9000.

The bright blue Covington/Cincinnati Suspension Bridge, just a few blocks west of the Licking Riverside Neighborhood, has been renamed the **John A. Roebling Suspension Bridge** in honor of the engineer who designed it. When it opened in 1867, after twenty-two years of construction, the bridge was the longest of its kind in the world (1,057 feet) and served Roebling as a prototype for his later Brooklyn Bridge in New York City.

## TRUE BLUE

The film *Rain Man*, starring Dustin Hoffman and Tom Cruise, was filmed in the Northern Kentucky/Cincinnati area.

Take Garrard Street south and look on the right for the **Amos Shinkle Townhouse Bed and Breakfast,** circa 1854. What was once a posh residence for one of Covington's early big businessmen, Amos Shinkle, is now an impressive bed and breakfast facility. Co-owners Bernie Moorman and Don Nash have taken pains to maintain such interesting features as the original murals on the walls of the front staircase. Rooms range from a master suite with a whirlpool to a converted carriage house that is ideal for families. Prices range from $77 to $130 and include a full breakfast. Call (606) 431–2118 or (800) 972–7012.

Another handsome place of lodging is the ◆ **Sandford House Bed and Breakfast** at 1026 Russell Street in an area known as the Old Seminary Square Historic District (from Eighth to Eleventh Streets). Built in the early 1820s for politician Thomas Sandford and sold in 1835 to the Western Baptist Theological Institute, the house was caught in the middle of one of Kentucky's hottest disputes. Northern and Southern trustees feuded so severely over the slavery issue that the seminary was forced to split into two separate schools, one in Georgetown and one in Findlay, Ohio. Hosts Dan and Linda Carter keep an award-winning garden and, in mild weather, serve breakfast in a gazebo surrounded by award-winning landscaping. The penthouse offers a beautiful view of downtown

## WILDER SPIRITS

Some of the wildest ghosts in Kentucky have been spotted at Bobby Mackey's (44 Licking Pike; 606-431-5588), a country-and-western club in Wilder, not far from Newport. Over the years, more than thirty people, employees and patrons alike, have reported seeing ghosts. And these aren't your friendly ghosts—one man claimed to have been attacked by a ghost in a club rest room. Local legend has it that the hauntings are the result of the building's use for satanic worship in the nineteenth century, and its speakeasy days during the 1920s. The owner has tried exorcism and has even posted warning signs so patrons know that not all the spirits at this nightclub come in bottles.

Cincinnati. Prices begin at $55 a night. Call (606) 291-9133 or (888) 291-9133 for reservations.

Although **Main Strasse** has been billed as a miniature German village in downtown Covington, historically the area is ethnically heterogeneous. German, Irish, and African Americans have lived in this architecturally fascinating neighborhood, which has been developed into a shopping district for tourists. You can find everything from antiques and doll boutiques to restaurants and bakeries. At the edges of the developed area are local pubs with Irish names.

One of the best restaurants in town is not German, but Cajun. **Dee Felice Café,** at 529 Main Street, next to the Goose Girl Fountain, is hot. The food is spicy and the jazz is cool. From a bowl of gumbo for about $5.00 to spicy blackened seafood and chicken (entrees range from $14.95 to $21.95), the flavor tugs at the southern palate. It's hard to believe that the ornate building was originally a pharmacy. No Super-X can hold a candle to these pressed tin ceilings and miniature Corinthian columns, details of which are preserved in the restaurant and painted audacious colors. Every night a live band plays Dixieland, blues, and lots of jazz on a stage behind the long bar. The founder, the late Dee Felice, was a jazz drummer in his own right; he used to play with James Brown, Mel Torme, Sergio Mendez, and others. Lunch hours are 11:00 A.M. to 2:30 P.M. Monday through Friday. Dinner begins at 5:00 P.M. nightly. The phone number is (606) 261-2365.

On the beaten path of Main Strasse, but worth your time if you have young children, is ✦ **The Village Puppet Theatre** at 606 Main Street. Puppeteers Linda Mason and Nancy Hundrup give "live" puppet and marionette shows year-round, Wednesday through Sunday. Great traditional stories like "Jack and the Beanstalk" and "The Elves and the Shoemaker" are scheduled along with musical shows featuring trick marionettes. The lobby has a concession stand and a small store featuring, of course, puppets—ranging from inexpensive hand puppets to giant, intricate marionettes. Tickets are $5.25 per person. Call for exact show times at (606) 291-5566.

Iron Horse history buffs, take note of the **Railway Exposition Company, Inc., Museum** at 315 West Southern Avenue. This museum has a number of immaculately preserved items, such as a 1906 Southern Railroad open platform business car, a diner built for the Golden Rocket, several locomotives, sleeping cars, post office cars, cabooses, and more. Guided tours of the museum are available May through October on Saturdays, Sundays, and holidays from 1:00 to 4:00 P.M. Admission is charged. Call (606) 491-RAIL for more information.

Unique knickknack nautical decor and more awaits you any hour of the day or night at **Covington's Anchor Grill** (438 Pike Street; 606-431-9498). Eating with neighborhood locals becomes a dining experience when you put a quarter in the jukebox. The mechanized C.C. doll band display comes to life in the corner of the grill while overhead a rotating ballroom star light sets the mood.

Across the Licking River and northeast of Newport is the **Weller Haus Bed and Breakfast,** in Bellevue's Taylor Daughters' Historic District at 319 Poplar Street (2 blocks south of Highway 8). For $75 to $130, you can eat a classy breakfast and sleep peacefully amid eighteenth-century antiques in an attractive, folk-style Victorian house. According to AAA, this is a three-diamond bed and breakfast. Call (606) 431-6829 or (800) 431-HAUS for reservations.

Since 1939 **Schneider's Sweet Shop,** at 420 Fairfield Avenue (Route 8), has been Bellevue's most exquisite temple of the sweet tooth. Using old-fashioned equipment and timeless craftmanship, Jack Schneider creates truly fantastic homemade ice creams and candies. The place is famous, especially during the winter holiday season, for its "opera creams," unusual little chocolate candies with rich, creamy centers, available in the Tri-State area only. Schneider's other famous originals include the summer top-seller, Ice Ball with Ice Cream, a scoop of vanilla ice cream with shaved ice packed around it and a healthy dose of specially concocted syrup poured over the top. They have won the award for best caramel apple in the Cincinnati area and have the popular vote for Jack's own favorite, Cookies 'n' Cream ice cream. This heaven is open Monday through Saturday from 10:00 A.M. to 9:00 P.M. and Sunday from noon to 9:00 P.M. Call (606) 431–3545.

## MORE GOOD LODGING

COVINGTON

**Carneal House Inn,** 405 East Second Street; (606) 431–6130. Six guest rooms in a Palladian-Georgian-style mansion. $100 and up.

**Embassy Suites Hotel Cincinnati at RiverCenter,** 101 East River-Center Boulevard; (606) 261–8400. Luxurious accommodations overlooking Cincinnati. $100 and up.

**Summer House Bed and Breakfast,** 610 Sanford Street; (606) 431–3121. Caribbean atmosphere with several rooms and suites. $75 and up.

NEWPORT

**Gateway Bed and Breakfast,** 326 East Sixth Street; (606) 581–6447. Spacious rooms in an Italianate-style townhouse. $75 and up.

## MORE FUN PLACES TO EAT

COVINGTON

**Brewworks,** Twelfth Street at I–71/75 exit 191; (606) 581–BREW. Multilevel restaurant and microbrewery in renovated turn-of-the-century building.

**Gumbo Charlie's,** 1 Madison Avenue; (606) 491–3100. Seafood in a casual atmosphere.

**Mike Fink's,** Greenup Street at Ohio River; (606) 261–4212. Dine aboard an authentic sternwheeler.

**Wertheim's,** 514 West Sixth Street; (606) 261–1233. Traditional German fare plus pasta and chicken dishes.

NEWPORT

**Crockett's River Cafe,** 101 Riverboat Row; (606) 581–2800. Seafood in an art deco setting along the river.

# BUFFALO TRACE AREA

The river towns strung along the mighty Ohio and the areas that spread away from them are usually historically significant and, for that reason, often a touch schizophrenic, caught between the stillness of the past and the fluid present. **Augusta**, in Bracken County, is one of the few such towns that has struck a happy balance while remaining scenic. From Covington or Newport, either hug the banks of the Ohio River by following Highway 8 east, or buzz along the newer "AA" Highway 546, which connects Alexandria and Ashland. If you take the AA, watch for its intersection with Highway 1159. Turn left (north) and meander around for a moment at the **Walcott Covered Bridge**, a 75-foot wooden bridge spanning Locust Creek, which was active from 1824 until 1954. Walk into the bridge and read the descriptions of bridge types, definitions of terms, and explanations for methods of construction.

You may have already seen Augusta if you watched the television miniseries "Centennial" because the town was used to film scenes taking place in St. Louis, Missouri, in the 1880s. Because Augusta has no flood wall, Water Street (or Riverside Drive) was a ready-made set, except

## TRUE BLUE

The only replica of the tomb of Jesus in the United States is in the Garden of Hope in Covington.

for a few details—the film crew put down 4 inches of dirt on the street to cover the pavement and pulled down power lines and business signs. The houses along the river were, as they always are, picture perfect. Since then, several Public Broadcasting System (PBS) productions have been filmed in Augusta, including the classic *Huckleberry Finn.*

❧ **The Beehive Tavern,** on the north corner of Main Street and Riverside Drive, is an elegant Colonial-style restaurant and bed and breakfast located in a 1790s row house facing the river. Drinks are served from noon until closing Wednesday through Saturday on the upstairs balcony, which has a perfect river view. Inside, lunch and dinner are served between noon and 8:00 P.M. Wednesday and Thursday, between noon and 9:00 P.M. Friday and Saturday, and from 1:00 to 7:00 P.M. Sunday. The menu changes every two weeks and includes items such as roast pork with fried apples, cornbread stuffing, and some Spanish dishes, reflecting the heritage of owner Luciano Moral, who was born in Cuba to Spanish parents. Entrees range from $10.95 to $16.50. Be sure to save room for desserts; the blueberry trifle cake and caramel flan are primo.

Directly across the street is the **Augusta Ferry** (606-756-3291), one of the very few functional ferries on the Ohio River. It's operational year-round during daylight hours and, although a trip schedule exists, the captain will carry you across any time. The ride costs $5 per car. Imagine yourself crossing the water when the town was new and the ferry was powered by mules. One block east of the ferry is the **Riverside House 1860 Bed and Breakfast,** a meticulously renovated Victorian home. Starting at $72 a night you get the full Victorian treatment—bedrooms decked out in period antiques, English breakfast, high tea at 4:00 P.M., and one of the most serene views of the river in town. Call (606) 756-2458 for reservations.

A popular event in the area is **"The Old Reliable" Germantown Fair,** held the first week in August at the Germantown fairgrounds on Highway 10. No one seems to be able to explain the "Old Reliable" aspect beyond the fact that it happens every year. Germantown straddles the Bracken–Mason county line. Thirty-three yards from that county line, in Germantown, is a classic country cooking restaurant called **Bonnie's Ole Country Inn** (606-728-2912). There's nothing particularly German about the place, but fast food can't hold a candle to the speed of the cooks, and you get a real meal to boot. Hours are 7:00 A.M. to 7:00 P.M. Monday through Saturday and 7:00 A.M. to 3:00 P.M. Sunday.

Follow Highway 8 along the river to Maysville. If you arrive from the west, there is a functional **covered bridge at Dover.** Highway 1235 crosses Lee's Creek by means of this 61-foot-long "Queensport truss" bridge, which had a toll booth at one end when the oldest part was built in 1835.

Maysville is the next town upriver, the site of the closest bridge to the north, and the hub of activity for the whole area. To steep yourself in area history, go to the **Mason County Museum** (606-564-5865), at 215 Sutton Street, in an 1878 structure originally built to be the town's first library. Because of the historic significance of the area as an early point of access to the west, the little museum tells the bigger story of the expansion of America. Hours are 10:00 A.M. to 4:00 P.M. Monday through Saturday.

In downtown Maysville, right next door to the Ohio River bridge, the visitors bureau shares space with the ◆ **National Underground Railroad Museum** (115 East Third Street; 606-564-9411), which displays documents, photographs, and other items relating to the flight to freedom slaves through a network of brave abolitionists. Maysville was a key point along the railroad, from which escaped slaves from Kentucky and points farther south crossed the Ohio River. Right now the museum's collection is small, but plans are that it will grow and eventually move to its own location. The museum is open Monday through Saturday from 10:00 A.M. to 4:00 P.M. A small admission fee is charged.

Follow Second Street past Sutton and park anywhere. On the north corner of Sutton and Wall Streets is the shop of a fine furniture maker. ◆ **Joseph Byrd Brannen & Co., Antique Furniture Reproductions** is an inspirational one-person operation. Joe Brannen is asked to make all manner of hardwood furniture, but his true love is for traditional eighteenth- and nineteenth-century American furniture in cherry, walnut, mahogany, and curly maple, a wood with delicious figuring and a mean grain from which many woodworkers keep a respectful distance. Joe does use power tools, but he finishes all of his work by hand, using planes or scrapers that are fueled by pure elbow grease. The difference is noticeable and worth the extra cost. He always has a few finished pieces of furniture on hand and welcomes visitors Monday through Saturday from 9:00 A.M. to 5:00 P.M., except on Thursday. Write for a brochure and price list at 145 West Second Street, Maysville 41056, or call (606) 564-3642.

Directly across the street on the corner is **Gantley's Shoe and Harness** (144 West Second; 606-564-9875), another impressive one-craftsperson operation. Joe Gantley can do just about anything with leather. Although he is set up for small work like making belts and repairing shoes and purses, he prefers working on equine equipment. Joe and his wife, Deedee, are known all over the state as fine riders and trainers of American saddlebreds, standardbreds,

## SPEAKING FIGURATIVELY

You know that polite-but-blank stare your children sometimes give you when you're trying to tell them something? Imagine a whole room of it, and you have an idea of what awaits you at **Vent Haven Museum** in Fort Mitchell (33 West Maple Avenue; 606-341-0461). Vent Haven is home to more than 500 ventriloquistic figures (the world's largest known collection), left as a legacy by one William Shakespeare Berger, a Cincinnati businessman and amateur ventriloquist. Assembled between 1947 and Berger's death in 1972 at age 94, his collection includes figures of all shapes, sizes, and heritages, some predating the Civil War; others able to walk, move their noses, spit, and smoke cigarettes. It's a little disconcerting but fascinating, and a tour (by appointment only, May through September) will sure be something to talk about.

and Hackney ponies. Ask him about the horse show photos in his shop. Joe's shop is open weekdays 9:00 A.M. to 5:00 P.M.

Drive west another 2 blocks to Rosemary Clooney Street, so named when her first motion picture premiered in Maysville, her hometown. Go toward the river and you'll find the only active Amtrak station in Kentucky and a great place to eat called **Caproni's Restaurant.** Its national fame began in the 1930s, when it was just a cafe at which eastbound soldiers stopped during train layovers. Today, two long balconies look out over a wide, slow-moving part of the Ohio River. The other selling points are super food, high-quality local and foreign wines, and imported beers. You can have the usual range of country cooking, done with unusual class, or you can indulge in a savory plate of fettuccine Alfredo for a mere $5.95, a New York strip steak for $12.95, or a variety of seafoods. Call (606) 564-4119.

Another of Kentucky's few remaining covered bridges is east of Maysville in Lewis County. From Maysville, take Highway 10 through Plumville and turn left (east) onto Spring Creek Road. Just as you cross the county line at the intersection with Cabin Road you'll see the **Cabin Creek Bridge** on the south side. The 114-foot-long bridge was built in 1897 and closed to traffic in 1983. Call (606) 796-6311 for more information.

Driving the 4 miles straight uphill on Highway 68 between

Maysville and ◆ **Washington** will take you a matter of minutes. In the eighteenth century, however, the climb consumed a whole day. Heavily loaded wagons and carts that had just come across the Ohio River at Maysville (then called Limestone) were worn out by the time they reached the ridge, so they stopped at Washington for a rest. I wouldn't call these pioneers tourists, but their patronage caused the town to grow from a few humble cabins into a bunch of humble cabins.

The area was settled by Simon Kenton, who first claimed the land. Kenton later sold it for 50 cents an acre to Arthur Fox and William Wood, who laid out the town of Washington. Like a good imperialist, Kenton had come to the area in search of sugar cane so that he could get rich making Jamaican-style rum. The hills were indeed covered with cane, but it was wild Kentucky cane, a tall, woody native grass, the only bamboo species native to North America. Nothing sweet about it. Like a good capitalist, Kenton realized his error and went on to exploit some other aspect of the land. He eventually opened a small store in a cabin in Washington; that cabin now stands next to the visitors center. Legend has it that Kenton couldn't pay his bills and was thrown into debtor's prison in Washington, the very town he founded. The tables do turn. . . .

When Kentucky joined the Union in 1792, people west of the Alleghenies thought that Washington, population 462, might become the capital of the United States. (Obviously the other Washington got the vote.) If time could have frozen at that moment, you probably would have seen a town much like the historic restoration that stands today. You can get a more complete story of the town and its characters from one of the tour guides at the visitors center between May 1 and early December, Monday through Saturday from 10:00 A.M. to 4:30 P.M. and Sunday from 1:00 to 4:00 P.M. Rates are $2.00 for adults and $1.00 for students. Call (606) 759-7411 for more information.

Washington is full of small antiques and specialty shops selling everything from rare books to homemade candies to clocks, yarns, dried herbs, and copper lamps. The place to eat in town is ◆ **Brodrick's Tavern Food & Spirits** (606-759-5225) at the corner of Main and "C" Streets. This place has been licensed since 1789, when the first court of the new Mason County, for which Washington served as county seat, granted David Brodrick permission "to keep an ordinary in his home." This is where those tired hill climbers rested before heading down the buffalo trace, the place where the buffalo crossed the river. Lunch is usually served from 11:30 A.M. to 5:00 P.M. Weekend dinner hours begin at 5:00 P.M.

Just a few miles from Washington off Highway 68 is the community of ◆ **Mays Lick.** Founded in the late 1700s, this tiny community has numerous historic buildings and churches. In 1995, Donna and Michael Burkart moved to the town and liked the downtown historic district so much, they bought it, restoring several of the old buildings. Today you can spend a pleasant morning or afternoon strolling through town. At Bootknife Forge and Wiccan Wares (606-763-6308), Bill and Linda Perkins sell handmade iron fences, candleholders, leatherwork, and candles. At The Old Hardware Store (606-763-6506), Bob Hubbard restores antiques and takes custom orders for old-fashioned tin lanterns. There are also a country pine furniture shop and several antiques shops. Coffee, sandwiches, and homemade desserts are on the menu at Izzy B's (606-763-6177). Shop hours vary somewhat, but most are open Tuesday through Saturday from 10:00 A.M. to 5:00 P.M. and Sunday from 11:00 A.M. to 5:00 P.M.

Highway 68 follows a north-south path made by buffalo traveling to and from the salt deposit at Blue Licks. From Maysville, go south on the buffalo trace to the ◆ **Blue Licks Battlefield State Park** (606-289-5507). The place had always been one of importance to the native people as well as to the settlers who mined salt there. Its connotation darkened when in August 1792 more than sixty Kentucky pioneers were killed in a bloody Revolutionary battle against Indians and Canadian soldiers ten months after the British surrendered at Yorktown. All this in a fifteen-minute battle! A large granite obelisk at the park marks the area where the fighters, including Daniel Boone's son Israel, were buried in a common grave.

Take a hike along the buffalo trace beginning in the parking area. This fifteen-acre area is set aside as a state nature preserve in order to protect one of the last and largest stands of Short's goldenrod, a federally endangered species. Notice how the goldenrod grows thickest in

## PREMIUM HOSPITALITY

Had I driven into a time warp? At Henderson Chevron in Tollesboro (east of Maysville), there were no self-service pumps. "Fill her up?" the attendant asked. I hadn't heard those words in years. Owner Paul Henderson even checked under the hood for free. A big orange tabby dozed in the front window. "That's Ol' Yellow—he just came around one day," explained Henderson. Across the road, there was a miniature golf course behind the "White's Hams" building. Nobody was around, but there was an honesty jar to leave the money in if you wanted to play. Small things like these are one of the reasons traveling the backroads is so enjoyable, and Kentucky has many small towns like Tollesboro where you'll find old-fashioned values and friendliness. Folks like Paul Henderson like it that way. "Some folks have told me I ought to go self-service. But we've always done it this way since I started in this business with my dad in '64, and I think we'll just keep it that way."

the open areas. It is speculated that grazing and trampling by buffalo, now nonexistent in Kentucky, helped the plant survive; the buffalo also may have carried the seeds in their thick fur and thus spread the graceful yellow plant. (Goldenrod, by the way, is not responsible for your hay fever. Blame ragweed.) Goldenrod blooms in September, but as tempting as it is, please don't pick any.

The displays in the park museum are concerned with the cultural and geographic history of the area. Several original pieces of Daniel Boone's salt-making equipment are in the museum, donated by descendants of Simon Kenton. In 1778 Boone and a few others made a salt expedition and were taken prisoner by the Shawnees, who adopted many of the white men into their families. Boone was adopted by the chief, Blackfish. Later Simon Kenton retrieved the equipment. Today the park has fishing facilities and all the usual recreational trappings. In mid-August the park sponsors a historic reenactment of the battle during a festival that features period demonstrators and other related entertainment.

This is definitely the region of covered bridges. **Johnson Creek Covered Bridge** crosses the creek on the original buffalo trace just north of Blue Licks Battlefield State Park. Built in 1874, the dilapi-

**Covered Bridge**

dated structure is 114 feet long and 16 feet wide, with Smith-type trusses. Take Highway 68 east from the park, then take Highway 165 north to Highway 1029 and watch for the bridge, which is closed to traffic.

In Fleming County, south of Maysville, there are three covered bridges. The first is the 60-foot-long ◆ **Goddard (White) Covered Bridge,** the only surviving example of Ithiel Town truss design in the state, a latticelike design that uses rigid, triangularly placed beams as supports. Photographers love this spot because a picturesque country church can be seen through the bridge. From Maysville, go to the county seat, Flemingsburg, by way of Highway 11 south. Then follow Highway 32 east almost 6 miles to Goddard. This time, you can drive over the bridge. For more information, call (606) 845-5951.

Follow Highway 32 down the road a piece and turn right (west) on Rawlings Road, or north on Highway 1895 (Maxey Flats Road). At **Ringos Mills** you'll find an 86-foot bridge built in 1867 that was part of a large nineteenth-century gristmill.

A more utilitarian-style covered bridge is a few miles away near Grange City. The 86-foot-long **Hillsboro Bridge** is roofed and sided with corrugated tin, and the abutments are made of "red stone." The construction is of the burr truss-design with multiple king posts. It's a sight! It's also a shame that it's too run-down to use. To get there from Flemingsburg, drive south on Highway 111, pass Hillsboro, and watch the right side of the road.

## MORE GOOD LODGING

### HILLSBORO

**DH Mountain Lake Manor,** Stockton Creek Road; (606) 876–5591. Four rooms in a luxurious manor house on a 1,500-acre riding and fishing resort. $75 to $95.

### MAYSVILLE

**French Quarter Inn,** 25 East McDonald Parkway; (606) 564–8000. $69 and up.

**Kleier Haus,** 912 Highway 62; (606) 759–7663. Three rooms in a renovated turn-of-the-century house. $75.

**Super 8 Motel,** Highway 68; (606) 759–8888. $50 and up.

### AUGUSTA

**White Rose Bed and Breakfast,** 210 Riverside Drive; (606) 756–2787.

### MAYSVILLE

**deSha's Restaurant,** 1166 Highway 68 South; (606) 564–9275. Varied menu with wide selection of appetizers; homemade meat loaf and other specials.

**Tippedore's,** 25 East McDonald Parkway; (606) 564–8000. Seafood and Cajun dishes.

### WASHINGTON

Marshall Key's Tavern, 2111 Old Main Street; (606) 759–5803. Homemade soups, sandwiches, daily specials, and pies.

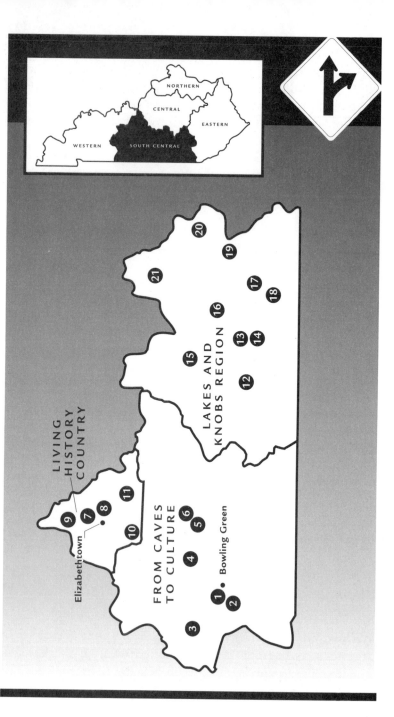

# SOUTH CENTRAL KENTUCKY

1. The Kentucky Museum
2. Riverview at Hobson Grove
3. Woodbury
4. Mammoth Cave National Park
5. The American Cave Museum and Hidden River Cave
6. Wigwam Village
7. Schmidt's Coca-Cola Museum
8. Emma Reno Connor Black History Gallery
9. Patton Museum of Cavalry and Armor
10. Nolin River Nut Tree Nursery
11. Abraham Lincoln Birthplace National Historic Site
12. Lake Cumberland
13. Dunagan's Grocery & Supply
14. Mill Springs Mill
15. Bluegrass Wood and Leather Craft
16. Burnside
17. Cumberland Falls
18. Blue Heron
19. The Harland Sanders Café & Museum
20. Levi Jackson State Park
21. Renfro Valley

# SOUTH CENTRAL KENTUCKY

Kids aren't the only people who need to play and learn. This region's parks and large dammed lakes are like big playgrounds for adults. There are two of the world's natural wonders, Mammoth Cave, which highlights the most spectacular manifestations of Kentucky's unique karst geography, and the breathtaking Cumberland Falls, the second largest cataract in this hemisphere and one of two in the world with a moonbow. South central Kentucky is also associated with history. The north is Lincoln country and home to the state's only African American history gallery, and the south boasts the beautiful Big South Fork National Park. Bowling Green, the largest city, is known, in part, for having the world's only Corvette plant. The whole region is spiced up with amusing town names, quirky craftspeople, and zany festivals.

## FROM CAVES TO CULTURE

Being in the heart of Western Kentucky University's campus on Adams Street in Bowling Green, ◆ **The Kentucky Museum** is not off the beaten path, but its contents are unique. This is one of the best collections of objects pertaining to Kentucky history and culture housed in one place. The museum also makes a special effort to exhibit fine traveling shows and to put together displays using borrowed objects that otherwise would never be in the public view. Traditional Kentucky quilts are the museum's forte. There's a Christmas crazy quilt made of silk hat liners, for example. During the holidays, a houseful of relatives were snowbound for several weeks, so instead of flipping on the tube and watching game shows, they made a quilt together. Some of the quilts are political, such as the 1850 Henry Clay quilt with his portrait in the middle in crewel work, which was a presentation piece from Mrs. Henry Clay to the wife of Senator John Jordan Crittenden. And some quilts are downright fascinating, for example, the dizzying 66,000-piece Spectrum Quilt, which is rare in that it was made in the 1930s by a man, a jeweler who had heard that the work would keep his fingers nimble. The list goes on.

You can't help liking Curiosity Hall, a narrow hall on one side on the museum filled with unusual relics with unusual ties to Kentucky. The oddities include things like doll heads supposedly used during World War I to transport spy messages, and an item known as a "death crown," a ring of feathers found inside the pillow of a deceased person. Some say that the crown means that the person has gone to heaven. Others say that the feathers form a ring slowly during one's life and when the ring is complete, the time has come to die. A friend told me that this belief was so deeply instilled in her during childhood that, despite her logical nature, she still beats her pillows every morning to fight fate and destroy the feather ring. After a year of marriage, her husband got irritated enough with the habit to ask why in tarnation she did it. When she explained, he answered, "That's pathetic, honey. These are foam pillows." Museum hours are 9:30 A.M. to 4:00 P.M. Tuesday through Saturday and 1:00 to 4:00 P.M. Sunday. Admission is charged. Call (502) 745-2592 for further information.

## TRUE BLUE

The world's largest collection of millstones is found at McHargue's Mill near London, Kentucky.

Another downtown museum in Bowling Green is ◆ **Riverview at Hobson Grove,** which grandly overlooks the Barren River. In the late nineteenth century the river was bustling with commerce, so that homes facing the river had to be worthy of the attention they received. The Hobsons built a magnificent, three-story, brick Italianate mansion, which has been restored and filled with period antiques. Excellent guided tours are given from 10:00 A.M. until 4:00 P.M. Tuesday through Saturday and from 1:00 to 4:00 P.M. Sunday. Riverview is closed in January. The house comes to life for visitors, thanks to an award-winning photographic and oral history exhibit called "If Only These Walls Could Talk." To get there, follow Main Avenue north to the outside of the Victoria Street bypass (Hobson Lane), pass the Delafield School, and watch for the sign. Call (502) 843-5565 to find out about the popular seasonal interpretive programs, such as "Victorian Valentine's Day Celebration" and "Nineteenth Century Servant Life."

**Mariah's Restaurant,** downtown at 801 State Street (502-842-6878), is located in Bowling Green's oldest brick house, the circa 1818 home of Mariah Moore, daughter of the town's first

**National Corvette Museum**

white settlers. The Southern-style food is very good, and the restaurant is famous for its homemade appetizers, sauces, and more than thirty variations on the theme of delicious chicken. Open from 11:00 A.M. to 10:00 P.M. daily.

Corvette devotees are already aware that the only Corvette assembly plant in the world is in Bowling Green. The fascinating, hour-long tour of the plant itself is offered at 9:00 A.M. and 1:00 P.M. Monday through Friday, except during model changes and on holidays. It's best to call and confirm at (502) 745-8419. The **National Corvette Museum** at exit 28 off I-65 gives fans a good look at the history and glory of the racy, powerful, best sports car made in America. There are nostalgic displays and lots of souvenirs. One thing sure to spark your curiosity is the building itself, an unusual asymmetrical, yellow, almost conical structure with a huge red spire.

A query about the design to a museum employee elicited the following explanation: "Well, when the museum opened, the newspaper said that some Corvettes of the '50s and '60s had a red cone coming out of the back light. Later, someone told us that from the air, the building looked like part of the dashboard. Finally we called the architect, who said that neither was the case; he had simply wanted to create a building that was completely different." Which it is. Admission is $8.00 for adults, $4.00 for ages 6–16, and $6.00 for ages 55 and over. Hours are 9:00 A.M. to 7:00 P.M. daily. For museum information, call (502) 781-7973.

In its heyday ❖ **Woodbury** was a busy little town on the Green River at the site of Lock and Dam Number 4. After the log structure, which was finished in 1841, washed away in 1965, the Butler County Historical and Genealogical Society developed Woodbury into a museum complex. What was formerly the lock keeper's home has been transformed into The **Green River Museum** (502-526-2133), a visual history lesson about the riverboat era in Woodbury. The remains of the lock and dam structure are visible from the museum's big porch. From mid-April through Labor Day, the museum is open on weekends or by appointment. Woodbury has a very unusual way of celebrating Mother's Day. Every Mother's Day weekend, about 500 flintlock rifle enthusiasts gather in Woodbury for the **Annual Rifle Frolic.** Dressed in pioneer garb, they spend two days demonstrating the fine points of early skills such as flintlock rifle shooting and tomahawk throwing.

Notice on your map how the Kentucky border bulges just a bit to the south in this area. Legend has it that when the border was surveyed and this land was to be relegated to Tennessee, a farmer named Sanford Duncan invited the surveying team to a party at the Duncan Tavern, a popular spot for travelers on the Louisville-to-Nashville trek because of the fine food and Kentucky liquor served there. The surveyors were so appreciative (and drunk) that they agreed to survey all of Duncan's land into Kentucky. The heck with straight lines.

If you travel northeast of Bowling Green, you will be in some of the most spectacular cave country in the world. Second to the Kentucky Derby, ❖ **Mammoth Cave National Park** is the best nationally known tourist attraction in the state, and for that reason, travelers can get information about cave history and trips anywhere within a hundred-mile radius. While definitely a well-beaten path (about 2.1 million people visit every year, and during the summer months it can be incredibly crowded), Mammoth Cave does have lesser known aspects. Explore the cave in an old-fashioned light on a Gothic Lantern Tour. Or take a Wild Cave Tour and crawl through tight passages. Whatever tour you decide to take, if you're coming in the summer, especially on weekends, it's a good idea to reserve your cave tour well in advance. Call (800) 967-2283.

Above ground, there are more than 70 miles of wonderful hiking trails. Visit the **Old Guides Cemetery,** near the Heritage Trail near the Cave's Historic Entrance. Among those buried here is Stephen Bishop, the cave's preeminent explorer in the 1800s. Bishop, like many of the people who helped map underground passages and served as tour guides in antebellum days, was a slave. His owner purchased Mammoth Cave about 1838. Bishop's many discoveries led to national renown and resulted in his gaining his freedom in 1856. He hoped to purchase the freedom of his wife and son and emigrate to Liberia but was unable to do this before his death in 1857. Mammoth Cave is open every day but Christmas. Call (502) 758-2251 or 758-2328 for more information.

To date, the navigable cave system in this area is more than 300 miles long. Ask about some of the odd projects the cave provoked, such as an underground hospital for tuberculosis victims. The cool, clean cave air would have been good for any victim of lung disease, but smoke from the cooking fires accumulated in the chamber where they lived and killed them quickly. What the doctors needed was more basic than holistic thinking—they needed common sense. Other cave project artifacts include leaching vats, which remain from the time when saltpeter (sodium nitrate or potassium nitrate) was extracted for making gunpowder during the War of 1812. Also make sure you hear the whole story of the explorer Floyd Collins. For many years his casket was on display in the Crystal Onyx Cave, to which he had been searching for a new entrance when he died. In 1929 when local cave owners were competing fiercely for tourists, someone stole Collins's body and dumped it in the Green River because it was a popular attraction. His remains have since been reinterred in a less public place.

◆ **The American Cave Museum and Hidden River Cave** on Main Street in Horse Cave is an environmental education museum developed by the American Cave Conservation Association, Inc. The association's worthy mission is to educate people, especially those who live on karstlands, about how the land works and about how our actions affect the health of the system. Venial sins like

dumping trash in sinkholes become mortal sins in karst areas, where the whole groundwater system can easily be contaminated. Just the entrance to Hidden River Cave is accessible through the museum (for the first time since 1943). Previously, no one wanted to go near the cave and its underground stream because it reeked of raw sewage.

Other exhibits in the museum include a whole wall display devoted to bats, a large cross-section of a karst region, and stories and artifacts from mines, bootlegging operations, early tourist endeavors, prehistoric shelters, and ceremonial sites. For more information, contact: ACCA, Main and Cave Streets, P.O. Box 409, Horse Cave 42749, or call (502) 786-1466. Museum hours are 9:00 A.M. to 5:00 P.M. Monday through Friday and 1:00 to 5:00 P.M. on weekends from Memorial Day through Labor Day.

**The Horse Cave Theatre** is one of only eight professional theaters in rural America. From late June through October, the company stages six productions per season. The range of genres is broad—Shakespeare, modern comedies, thrillers, and experimental theater by regional playwrights—and the theater thereby maintains a loyal local audience in addition to tourists. Performances run every evening except Monday at the large open-thrust stage in downtown Horse Cave at 107-109 East Main Street. Weekend days also feature matinees. Call (502) 786-2177 or (800) 342-2177.

After spelunking or theatergoing you'll probably be irresistibly tempted to retire to your own personal concrete wigwam motel room, complete with rustic hickory furniture, color television, and fake smoke hole and tent flaps at ◆ **Wigwam Village.** Take exit 53

**Wigwam Village**

off I–65 and turn left; at the second stoplight, head north on Highway 31W and go 1 mile until you see a semicircle of fifteen white wigwams with a red zigzag design on the side. In the center is the 57-foot-high office wigwam, all built in 1937, way before the interstate existed and before concrete construction was very sophisticated. Before Americans got their kicks on the now-legendary Route 66, these maverick lodgings rose boldly from the flat plains of south central Kentucky. The first wigwam village, which has been demolished, was 12 miles away, and there's one other group existing in Holbrook, Arizona. If you want to lodge in these little gems, especially on a weekend night, you'd best plan about six months in advance. Prices range from $35 to $45 per night. Groups can reserve the whole village. Call (502) 773-3381 before 10:00 P.M. for information and reservations. The village is closed from mid-December until April 1.

Kentucky was a state deeply divided during the Civil War, and exhibits at the **Hart County Museum** (109 Main Street; 502-524-0101) in Munfordville, 3 miles north of Horse Cave, demonstrate this point well. Among the Civil War artifacts at the museum are items belonging to two Hart Countians who fought in the conflict. Confederate General Simon Bolivar Buckner and Union Major General Thomas Wood were childhood friends and West Point classmates who later found themselves fighting on opposite sides of the conflict. The Munfordville battleground site is being preserved by the county historical society. A museum staff member can guide you there.

Several Amish communities are located in Hart County, and in summer months, you can buy fresh produce and other items on the courthouse lawn. Year-round, it's worth a drive out Logdson Mill Road to **Anna's Kitchen.** Anna Miller makes delicious jellies and relishes; stop by any day except Sunday. There's no phone; watch for the sign on the left.

East of Bowling Green, the next sizable town is Glasgow, host of the **Highland Games and Gathering of Scottish Clans,** held near the end of May or in early June at Barren River Lake State Resort Park east of Glasgow on Highway 31. The games begin with a musical extravaganza called the Tattoo, then clan and society members get together for a Tartan Ball and Scottish Country Dancing. Last but not least exciting are the athletic and battleax competitions, which originated as martial exercises under King Malcolm Canmore in Scotland around 1060. The best-known aspect of the gathering, however, is the Ceilidh, another set of musical performances by American and international musicians—praised by Fiona Ritchie of National Public Radio's "Thistle and Shamrock" show. For more information, contact: Glasgow Highland Games, Inc., P.O. Box 1373, Glasgow 42142, or call (502) 651-3141.

The **Hall Place Bed and Breakfast** is a handsome place to spend the night and have a big country ham breakfast. From downtown Glasgow, take Highway 31E south (South Green Street) for a block and a half and look for the sign on the right. Although the house was built in 1852, the three B&B rooms have modern, private baths, phones, and televisions. Rates are

$45 per night single, $50 double. Call (502) 651–3176 for more information.

From Glasgow, take Highway 63 south to Tompkinsville, the Monroe County seat. Follow Highway 1446 south of town for about 3 miles to the **Old Mulkey Meeting House.** Built in 1804, it is not only the oldest log meeting house in the state, but it is probably the only example of highly symbolic log architecture. The building's twelve corners represent the twelve Apostles and the three doors are meant to be reminders of the Trinity. Daniel Boone's oldest sister, Hannah, is buried in the cemetery alongside other early settlers.

## TRUE BLUE

Although Kentucky never left the Union during the Civil War, a Confederate capitol was established at Bowling Green.

Unassuming as it looks, Tompkinsville has a bizarre reputation to uphold. In early September this town hosts the most popular event in the **Monroe County Watermelon Festival,** the Privy Grand Prix. Yes, it's an outhouse race, and it's professional. The outhouses (3-by-30-by-6 feet from the ground) must be made of wood, except for the wheels and roofs, and teams must consist of two people pulling, two pushing, and one sitting on the john who must wear a seat belt and crash helmet and weigh at least 100 pounds. Contestants dream of breaking the toilet paper ribbon in a shower of glory. The festival's main theme is watermelons, however, so there has to be a seed-spitting contest. In 1982, the first year of the Privy Grand Prix, the announcer for the spitting contest got tongue-tied and made a first call for "speed-sitting." Thus, serendipity gave birth to a new, perfect name for the outhouse race. Call (502) 487–9548 for more information.

## MORE GOOD LODGING

### BOWLING GREEN

**Best Western Motor Inn,** I-65 Exit 122; (502) 782–3800 or 800–343–2937. About $60 per night.

### GLASGOW

**Four Seasons Country Inn,** 4107 Scottsville Road; (502) 678–1000.

Twenty-one guest rooms with private baths. $64 to $109 per night.

**Mammoth Cave Hotel,** Mammoth Cave National Park; (502) 758–2225. Rooms and cottages; pet kennel available. About $75 per night.

### BROWNSVILLE
**The Mello Inn,** 2856 Nolin Dam Road; (502) 286–4126. Newly constructed Victorian-style house on twelve acres. $65 to $75 per night.

### SMITHS GROVE
**Victorian House Bed and Breakfast,** 130 Main Street; (502) 563–9403. Four rooms with private baths and fireplaces; located in antiques district 10 miles north of Bowling Green. About $85 per night.

# MORE FUN PLACES TO EAT

### CAVE CITY
**Happy Days Diner,** Highway 31W North; (502) 773–5851. A 1950s jukebox sets the tone for breakfast, lunch, and dinner. Near Wigwam Village.

**Sahara Steak House,** 413 Happy Valley Road; (502) 773–3450. Steaks, seafood, and country ham dishes.

### HORSE CITY
**Trees Restaurant,** 114 East Main Street; (502) 786–1717. Barbecued ribs and a lavish seafood buffet.

### BOWLING GREEN
**The Parakeet Café,** 951 Chestnut Street; (502) 781–1538. Pasta and traditional beef and chicken dishes served in a refurbished blacksmith's shop.

**440 Main Restaurant and Bar,** 440 East Main Avenue; (502) 793–0450. Elegant dining in a restored historic home.

# LIVING HISTORY COUNTRY

"The pause that refreshes will make husband more helpful." Wives everywhere want to know: What kind of pause? At what price? Every experienced consumer knows that it's Coca-Cola, at the cost of 5 cents per pause in 1934 when the phrase was printed on a drink tray. ◆ **Schmidt's Coca-Cola Museum** in the Coca-Cola Bottling Company of Elizabethtown is an I-remember-that-one experience with a dark twist. Go north of town on Highway 31W. In the museum you'll find yourself growing curiously thirsty. These Coca-Cola memorabilia are antiques, but it seems that subliminal (and overt) messages were being employed by advertisers from the beginning. The color red is pervasive, and the "Coca-Cola Girls" smile out from every wall, eternally in full bloom. In the beverage's early days, it was advertised as a virtual panacea. One poster reads: "The slightly tonic effect of Coca-Cola relieves fatigue and calms overwrought nerves without undue stimulation. It is genuinely good to the taste and aids digestion." Though it is never mentioned in the museum, keep in mind that Coke was originally, in 1888, sold as a mouthwash and contained a small quantity of cocaine, an ingredient eliminated in 1905. Now we have only sugar (or Nutra-Sweet) and an almost patriotic penchant for the stuff. Come see one of America's favorite seducers. Hours are Monday through Friday from 9:00 A.M. to 4:00 P.M. There is a small admission fee. Call (502) 737-4000 for more information.

Polarities can be wonderful teachers. Leave the Coke Museum and please, please, please take time to get an education at the ◆ **Emma Reno Connor Black History Gallery.** Go southeast of the courthouse on East Dixie Avenue, veer left onto Hawkins Drive, and look immediately for a white stucco house on the right with a sign that says BLACK HISTORY GALLERY painted on a set of black concrete steps in the front yard. This was the childhood home of the late Emma Reno Connor, a teacher who recognized a disgraceful dearth of information about the lives and accomplishments of African Americans. She supplemented her lesson plans with pictures, articles, and stories of African Americans and later organized these teaching materials into museum displays.

An amateur museum that comprises well-organized cutouts from magazines, original pen-and-ink portraits of great people, poems by Ms. Connor, and newspaper articles, this is also a powerful place full of love, knowledge, and opportunities to see our culture from another true angle. You'll enjoy learning about the lives and accomplishments of Satchmo (Louis Armstrong), Josephine Baker, Langston Hughes, Sojourner Truth, Gwendolyn Brooks, Frederick Douglass, and Martin Luther King, Jr., to name a few outstanding people. Hours are noon to 5:00 P.M. Saturday and Sunday or as posted. On weekdays, make an appointment with Charles Connor, Emma's widower, at (502) 769-5204 or with her sister Ruby Williams at (502) 765-7653. A tour of the gallery with Mr. Connor brings nationally known figures to life, and Ms. Williams knows the personal histories of local heroes. Together they could change your life.

Many towns of historic significance offer walking tours of their downtowns, but few resurrect the characters in living color. In the summer, try the **Elizabethtown Historic Walking Tours,** during which you meet and see a brief "performance" by Sarah Bush Johnston Lincoln (Abe's stepmother), P. T. Barnum, Jenny Lind, Carrie Nation, and eight other historical figures portrayed by local people dressed in period costumes who are well versed in their figure's history. Carrie Nation, for example, runs down the street with a Bible in one hand and her famous hatchet in the other to shut down Jim Neighbor's bar. (In real life she was prevented from destroying the joint when someone knocked her out with a bar stool.) The tour covers twenty-five buildings and takes about an hour. Tours are scheduled for Thursday nights at 7:00 P.M. and start at the Elizabethtown Visitors and Information Commission, 24 Public Square. You can also call (502) 765-2175.

Elizabethtown has another unusual seasonal event worth the trip to town. From the Wednesday before Thanksgiving until January 2 every year, Freeman Lake Park (directly behind the Coca-Cola plant on Highway 31W North) is transformed into a glittering wonderland during **Christmas in the Park.** Cut your headlights and take the luminaria-lined drive around the lake past more than seventy lighted Christmas displays built and donated by local businesses,

## TRUE BLUE

The Squire Pates House on Highway 334 near Lewisport was the site of Abraham Lincoln's first trial. He defended himself against charges of operating a ferry across the Ohio River without a license.

including a huge swan floating in the water and Santa in a boat. The show is on from dusk until 11:00 P.M. nightly.

North of Elizabethtown via Highway 31W is Fort Knox Military Reservation, with a couple of attractions worth seeing. To America's World War II generation there was perhaps no greater hero than General George S. Patton. The ◆ **Patton Museum of Cavalry and Armor** (502-624-3812) at Ft. Knox was dedicated in the general's honor on Memorial Day 1949, four years after Patton's death. In addition to a special section dedicated to Patton's life, the museum also includes a display of tanks and a variety of other military items—even a section of the Berlin Wall. The museum is on Fayette Avenue near the Chaffee Avenue entrance to the base. It's open weekdays year-round from 9:00 A.M. to 4:30 P.M. It opens at 10:00 A.M. on weekends, closing at 6:00 P.M. May through September and at 4:00 P.M. October through April. Admission is free.

Not far from the Patton Museum is the **United States Treasury Department Gold Depository,** America's "Gold Vault." Although no visitors are allowed inside, you can view the building from the outside and let your imagination run wild at what it looks like inside, where a two-level vault protected by a twenty-ton door and armed guards stores the nation's cache of pure gold bars.

A great place for lunch or dinner is south of Elizabethtown in a little railroad community called **Glendale.** Go south of town on Highway 31W for about 5 miles, then take Highway 222 west to Glendale. In the early 1970s James and Idell Sego transformed the old Glendale hardware store, which is smack-dab next to the railroad tracks on Main Street, into **The Whistle Stop Restaurant** (502-369-8586), where they now serve really really good Southern food for reasonable prices in a cozy, depot atmosphere. Famous for its open-faced hot brown sandwich—a mountain of roast beef on bread, smothered with a rich cheese sauce—the restaurant's menu ranges from homemade soups to ham and asparagus rolls to fried chicken and taco salad. Desserts clarify the meaning of sin. Hours are 11:00 A.M. to 9:00 P.M. Tuesday through Saturday.

All of Glendale seems to be in a time warp. Though the village is small, it has a functional general store and several antiques and gift shops. During the first weekend in December, every building is decked out for a **Christmas in the Country** event, open to the public. Or come to Glendale on the third Saturday in October for the **Glendale Crossing Festival** when the spirit of the old-time trading days pervades the town.

In the midst of this pretend atmosphere is an 1870s farmhouse with a big inviting front porch. This is the **Petticoat Junction Bed & Breakfast** (223 High Street; 502-369-8604). Six overnight rooms are available, two of which have private baths (one bath has an old-time claw-foot tub and the other a state-of-the-art Jacuzzi). Two rooms are in a small private cottage out back. Walk-ins are welcome.

The **Official Kentucky State Championship Oldtime Fiddling Contest** is an event for beginner and virtuoso musicians or for anyone who just likes to listen to bluegrass music. Fifteen to twenty different contests, including harmonica, flat-top guitar, mandolin, banjo, bluegrass band, and even jig dancing, are held annually at Rough River State Dam Park in northern Grayson County during the third week in July. This is a recommended place to have a breakdown—take your choice of "Tennessee Breakdown," "North Carolina Breakdown," "Straw Breakdown," or "Cheatum County Breakdown." When the region's hottest fiddlers compete in the Governor's Cup Fiddle Off, you'll want to cry at the music's sweetness—but the wind from the musician's lightning-quick bow action will dry your tears before they can hit your cheeks. Camping is available, and folks are invited to come early for the informal jam sessions that go on all week prior to the main contest. For more information call contest director Brent Miller at (502) 259-2311. Also ask about the park's other special events such as the "Dulcibrrr" in February, a weekend for fans of lap and hammered dulcimers.

Not everything in the area is caught in the past. John and Lisa Brittain of the ◆ **Nolin River Nut Tree Nursery** have become famous for performing nutty modern-day miracles. Of the more than one hundred varieties of nut trees grown in their nursery, most are grafted. You're not supposed to be able to graft most nut trees because the sap tends to run so much that the grafts don't take—that is, heal and fuse to the rooted tree—yet these growers make expert use of an obscure method called a coin purse graft. They also are able to dig and ship nut trees up to 5 feet tall, that's 4 feet taller than the "rules" claim to be possible without fatally damaging the taproot.

The Brittains can probably answer any question you have about nut trees and sell you just about any variety your heart desires. They now have more than 175 varieties available, plus fifteen kinds of persimmons and four varieties of pawpaw. For between $16 and $30 per tree, you can choose from a number of walnuts, heartnuts, butternuts, chestnuts, hickories, pecans, and hicans (a cross between hickory and pecan). Order as far in advance of spring as possible, and call if you plan to visit. For a catalog write: Nolin River Nut Tree Nursery, 797 Port Wooden Road, Upton 42784, or call (502) 369-8551.

Abraham Lincoln has put Hodgenville on the map and kept it there. From Elizabethtown, take Highway 61 south to Hodgenville and follow signs to the ◆ **Abraham Lincoln Birthplace National Historic Site** (502-358-3137), just south of town. The humble log cabin in which Abe was born on February 12, 1809, is enshrined in a huge, stone-columned building prefaced by fifty-six steps, which represent the years of Abe's life. The park is open all day, every day. Go through town on Highway 31E to tour Lincoln's boyhood home on **Knob Creek Farm,** open daily from April through October. There is a replica of the cabin where young Abe's first memories were formed; this was the last place he lived in Kentucky. Admission is $1.00. Call (502) 549-3741 for more information.

Downtown on Lincoln Square near the bronze statue is a small **Lincoln Museum** (502-358-3163) open Monday through Saturday from 8:30 A.M. to 5:30 P.M. and Sundays from 12:30 to 5:00 P.M. Admission is $3.00. The museum features twelve scenes from Lincoln's life (with wax figures) and a display of memorabilia. Ask about the **Lincoln Days Celebration** held in town during the second weekend of October. The festival features a few odd events, including Lincoln look-alike contests and a very manly railsplitting tournament. Call (502) 358-3411 for more information.

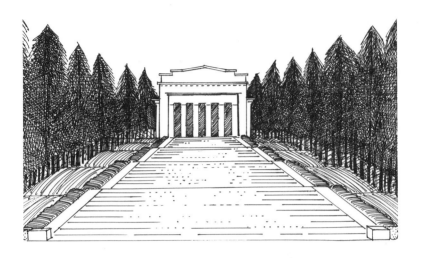

**Abraham Lincoln Birthplace National Historic Site**

Heading south past the Lincoln Birthplace, turn left on Highway 61 to Highway 470 and you'll come to the **Buffalo Antique Mall** (502-325-3900). Owner Allene Hager said her wonderful building with tin ceilings is pretty typical for a turn-of-the-century general store, which is what it was built as. The balcony that runs the perimeter of the front room gave the store owner a pretty clear view of what was going on in just about every nook and corner, she explained. For her, the railing is the perfect display rack for a type of collectible she especially loves: quilts and coverlets. Dozens hang in the shop, their bright colors a pleasing contrast against the white walls. Hager is herself a quilter. Stop by to see her latest quilt top, browse the three levels of just-about-everything, and chat about quilts or antiques. Hours are Monday through Saturday 9:00 A.M. to 5:00 P.M. and Sunday 1:00 to 5:00 P.M.

# MORE GOOD LODGING

FORT KNOX
**Best Western Gold Vault Inn,** 1225 North Dixie Highway; (502)
351–1141. About $60 per night.

BRANDENBURG
**Doe Run Inn,** Highway 448, northwest of Fort Knox; (502) 422–2982.
Rustic country inn decorated with antiques. About $50 per night.

ELIZABETHTOWN
**The Inn at Tara Dawn Farm,** 14600 Boston Road; (502) 833–4553.
Antebellum farmhouse on seventeen acres. $85 per night.

LEITCHFIELD
**Rough River Dam State Resort Park,** Highway 79; (502) 257–2311.
Lodge and cottages. About $75 per night.

# MORE FUN PLACES TO EAT

BRANDENBURG
**Doe Run Inn,** Highway 448, northwest of Fort Knox; (502) 422–2982.
Country ham, skillet-fried chicken, and other regional favorites.

LEITCHFIELD
**Rough River Dam State Resort Park,** Highway 79; (502) 257–2311.

ELIZABETHTOWN
**Stone Hearth Restaurant,** Highway 62; (502) 765–4898. Home
cooking.

# LAKES AND KNOBS REGION

Going east from Glasgow, the high road leads to **Columbia,** the
low road to Burkesville. Take Highway 80 or the Cumberland Parkway to Columbia. Everyone knows that Lindsey Wilson College is in
Columbia, but few people know about the **Adair County Bell Pepper Festival,** winner of the Kentucky Festival Association's "outstanding festival for its size" award. In many ways, it's a good old
county fair, but there's more. How about a Bed Race or an Ugly
Man Contest, or tests of real vocational skill, like the Hay Bale

Throwing Contest or Nail Driving Contest? They have a darn good square dance on Monday night. The festival is held the week after Labor Day.

Few people know that on April 29, 1872, Jesse James and his gang held up the Bank of Columbia and killed a cashier, R. C. Martin. Nor do most know that Mark Twain's parents, Jane Lampton and John Marshall Clemens, were married in Columbia in 1823. Fewer still realize that Maxwell House coffee was developed by a Burkesville boy named Joel Owsley Cheek. After a brief career as a traveling (by horseback) salesman, Cheek started experimenting in the late 1870s with roasting and mixing blends of coffee that were usually sold to the stores green and unground. The first place to sell the expensive blend was at the Maxwell House hotel in Nashville, Tennessee. The rest is history.

**Dale Hollow** is a large man-made lake that straddles the Kentucky-Tennessee line. From Burkesville, take any road to the south and watch for signs. The area is full of small marinas, motels, and fishing camps. It is said to be one of the cleanest lakes in the state, and since there are myriad inlets and islands, Dale Hollow is good place to swim. Another thing shared by the two states is a little town with a rowdy reputation called Static, which sits directly on the border where Highway 127 goes through. Kentucky says Static belongs in Tennessee, and Tennessee says the town is all Kentucky's. With a town name that means "showing little change," it's no wonder no one claims the place. To make things worse, legend has it that Static was named after a local farmer's one-eyed bulldog.

To the north is ◆ **Lake Cumberland,** one of the largest man-made lakes in the United States; its peak surface area is more than 55,000 acres. It is also said to have more walleye, bass, and crappie than any other American lake. Although there are water-oriented businesses all around the lake, you may want to stop by the headquarters of the Lake Cumberland State Resort Park (off Highway 127 just south of Jamestown; 502–343–3111) to get specific information. If you boat around the big, clear lake, you'll find endless little coves to explore, places to swim, fossils over which to ponder, and almost no commercial development to distract you.

A town named **Touristville** makes a person suspicious, and

**Dunagan's Grocery & Supply**

rightly so. Some chamber of commerce type was on the ball that hot summer day in 1929 when the post office was named. For a time Touristville did profit from the flow of vacationers through nearby Mill Springs, which sits very near what is now Lake Cumberland. ◆ **Dunagan's Grocery & Supply** in Mill Springs now serves as post office for both towns. The anachronistic store really is an attraction for nostalgia buffs and curiosity seekers. In 1935 Everette Dunagan's father moved the store to its present site from about a hundred yards across the road employing one pair of mules, a bunch of logs used as rollers, some cable, and two days worth of ingenuity. Since then precious little has changed. He carries a little bit of everything, as a good country store must; there's even a great little photo postcard of Dunagan's. Take your own picture or make a sketch. The place has been painted by several artists. Mr. Dunagan keeps his place open from 8:00 A.M. to 5:00 P.M. every day but Sunday. To visit, take Highway 90 to Highway 1275 and go 1 mile west. Trust me—you'll love it.

To get to Mill Springs, go to Monticello in Wayne County and follow Highway 90 to Touristville. Turn west on Highway 1275 and you'll see signs for the ◆ **Mill Springs Mill,** "largest over-shot waterwheel in the world." That's a slightly overrated waterwheel, but as it turns out, the wheel is 40 feet, 10 inches in diameter, making it the third largest in the nation and among the top ten in the world. It may be the only one of the biggies to still be functioning as a gristmill. The first cereal grinding mill was built around 1817 at this site where thirteen springs gushed out of the hillside. The waterwheel also powered a cotton gin, carting factory, and wagon production line. After a fire and several remodelings, in 1908 the Diamond Roller Mills' 40-foot wheel was installed. Today the mill is open at no charge to the public from Memorial Day to Labor Day, from 11:00 A.M. to 5:00 P.M. daily. On weekends they grind cornmeal with the old equipment. For specifics, call (606) 348-8189.

> **TRUE BLUE**
>
> The state bird of Kentucky is the cardinal.

The mill is the site of a tide-turning Civil War battle in January 1862. Confederate General Felix Kirk Zollicoffer set up camp at a house near the mill, the Metcalfe House. Zollicoffer lost the Battle of Logan's Crossroads and thereby left the first gap in what was a long, strong rebel defense line in Kentucky. Just west of Somerset on Highway 80 in a town called Nancy are the **Mill Springs Battlefield** (606-679-5725) and the Zollicoffer burial site, where more than a hundred rebel troops are buried under one stone, all from the Mill Springs battle. From the cemeteries, you can see (and smell and taste and climb) the fruit trees at the adjacent **Haney's Appledale Orchard** (606-636-6148), one of the state's best and largest apple orchards. The orchard is open mid-June through Christmas.

If you leave Jamestown and Russell Springs to the north, you leave the lake area and enter the Knobs again. Take Highway 127 north into Casey County, known as the **"Gate Capitol of the World."** Most gates, truck racks, and round-bale feeders are made of tubular steel, a concept first developed in 1965 by Tarter Gate in Dunnville, the first and largest of the gate companies in the county, producing more than 1,000 gates a day.

Due to the isolation and beauty of this hilly country, a large number of Mennonites have moved into the area. It's always inspirational to see their neat, well-tended farms, but these people are not interested in intrusion from the outside world. This community has two businesses that are open to the public. Going north on Highway 127 from Russell Springs, turn southeast on Highway 910. Go about 3¹/₂ miles and turn east onto South Fork. This is a beautiful drive past both secular and Mennonite farms (watch for "shocked" corn and draft horses in the field). It's hilarious to see the contrast in styles: Watch to the right side of South Fork for the gaudiest house in the world; the obviously secular yard is thick with whirligigs, holiday yard art, and endless junk.

At the other extreme and just a few miles away, ◈ **Bluegrass Wood and Leather Craft** (Furniture, Chairs, Tables, Harnesses and Leather Goods) is a remarkable place run by remarkable people. The store is a large building on the right filled with furniture (mainly in oak) upstairs and leather goods downstairs, all of excellent quality. Due to the fact that the Mennonites in the area do much of their farming with horses and mules, the leather items are primarily horse-related, but there aren't many limits to this craftsman's ability. The fellows in the shop are more than willing to answer questions, and if you're serious about a purchase, they are glad to take a special order as long it falls within their way of working. There's no phone, but they are usually open on weekdays during business hours.

Back on Highway 910, go "just a little piece" farther south to **Dutchman's Market,** a small Mennonite general store in the basement of their community elementary school. To remain apart as much as possible from the corrupt aspects of our culture, these Mennonites often employ low-technology methods for farming, building, and living in general. So, if you are in search of something unusual, a modern instance of an old model of any kind of equipment, like a hand-pump for your cistern, inquire about it at Dutchman's. Let me also recommend the local sorghum molasses. Alan Oberholtzer,

## MYSTERIES OF DARK SKIES

If you happen to be driving along Kentucky Highway 78 near Liberty after dark, take a few moments to glance skyward. You are at the site of a true unsolved mystery. It happened on January 6, 1976. Three Casey County women, two of them grandmothers and all avid churchgoers, were returning from dinner at a Stanford restaurant. Between Hustonville and Liberty, they saw what they thought was a plane about to crash. Next thing they knew, it was an hour and twenty-five minutes later and they were 8 miles down the road, with severe headaches and burnlike red marks on the backs of their necks. The car's electrical system was malfunctioning and the paint on the hood was blistered. Shaken and confused, the women returned to Liberty, where a neighbor asked them to draw what they had seen, and their aircraft looked suspiciously like a UFO. Soon, a veritable army of UFO investigators, and the national tabloids, descended upon this small Kentucky town. Under hypnosis the women told a story that seems almost commonplace today, but was then quite rare: They had been taken aboard a spacecraft and examined by creatures with huge pale-blue eyes. Later they even passed a polygraph test. These unlikely UFO abductees have long since moved away from Liberty, Kentucky; they grew tired of hearing the ridicule and laughter. The case, however, remains unsolved, a mystery to be pondered by those who gaze upon the night skies of Casey County.

the local molasses meister, keeps this store well stocked. You'll want to speed home to make a mess of biscuits just to have an excuse for draining what promises to be the first of many jars.

Return to Highway 127, head south again, and make your way toward Somerset. Along the way, if you want to stop for lunch or dinner, try the **Yosemite** (pronounced YO-seh-mite) **Country Store.** The homemade chili is hot—a liquid atomic fireball. This is one of those groceries that makes their own pickled eggs. What's funny is that they keep the homemade eggs next to a jar of commercial eggs, which are dyed a sickening hot pink. The manager told me it increases sales of the homemade ones. Smart. Yosemite is on Highway 70 going southeast from Liberty. You can stay on

Highway 70, which becomes Highway 635 and runs into Highway 27, which leads into Somerset.

◆ **Burnside,** just south of Somerset on Highway 27, is not only the only town on Lake Cumberland, it is the only town under the lake. In the late 1940s the U.S. Army Corps of Engineers moved the entire town to higher ground because the lake area was being impounded. The durable remains of old Burnside become visible during the winter when the lake's level lowers. It's eerie seeing foundations, porch steps, and sidewalks emerge from the mud and debris. Nearby is **General Burnside State Park,** a 400-acre island surrounded by Lake Cumberland. The park is used for camping, fishing, boating, and all the usual lakeside fooling around.

If you aren't camping and need lodging, try **The Shadwick House Bed and Breakfast** at 411 South Main Street in Somerset. It has been a guest house for more than seventy years and has remained in family hands. The present owners are the great-grandchildren of Nellie Stringer Shadwick, who built the place in 1920. Six rooms are available at the reasonable nightly rate of $40, including breakfast. For reservations, call (606) 678-4675.

**Stab,** a short name for a small town with a short creek, is 10 miles east of Somerset along Highway 80 near the Pleasant Run Baptist Church. Short Creek emerges from a hillside cavern at an impressive width of about 25 feet. It flows in a semicircle for maybe 150 feet and ducks back underground in a small cave. There's no doubt, this is the shortest creek in the world. Elwood Taylor, who owns the creek, says that there was a a gristmill at one end and that the creek formerly was used for wintertime baptisms because the water is always 54 degrees Fahrenheit. The Taylors own the small grocery at Stab. Stop by their store and ask permission to have a picnic by the creek. You may hear some good stories.

◆ **Cumberland Falls** is not really off the beaten path, but it's such a flamboyant, unusual cataract that it must be recognized. Follow I-75 to Corbin, get off on Highway 25W, veer west on Highway 90, and follow the signs to Cumberland Falls State Resort Park (606-528-4121). The wide, humble Cumberland River explodes dramatically as it crashes over the curving precipice and becomes the largest American waterfall east of the Rocky Mountains, except for

## KILROY'S ANCESTORS

The **Old Simpson County Jailer's Residence** in Franklin was being renovated, and since it was expected that little if any original plaster could be repaired, workers weren't being terribly careful as they ripped out old paneling and wallpaper. Until they found, in a second-story room of the building, something that made everyone stop and stare in astonishment: Drawings, possibly in charcoal, some almost life size, portraying Civil War soldiers, both Union and Confederate, including a portrait of the famous Confederate raider General John Hunt Morgan. Though it may never be known exactly who created these sketches, it is known that the building was occupied by Union troops and used to house Confederate prisoners of war, and it is thought that what is left on the walls is authentic and rare Civil War graffiti. The building, now home to the Simpson County Archives and Museum, is at 206 North College Street in Franklin, about 21 miles south of Bowling Green. Hours are Monday through Friday 9:00 A.M. to 4:00 P.M. Admission is free. Call (502) 586-4228 for more information.

Niagara. When the entire disk of the moon is illuminated and the skies are clear, a long moonbow arches from the top of the falls to the turbulent waters below. The only other moonbow in the world is at Victoria Falls along the Zambezi River in southern Africa. The Cumberland Falls are so powerful that the mist fans way out and above the water; when the wind is right, you get a gentle shower on the rocks at the top. More than 65 feet high and 125 feet across, the falls are believed to have retreated as far as 45 miles upstream from their original position near Burnside. In a process that takes many millennia, the water wears away the soft sandstone under the erosion-resistant lip at the top.

The park, which is open all year, has another smaller but beautiful falls called **Little Eagle Falls.** If it's hot, the pool below Little Eagle Falls is a divine swimming hole. Ask for information at the park lodge about hiking trails, rooms, cabins, and special events. Within the park is a state nature preserve left to its wild state. It boasts more than fifteen species of rare plants and animals including endangered mussels and plants like the box huckleberry, brook saxifrage, goat's rue, and riverweed. A guided hike can be a real education.

Another way to "get into" the river, and to have a rip-roaring good time, is to hook up with a guided canoeing or whitewater rafting trip down the river. Write: **Sheltowee Trace Outfitters,** P.O. Box 1060, Whitley City 42653, or call (800) 541-RAFT.

The other big playground in this region is at the **Big South Fork National River and Recreation Area** in McCreary County and below the border. Take Highway 27 or I-75 south to Highway 92 and go west to Stearns. If you're arriving via Highway 27, check out the natural rock bridge just off Highway 927, which goes to Nevelsville. You can also get to Big South Fork on Highway 700, which intersects Highway 27 near Whitley City. The latter route brings you directly to **Yahoo Falls,** Kentucky's highest.

The whole Big South Fork area is beautiful. Deep, jagged gorges are frequent surprises, and the variations in the landscape, from cool woods to hot, high, open-faced rocks, are endlessly pleasing. That the area was once extensively logged and mined is apparent. From early April through the end of October, the U.S. Forest Service operates the **Big South Fork Scenic Railway,** which takes visitors into an abandoned coal mining camp called ◆ **Blue Heron,** or Mine 18. The remnants of the isolated community are eerie and bring to life some of what you may know about company towns. The **Stearns Museum** (606–376–5730) fills out the picture with historic artifacts. The sandstone tree stump in front of the museum was recently unearthed in a strip mine just below the Tennessee line. Apparently the two-ton stump is not petrified wood but a sandstone cast of a tree (possibly an oak) that died about 315 million years ago. When the tree rotted or dissolved, the space was filled with sandstone silt, which then hardened.

Take exit 11 off I-75 and keep an eye peeled for a new brick Colonial-style building on the campus of Cumberland College in Williamsburg. This is the **Cumberland Museum, Lodge, and Center for Leadership Studies.** Students work in the facility to help pay for their tuition and to learn real-world skills in hotel manage-

## LOST AND FOUND

Unless I'm in a big hurry, I rarely worry about getting lost, because I know that almost any Kentucky road is going to end up somewhere interesting. And if it doesn't, well, you just turn around. So I wasn't too concerned that my directions to the Amish store near Munfordville that April Saturday were somewhat vague. "It's outside of town a little piece," the quilter who told me about the store said.

"I'm not sure which store you mean, but if you turn left at the yellow flashing light and head out of town, then turn left again after a ways, you'll come to an area where a lot of Amish people live," offered a gas station attendant. Now that was something to go on. When I saw the sign at Logsdon Mill Road for Yoder's Harness Shop, I figured that had to be the turn.

"Look, Mom, something's going on over there," my daughter exclaimed, a few miles down the road. Indeed, there was. Dozens of vans, trucks—and even more horsedrawn carriages—were parked in a field, and hundreds of people, Amish and "English" of all ages, were gathered under a tent. It turned out to be a consignment auction to benefit the Amish community school, with everything from handmade bookshelves to goats going on the block. In between bidding, you could fill up on just-grilled hamburgers and homemade baked goods. Best bad directions I ever had.

ment. The restaurant and lodgings have a great view of the surrounding mountains. Call (606) 539-4100 for information. Among other things, the eclectic Cumberland Museum has an Appalachian lifestyle exhibit, a Native American artifacts collection, a very unusual collection of more than 6,000 Christian crosses, and a "life science" collection that consists of actual, preserved animal specimens, such as polar bears and shrews, shown in displays that mimic their natural habitats. There is an admission charge. For more information, call (606) 549-2200, extension 3333.

Jellico, Tennessee, just across the border on I-75, is (or was) the number one place for underage Kentuckians to get hitched. In Jellico they do it fast, legal, and without parental or priestly consent: "I do and he does too."

Just east of Williamsburg is **Mulberry Friendship Center,** one of many fruitful mountain craft cooperatives in the Appalachian region. Because this one is near a beaten path, the folks are prepared to show visitors around. For example, women who quilt together regularly often have some beauties for sale at the center. Activities change, so call ahead at (606) 549-1617. From Williamsburg, go 9 miles east on Highway 92, turn right (southeast) on Highway 904, and watch for the sign.

**Corbin** sits on the adjoining corners of Whitley, Laurel, and Knox counties and serves as the commercial hub for the whole area. Although Corbin is not famous the world over, its native son, Colonel Harland Sanders, is. From Tokyo to Moscow to London, England, and London, Kentucky, the Colonel's red and white portrait, complete with the almost sinister goatee, smiles out on chicken consumers everywhere going through the doors of Kentucky Fried Chicken. Corbin is the home of the original restaurant—it's even listed on the National Register of Historic Places! At ◈ **The Harland Sanders Café & Museum,** see Harland's kitchen as it was in the 1940s and eat in a dining area restored to resemble the original restaurant. Go north of Corbin and take Highway 25E south; turn right at the second traffic light.

London, the next town to the north, is trying to get in on the chicken action, too, and holds an annual **World Chicken Festival** downtown at the end of September. In addition to the usual festival activities, all the great cooks in town compete for coveted cook-off prizes. The real winners are the tasters. Call (606) 878-6900 for specifics.

If you think the interstate near London looks busy now in a postindustrial, highway-laced world, ponder the years between 1775 and 1800, when more than 300,000 people came into Kentucky from the east through this area when it was wild. The ◈ **Levi Jackson State Park** is situated at the intersection of the Wilderness Road and Boone's Trace, the two main frontier "highways." The park is just 2 miles south of London on Highway 25. The Mountain Life Museum gives newcomers to the area a glimpse of pioneer history with a reproduction pioneer settlement stocked with period furniture and Native American artifacts. Also at the park is McHargue's Mill, a completely operational restored gristmill, circa 1812, that serves as a kind of mill museum and has what may be the world's largest collection of millstones. On park grounds is the only marked burial ground along the Wilderness Road (though historians believe that there are many other cemeteries lacking headstones). To ask about hiking, camping, or any park information, call (606) 878-8000.

The next town to the north is Mt. Vernon. Mt. Vernon is considered a kind of gateway to the Knobs, the serious hills that skirt the Appalachian Mountains. For a double delight—beautiful mountains and wonderful people—take a drive straight uphill from the caution light in downtown Mt. Vernon at the junction of Highways 150 and 1249. Exactly 10 miles later you'll find yourself on a hillside in front of a red brick ranch house on the left, home of **Betty Thomas Teddy Bears.** Betty works at home and welcomes visitors but requests that you call first at (606) 256-5378 to see her fine dolls and stuffed animals—everything from realistic Canada geese and goslings, decoy-sized mallard ducks, debonair foxes dressed in traditional hunt clothing and hard hats, Old World–style teddy bears, mice, cats, dogs, unicorns, soft-sculpture baby dolls, and on and on. Most of her pieces have hinged joints, and all are stuffed so tightly that they stand independently; all are made of high-quality wool, satin, or cotton in delicious colors.

Ms. Thomas's patience, persistence, and skill with her hands come by her honestly. Her parents raised thirteen children in a log cabin in a holler just across the road from her present home. Her father, William McClure, is rightfully considered a kind of legend among folk culture enthusiasts. For years his handmade wooden roof shingles were in constant demand in all the surrounding states, as were his handsome carved dough bowls. You can see some of his work on the roof of the Aunt Polly Hiatt house at Renfro Valley (coming up next). They say that although that roof has gaps in it so big you can see sky through them, it doesn't leak a drop. Long live the McClure family!

Here's the lineup: "Banjo Pickin' Gal," "Winking at Me," "Chicken Reel," "Cackling Hen," "Barbara Allen," "Poor Ellen Smith," "Tramp on the Street," "Matthew 24," and "Old Shep." These could be the names of Thoroughbreds in the starting gate at the Derby but are, in fact, some of the best country songs ever written and some of the first ever performed at ❧ **Renfro Valley,** "Kentucky's Country Music Capital." Many folks in the region remember when they first heard John Lair's silk-smooth voice in 1939 broadcasting an all-country music radio show live from his big tobacco barn in Rockcastle County. Those humble beginnings have led to the establishment of a large complex of buildings and year-round traditional music and entertainment programs at Renfro Valley; the radio shows are now transmitted to more than 200 stations in North America. In addition to performance events in the auditorium (a luxury barn), there are on the grounds a craft village with mountain craft demonstrators, a gift shop, the Renfro Valley Museum, a bakery, a hotel, and a restaurant. Go north from Mt. Vernon a few miles on Highway 25; for the more scenic route, to the Renfro Valley exit. Call for more information, show tickets, or reservations at (800) 765-7464.

# MORE GOOD LODGING

### CORBIN
**Best Western, I–75,** exit 25; (606) 528–2100. About $40 per night.
**Cumberland Falls State Resort Park,** Highway 90 southwest of Corbin, 606–528–4121. Rustic stone lodge and sixteen cabins, open year-round. About $75 per night.

### WILLIAMSBURG
**Cumberland Lodge Marriott,** 649 South Tenth Street; (606) 539–4100. About $70 per night.

### JAMESTOWN
**Lake Cumberland State Resort Park,** Off Highway 127; (502) 343–3111. Two lodges and thirty cabins; open year-round. About $75 per night.

### STEARNS
**Marcum-Porter House,** Highway 1561; (606) 376–2242. Bed and breakfast in historic house built by Stearns Coal and Lumber Company. $55 to $65 per night.

# MORE FUN PLACES TO EAT

CORBIN

**Cumberland Falls State Resort Park,** Highway 90, southwest of Corbin; (606) 528-4121. Wide variety of sandwiches and seafood entrees, plus regional specialties such as country ham, served in a family atmosphere.

**Dale Hollow Lake State Resort Park,** Highway 1206, south of Lake Cumberland; (502) 433-7431. Variety of American dishes and regional specialties. Dinner buffet Friday through Sunday.

### Somerset

**Lakeview Restaurant,** 5910 South Highway 27; (606) 561-5861. Indoor and outdoor dining overlooking Lake Cumberland. Lunch and dinner buffet daily, except Friday nights, when there's a big fish fry.

### RENFRO VALLEY

**The Lodge Restaurant,** I-75 exit 62; (800) 765-7464. Country cooking, with great soup beans, chicken and dumplings, and chocolate pie.

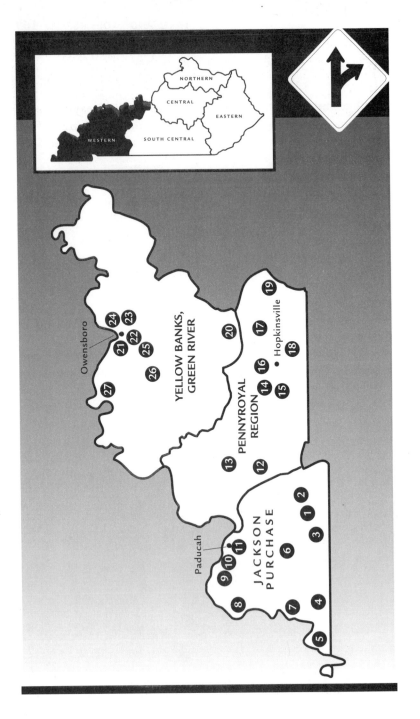

NORTHERN

CENTRAL

EASTERN

WESTERN

SOUTH CENTRAL

Owensboro

YELLOW BANKS,
GREEN RIVER

24 23
21 22
25
26
27

Hopkinsville

19

20 17
16
14 15
18

PENNYROYAL
REGION

13 12

2
1
3
6

JACKSON
PURCHASE

Paducah
10 11
9
8 7 4

5

# WESTERN KENTUCKY

1. National Museum of the Boy Scouts of America
2. House of Willow
3. Bell City Pottery
4. Henson Broom Shop Museum
5. Reelfoot Lake
6. The Wooldridge Monuments
7. Columbus-Belmont Battlefield State Park
8. The Wickliffe Mounds Research Center
9. Metropolis Lake
10. *Wacinton*
11. Museum of the American Quilter's Society
12. Land Between the Lakes
13. Adsmore Museum
14. Pennyroyal Area Museum
15. The Trail of Tears Intertribal Indian Pow Wow
16. Pete's Custom Saddle Shop
17. Jefferson Davis Monument State Historic Site
18. Penchem Tack Store
19. Shakertown at South Union
20. Everly's Lake Malone Inn
21. Bar-B-Q Capital of the World
22. sassafras tree
23. Owensboro Area Museum of Science and History
24. The Owensboro Museum of Fine Art
25. Mount Saint Joseph Center and Community of Ursuline Sisters
26. Diamond Lake Catfish Farm
27. John James Audubon State Park

The sky seems bigger in the vast, open land of this western region. Sunsets are beautiful, and you can see a storm coming for hours. There's plenty of room for everyone and everyone's here, from coal miners and bluegrass musicians to Amish farmers and master quilters. There must be something in the soil here because legendary figures have sprung up like weeds: Robert Penn Warren, Edgar Cayce, Casey Jones, Jefferson Davis, and John James Audubon, to name a few. Western Kentucky also boasts some of the best museums in the state, such as Shakertown at South Union, the most southern Shaker community, the Museum of the American Quilter's Society, and the Owensboro Museum of Fine Art.

Most dear to Kentuckians is the Land Between the Lakes, a clean, gorgeous, wild land surrounded by Lake Barkley and Kentucky Lake, a double paradise for fisherfolks. There must be more resorts and marinas per square mile around the Land Between the Lakes area than anywhere else in the state. Stop and ask about camping, cottages, fishing, restaurants, or anything else your heart may desire. American bald eagles also find this region attractive and make their homes here and along the shore of the Mississippi River in the far southwestern region. You'll find western Kentucky quiet, not overdeveloped, yet full of fascinating surprises. The fact that people here have uniquely open spirits gives the traveler a chance to absorb and deeply enjoy the culture of this place.

## JACKSON PURCHASE

On the fourth Sunday in May, if you are anywhere near Benton, west of the lakes on Highway 641, plan to attend "Big Singing Day," the only American singing festival that uses the 1835 Southern Harmony Book of shape note tunes. (Shape note singing is a traditional form of a capella that represents the four notes—mi, fa, sol, la—on the staff by a different shape, i.e., diamond, triangle, circle, square, respectively.) This wonderfully nonhierarchical group singing event has been happening here since 1843. There is no leader, no instrumental accompaniment, and the songs, usually traditional Welsh hymns, are arranged in parts such that no one sings beyond his or her range. Weather permitting, the singing happens outdoors on the courthouse lawn. The other big event is Benton's **Tater Day,** held on the first Monday in April since 1843 and the world's only event dedicated to the sweet potato. Pay your homage to a great food and enjoy a friendly small-town festival.

Going south on Highway 641 brings you to the peaceful town of Murray, which Rand McNally ranked "number one retirement location in the country" because of the proximity of outdoor recreational areas, the low crime rate, and the low cost of living. On the Murray State University campus, you can get a free crash course in the history of the region by visiting the Wrather West Kentucky Museum (502-762-4771). Hours are Monday through Friday from 8:30 a.m. to 4:15 p.m. and Saturday from 10:00 a.m. to 2:00 p.m. The Clara M. Eagle Gallery (502-762-3052), on the sixth floor of the Doyle Fine Arts Building on the corner of Olive and Fourteenth Streets, features a wide variety of exhibits from faculty shows, plus nationally touring exhibitions of fine art and craft.

### TRUE BLUE

Kentucky is one of only four states to use the designation _commonwealth,_ meaning government based on common consent of the people.

One of Murray's best-known attractions is the ❖ **National Museum of the Boy Scouts of America** at the corner of Calloway Avenue and Sixteenth Street. For youth, the best part will be the Gateway Park, an outdoor ropes and teams course (like the COPE courses). Boy Scouts, Cub Scouts, or any other group can test their skill and agility on the course (reservations recommended). The museum owns more than sixty original Norman Rockwell paintings and sketches-the world's second largest Rockwell collection. In 1912, when Rockwell was only eighteen years old, he was hired as an illustrator by _Boys' Life_ magazine. From 1912 to 1976 he painted hundreds of idealistic, humorous, all-American Scout scenes. For kids, the indoor museum includes high-tech, robot-guided exhibits, low-tech storytelling by professional actors, decision-making games, and simulated adventure courses. The museum is open Tuesday through Saturday from 9:00 A.M. to 4:30 P.M. and Sunday from 12:30 to 4:30 P.M. from March 1 to

November 30. It is closed Thanksgiving and Easter. Admission is $3.50 to $5.00 according to age. Gateway Park costs extra. Call (502) 762-3383.

For classy lodging in Murray, consider the **Diuguid House Bed and Breakfast** (603 Main Street; 502-753-5470). Hosts Karen and George Chapman serve a full breakfast, avoiding what they refer to as the four basic elements of Southern cooking: "salt, sugar, grease, and grit." The very Victorian house, which is now on the National Register of Historic Places, affords guests all kinds of spaces for living, from private nooks for reading to a large veranda for socializing. Rooms start at $35 per night.

Speaking of socializing, **Rudy's Restaurant** (502-753-1632) on the west side of the courthouse square is so crowded at lunchtime that you may have to sit with a stranger if you're determined to have a fresh hamburger and home-made onion rings. This little place has been open since the early 1930s, when the original Rudy made it famous for its consistently good country cooking and cutting-edge gossip. Rudy, a short, roly-poly fellow whose lip never knew the absence of a cigar, collected money and spread the news of the day from a stool behind the big brass cash register. Monday through Friday breakfast starts at 6:00 A.M., and lunch ends at 2:00 P.M. Supper is now served on Friday nights.

Take Highway 94 East and go about 8 miles out of downtown Murray. Watch for a shop on the right side of the road with curving bent willow chairs in the yard and a sign by the driveway indicating ◆ **House of Willow.** This is the workshop of Alfred Duncan, an extraordinary, thrifty chairmaker. Regardless of the fact that this style of outdoor furniture, sometimes called "stick furniture," is in vogue at the moment, this craft has lasting integrity. Just like the gypsies who sold willow chairs in this area in the early 1930s, Alfred and his master-teacher from down the road a piece, George Beard, go to riverbanks in Kentucky and all over swampy areas of the

## TRUE BLUE

In addition to an official state song ("My Old Kentucky Home" by Stephen Collins), Kentucky also has an official bluegrass song, "Blue Moon of Kentucky" by Rosine, Kentucky native Bill Monroe.

South to gather red and white willow trees, which are bent and nailed into place while green. Nothing is wasted; the large stock is used for heavy supports, thin branches are twisted into decorative backs or armrests, and the very thinnest trees, some as young as six months, are used as "benders," pliable pieces that make accommodating seats. Sit in any chair, love seat, or rocker and your body will understand that the Shakers couldn't have designed them better. The choices of branch size and spacing create a simple and visually stunning effect. Beard has become something of a regional treasure. In 1978 the Smithsonian bought one of his hooded chairs in red willow for its permanent collection; a dark red Indian willow love seat is in a museum in Utah; and the Kentucky Museum in Frankfort exhibits a settee and child's chair. George claims not to be able to tell his own work apart from Alfred's. These are craftsmen not to miss. Alfred works every day during business hours, including weekends. For more information, call (502) 759-9595.

To find a pottery, look for a chimney. From Murray, take Highway 94 west to Tri City, turn south on Highway 97, and look for ✥ **Bell City Pottery.** Stacks from huge, sixty-year-old, gas-fired kilns rise high behind a rambling cement-block building on the left side of the road. The James Nance family has owned and operated this pottery for about seventy years. In the past, most of the pieces were wheel thrown, or "turned," as they say in Bell City, but now production is geared toward slip-casting yard art like pink spray-painted "mingoes" (the local term for yard flamingoes), hoboes, and baby deer (Dish Barn style). Down the road another half mile are the distribution center for the pottery, a small retail sales area, and a concrete casting business run by Tommy Nance, nephew of James Nance II, the owner. With a few simple tools, Tommy makes hundreds of concrete bird baths and outdoor planters each year. Both the clay and the concrete businesses are somewhat modernized versions of America's oldest craft industry. Getting a detailed look at the daily-life realities of a production clayworks is worth your while. Bell City Pottery is a larger but lesser known version of Bybee Pottery (near Richmond), and because of its isolation, the craftspeople are also less dulled by tourism. Bell City Pottery is open Monday through Saturday from 9:00 A.M. to 5:00 P.M., but it's best to call ahead at (502) 382-2352 for a

## PLANTING IDEAS

Mike and Marci Bland own a shop in Owensboro that carries dresses, shoes, suits, hats, backpacks, paper, shampoo, lip balm, hammocks, pizza crust mixes, cooking oil, and a wide array of other products. Which wouldn't be unusual at all, except that the products are all made from industrial hemp (*Cannabis sativa*, but grown to include little of the psychoactive ingredient in the plant's marijuana form). Stop by **Common Sense Hemp** (1722A Sweeney, Owensboro; 502-926-4455) and you'll get a thought-provoking crash course in a hot Kentucky agriculture issue. The Blands are among a serious contingent of Kentuckians and others advocating industrial hemp, legal in some other countries as a versatile, environmentally friendly, profitable crop for Kentucky farmers. Actor Woody Harrelson came to Kentucky in 1996 and planted industrial hemp seeds to test the issue in court. Out and about in the state is the **Kentucky Hemp Museum,** an exhibit-on-wheels about hemp history and uses. Call its director, Craig Lee, at (606) 692-9775 to find out its schedule.

tour due to production schedules.

As you leave Bell City, going north on Highway 97, watch for **Murdocks' Mausoleum,** a semiunderground building with a sign on the top that reads, STOP SEE A ROAD MAP TO HEAVEN. Who wouldn't stop? On the wall of the porch is a large painted sign describing how one can get to heaven-the gospel of John is heavily quoted. Behind a decorative iron door and window one can view the burial area. The graves of two women take up perhaps a sixth of the burial space, leaving the rest free for future occupants.

The fence-sitting towns of Fulton, Kentucky, and South Fulton, Tennessee, host an annual **Banana Festival** during the third week in September. That's right, bananas in Kentucky. The festival, which was started in 1962, commemorates the spirit of an era when wholesalers from all over the country came to Fulton to buy bananas, which were shipped from South America to New Orleans and brought by rail to the largest ice house in the United States, in Fulton. From here the bananas were distributed throughout the North. In addition to the usual festival activities, the world's largest banana pudding travels the streets of both downtowns on a float during the grand parade and is then served to everyone free. Normally the pudding weighs one ton, but in order to make the pages of *The Guinness Book of World Records,* a two-ton pudding has been made. Follow Highway 94 west from Murray to Highway 45; go south into town and put on your best yellow tie.

Get back on Highway 94 and head west to Cayce. On the west side of town, look for the ◆ **Henson Broom Shop Museum.** What appears to be a perfectly maintained old country store is actually Richard N. Henson's broom-making shop. With a few simple pieces of equipment, three generations of skill, piles of sticks, heaps of broom straw, and lots of energy, Henson makes hundreds of graceful, functional brooms. His grandfather, also Richard N. Henson, started making brooms in 1930 when the American economy was faltering and the family needed more income. The elder Henson liked to say, "A Hoover put me into business, and a Hoover put me out of business," referring to the president and the vacuum cleaner, respectively.

Today the third-generation broom maker is rarely out of work. During the summer and fall, Henson converts his horse trailer into a portable workshop, dons a costume, and travels to festivals where he does historic craft reenactment, educating the public while he works. (He has been winning blue ribbons for his craftsmanship all over the country.) Brooms have changed very little during the past hundred years.

If you watch the television show *Dr. Quinn, Medicine Woman,* you will see Henson's brooms for sale in the show's general store and in use by the characters. To his array of old-fashioned kitchen, shop, whisk, cabin, Colonial hearth, Shaker, and parlor brooms, Henson has added a fancy, twisted-handled design he calls the "Jane Seymour Broom" in honor of the show's star. Prices range from $5 to more than $50. He's glad to have visitors, so stop by anytime. You can call him at (502) 838-6652, or write him at 2969 State Rt. 94 West, Hickman, 42050.

R. N. Henson likes his town, and although the mailing address is in Hickman, he puts Cayce on his business cards. Another young man who put this town on the map was the daredevil railroad engineer John Luther Jones (better known as Casey Jones), who was "yanked-up" here. When he got his first job with the Illinois Central, there were so many Joneses that his boss nicknamed him "Cayce." The legend that developed around him after his death somehow also corrupted the spelling to "Casey," but folks here haven't forgotten.

In downtown Hickman, next to the chamber of commerce, is the shop of **J. M. Cooper,** Old World-style tinkerer extraordinaire. Although he makes and repairs guns and jewelry, Cooper is best known for his work on clocks. The shop is filled with all kinds of modern and antique clocks, some of his own, some belonging to townspeople (the mayor told me that J. M. has had at least ten of her clocks for at least a decade), but his pride and joy-the courthouse clock-rises high above everything else on the bluff. In 1974 J. M. completely rebuilt the innards of the old Seth Thomas, originally installed in 1904. The clock parts weigh almost two tons, the bell about 2,800 pounds, and the striking hammer a hefty 40 pounds. Few such clocks are in operation, and fewer yet are still wound by hand; every eight days "Coop" climbs the long stairs of the clock tower and winds. On slow days, when he's feeling up to it, he'll take people up. His shop hours are by chance, so call the chamber ahead at (502) 236-2902 to find out if J. M. is in.

## TRUE BLUE

Mark Twain called Hickman "the most beautiful town on the Mississippi."

Follow Highway 94 west out of town to ◆ **Reelfoot Lake.** The part of the lake that is in Kentucky (most is in Tennessee) is wild, beautiful swampland. During the winter of 1811-1812, a series of earthquakes along the New Madrid fault shook the whole region so violently that the tremors made bells ring as far away as Pittsburgh, Pennsylvania. Reelfoot Lake was created when the quakes caused the Mississippi River to run backwards; when it returned to its usual flow, it straightened out and left behind one of its old curves. Look at your map and the abandoned bend will become obvious. Admire the large stands of bald cypress trees. Their lower trunks are broad, flaring like upside-down flying buttresses; the needles are feathery and fine; and they're surrounded by their own "knees," or cone-shaped roots, which seem to emerge from the water independently. These roots make it possible for the large trees to remain upright in the muddy soils. Follow Highway 94 southwest to the Reelfoot Lake National Wildlife Refuge and talk to the rangers about the local wildlife.

The only way to go farther west in Kentucky is to drive down Highway 94 into Tennessee, where it becomes Highway 78. From Tiptonville, Tennessee, follow the signs to the Madrid Bend, also known as Kentucky Bend or Bessie Bend. A few families have the peninsula to themselves to farm however they please.

In the center of the Jackson Purchase region is the town of Mayfield, known to outsiders for ◆ **The Wooldridge Monuments,** "the strange procession that never moves," in the cemetery. The entrance to the Maplewood Cemetery is in town at the intersection of the Highway 45 overpass and North Seventh Street. The eighteen-figure group in sandstone and Italian marble was erected in the late 1890s by an otherwise inconsequential bloke named Henry G. Wooldridge. Though he is the only person buried on the site, the figures represent him on his favorite horse, Fop; him standing by a podium; two hounds, a fox, and a deer; and his three sisters, four brothers, mother, and two great-nieces, one of whom, rumor has it, actually resembles Henry's first love, Minnie, who died in her youth. Legend has it that when the statues were en route from Paducah, a drunk climbed on the flat rail car and mounted the stone horse behind the stone Wooldridge to ride into Mayfield, the drunk king of a mute parade.

A great place to eat in town is the **Hills Drive Inn** (502-247-9121). Coming from Murray by Highway 121 north, it's on the left at the Y intersection of Cuba and Paris roads, next to McDonald's. In business since 1949, the place is known for homemade pies and any-way-you-want-it sandwiches. It has a big porch for summer eating, a drive-in window, indoor tables, and a long sociable counter. The decor has definite allure. I tried, in vain, to buy an old tin John Ruskin cigar sign—BEST AND BIGGEST. Hours are 7:00 A.M. to 2:00 P.M. Monday through Thursday and on Saturday. On Friday they're open until 7:00 P.M.

Fiery debates and pit barbecue are at the heart of the **Fancy Farm**

**Picnic,** perhaps the sole survivor of grass-roots political campaign picnics in America. *The Guinness Book of World Records* lists it as the world's largest one-day picnic, not surprising when more than 15,000 pounds of fresh pork and mutton are cooked annually. The first Saturday in August at 10:00 A.M., games and entertainment begin, country goods booths go up, and local, state and national political figures rile the crowds, one way or another. Speeches are given from a red, white, and blue bunting-covered flatbed wagon, just like in 1880, when the picnic was established as the last opportunity for candidates to meet before the August primaries. Because the primaries are now held in May, the picnic functions as a debate for the final candidates. Fancy Farm is 10 miles west of Mayfield on Highway 80, at its junction with Highway 339.

Due west on Highway 80 in Hickman County is the low-lying river town of Columbus. Slightly upriver, between Columbus and Clinton, the ◆ **Columbus-Belmont Battlefield State Park** (502-677-2327) perches on 200-foot-high palisades. The park marks the Civil War site of the westernmost Confederate fortification in Kentucky. Rebel soldiers installed a whopping mile-long chain, held afloat by wooden rafts, across the Mississippi River to prevent Union gunboats from moving south. Each link of the chain weighed fifteen pounds, and the anchor attached to it was six tons. Cannons were lined up on the face of the bluffs. Shortly after the fortification was complete, Union forces led by Ulysses S. Grant took the town in 1861 when Confederate forces were crumbling everywhere. It's a pleasantly dizzying picnic and camping site, and the park has a little museum of early Native American artifacts and Civil War relics including chain links, the anchor, and cannons from the river blockade. The museum is open only on weekends in April and October, daily May through September.

Hickman County is missing a tooth. Sometime between 1820 and 1870 a channel of the Mississippi River shifted to the east, leaving a 9,000-acre chunk of Kentucky land stranded in Missouri, nearly a mile west of the rest of the county. Despite its new location, in 1871 the Supreme Court awarded the land, now called Wolf Island, to Kentucky, thereby denying the big daddy of all waters the power to move official boundaries.

Follow Highway 123 north to Bardwell, then take I–51 north to Wickliffe. Every Memorial Day weekend from Wickliffe to Fulton, on the Tennessee border, Highway 51 is lined with flea markets and yard sales. If you can't find junk to your heart's desire on that weekend, you ain't never gonna find it.

Go through Wickliffe as if you were crossing the river to Cairo, Illinois, and look for signs to ❖ **The Wickliffe Mounds Research Center** (502-335-3681). You'll understand why the Mississippian Indians chose this site as a town or ceremonial grounds when you stand on the highest mound and look out toward the wide sparkling junction of two massive rivers, the Ohio and the Mississippi. The scene is exhilarating. In addition to the intact four-sided, flat-topped "ceremonial mound," three excavation areas have been preserved and interpreted for the public.

One of the most significant displays is in the cemetery. Without being eerie or morbid, the space is moving. The bodies were buried close together, each surrounded by a few significant belongings, each facing east as if to remain in contact with the cycle of days and nights. The display explains how archaeologists determine diet, illnesses, typical injuries, and physical appearances by analyzing the remains of people who weren't radically different from us. All the actual human remains and burial goods have been replaced with plastic replicas in their original positions. This seriously self-examining display deals with various points of view, including a Native American view, about the appropriate study and treatment of human remains. The curators and Native American advisers are working toward making Wickliffe Mounds into a ceremonial site, as it was thousands of years ago. Hours are 9:00 A.M. to 4:30 P.M. daily from March to November. Admission is charged. If you want to try your hand at excavation, check into summer field school at the Mounds. Write: Wickliffe Mounds Research Center, P.O. Box 155, Wickliffe 42087.

About 6 miles northeast of Wickliffe on Highway 60 is the town of Barlow, and in it a museum called the **Barlow House Museum,** on the corner of Broadway and Fifth Street, which pays tribute to

## TRUE BLUE

Kentucky Lake and Lake Barkley together form one of the largest man-made lakes in the United States.

the early history of Ballard County by preserving the home and belongings of a family that helped settle the region. In 1849, Thomas Jefferson Barlow bought land, but didn't want to farm, so he opened a general store and started selling lots for houses. Like many an American town, that's how Barlow was born. The fully restored 1903 Victorian home belonged to Thomas's oldest son, Clifton J. Barlow, and remained in the Barlow family until 1989. The house is open to the public for tours Friday, Sunday, and Monday from 1:00 to 4:00 P.M. or by appointment, and also for meetings, receptions, and so forth. Contact Della Johnson for more information at (502) 334-3010 or 334-3691.

If you've become hooked on digressions, here's an opportunity to indulge. Continue on Highway 60 east to La Center and take Highway 358 north, then go west on Highway 473 through Ogden (once called Needmore) to **Monkey's Eyebrow,** the most debated place name in the state of Kentucky. There is no post office, hence no official name, but we argue na'theless. Byron Crawford submits the idea that, if one looks at the shape of the northern boundary of Ballard County, the Ohio River forms a rough profile of a monkey in such a way that this community is just where the eyebrow would be. Others say that there was a store owned by John and Dodge Ray, the brothers who settled the sandy loam ridge in the late nineteenth century, and behind it a berm that resembled a monkey's eyebrow because it was covered with tall grasses. New theories are welcome fuel for the fire.

Back on Highway 60, go east until you reach Future City. Turn left (northeast) on Highway 996 and go almost 6 miles to where the road ends in a strange swampy landscape. The Kentucky State Nature Preserves Commission has purchased ◆ **Metropolis Lake** in order to protect this intriguing little naturally formed body of water and the river floodplain that surrounds it from destructive development. Fishing is permitted here because anglers drool over the lake's population of fish and because people take good care of the area. Although the lake area used to be a developed commercial recreation area, today it is more pure, an enchanted dreamscape with bald cypress and swamp tupelo trees casting strange shapes

**Wacinton**

against the sky and even stranger reflections on the water. Beavers, kingfishers, wildflowers, and seven rare aquatic species are among the many living creatures that share this special space. If you have questions, call the commission at (502) 564-2886.

Stay on Highway 60 and go east into Paducah, the urban center of the Jackson Purchase region. As you near the downtown area, look for Noble Park on the west side of the road. Stop when you are haunted by an enormous sculpture of a Chickasaw Indian. The piece, called ❖ *Wacinton,* or "to have understanding," was carved from a 56,000-pound red oak tree by Hungarian-born sculptor Peter "Wolf" Toth in 1985. Toth donated the piece to the city of Paducah and the state of Kentucky in honor of the Native American people who lived in the area before the Jackson Purchase, in 1818. In 1972, at the age of twenty-five, Toth decided to carve a giant

Indian sculpture for every state in the Union. He refuses pay. His "trail of whispering giants" is a gift to our national conscience. He identifies with the suffering of Native Americans because he and his family lost everything when they fled Hungary in 1956 just before the communist revolution. Paducah's *Wacinton* is his fiftieth sculpture. After the United States, he says he'll be carving in Canada, then Mexico.

The people of Paducah have renovated and preserved a once-dilapidated Classical Revival mansion by making it into the **Whitehaven Welcome Center,** south of town on I-24, and filling it with antique furniture from the area. Get travel information here, or call the center at (502) 554-2077. Tours are available from 1:00 to 4:00 P.M. daily.

In downtown Paducah between Broadway and Kentucky Avenues is the Market House, the hub of business and trade since 1836. Today the building houses three arts organizations. **The Market House Museum** (502-443-7759) is a regional history museum that includes the reconstructed interior of an 1877 drugstore. Hours are noon to 4:00 P.M. Tuesday through Saturday and 1:00 to 4:00 P.M. Sunday. Admission is $1.50. The **Yeiser Art Center** and gift shop (502-442-2453) hangs traveling exhibits of contemporary and traditional art. Hours are 10:00 A.M. to 4:00 P.M. Tuesday through Saturday and 1:00 to 4:00 P.M. Sunday. Admission is $1.00. Also in the building is the **Market House Theatre** (502-444-6828), a not-for-profit community theater—check its busy production schedule.

Across the street, the **Paducah Harbor Plaza** is a five-story yellow brick building with stained-glass windows and ornate sandstone cornices. Beverly McKinley has opened a bed and breakfast on the second floor, making accommodations available in high style as they were when the place was called the Hotel Belvedere. For between $55 and $75 a night, one or two people get a renovated bedroom appointed with antiques and handmade quilts, and a continental breakfast. In the morning, guests get first crack at the women's apparel and rich fabrics, buttons, and quilt and clothing patterns in Dogwood Lane, a store on the first floor of the plaza that caters to quilters. Call (502) 442-2698 or (800) 719-7799.

# AUTHENTIC TO THE END

Civil War reenactors (and Kentucky has a slew of them) often take their reenactment quite seriously, insisting on meticulous detail and authenticity in their uniforms and accessories, and often adopting the total identity of soldier from the past. Carrying this thought to its ultimate conclusion was one of the inspirations for **Bert & Bud's Vintage Coffins,** of Murray. Roy "Bud" Davis and Albert "Bert" Sperath, respectively the former and current director of the Clara M. Eagle Art Gallery at Murray State University, create nineteenth-century "toe-pincher-style" and other unique coffins at a studio in Sperath's garage. So far, business hasn't been exactly lively, but one Murray antiques buff ordered a coffin for use as a coffee table, and a Nova Scotia customer plans to use one in a theatrical production. Meanwhile, they're looking at lighter sidelines. They also built a whimsical coffin that looks like a dollhouse for Davis's wife. "She has no intention of using it for a long time," he noted. "Our market is really not for people who need a coffin now, but for people who want something different and tend to plan ahead." Give Davis a call at (502) 753-9279 if you're interested in stopping by while you're in Murray.

You can sleep with the ghost of a heroine at the **Farley Place Bed and Breakfast** (502-442-2488). From I-24, take exit 4 and turn east on Highway 60; follow the highway for 7 miles, then turn right on Farley Place and look for house number 166 with the bronze historical marker in the front yard. This big Victorian house was once home to Emily Gant Jarrett, a dyed-in-the-wool rebel who stole the Confederate flag from its pole minutes before General Grant took the city, and hid it, perhaps under her dress, while Union soldiers searched her house for it.

When people think of Kentucky crafts, quilts are often the first things that come to mind. Since April 1991, Paducah immediately comes to mind as the quilt capital of America, thanks to the ◆**Museum of the American Quilter's Society** downtown at the corner of Second and Jefferson Streets. Those of us who have grown up around (or under) handmade quilts and taken them for granted can't help but be awestruck with the beauty and variety of the quilts in the museum. Unlike many collections in the region, this museum is primarily devoted to the modern quilt. Those who appreciate abstract painting may find a new passion in the bold shapes and colors of these "canvases."

In addition to the main display area of quilts from the permanent collection and the two additional galleries with quilts from traveling exhibitions, the 30,000-square-foot building has a climate-controlled vault, a bookstore and gift shop, and classrooms. The museum is open Tuesday through Saturday from 10:00 A.M. to 5:00 P.M. year-round and Sunday from 1:00 to 5:00 P.M. from April through October. Admission is $5.00 for adults, $3.00 for students. For more information, call (502) 442-8856.

Also contributing to Paducah's position as Quilt City USA is the annual **AQS National Quilt Show** sponsored by the Paducah-based American Quilter's Society. This national quilt extravaganza is held in late April at the Julian Carroll Convention Center in downtown Paducah. More than 400 quilts from all over the world are displayed and judged to win a part of the $75,000-plus in cash awards. During that week the whole city is overflowing with quilts; special workshops and lectures are offered; and quilt supply vendors set up shop. Hotel space is at a premium during the show, so plan ahead. For show information, write: AQS, P.O. Box 3290, Paducah 42002-3290, or call (502) 898-7903.

Twenty-one miles north of Paducah on Highway 60 in the tiny town of Burna is the **World's Tiniest Itsy-Bitsy Bus Station.** Downtown, across the street from Jeannie's Food Market is a white clapboard building about the size of a big outhouse with windows and a red, white, and blue Greyhound sign hanging by the door. I guess there's room to sell a ticket. If you need a bus, don't lose faith—the hound will stop wherever there's a sign.

## MORE GOOD LODGING

PADUCAH

**Fox Briar Farm Inn,** 515 Schmidt Road; (502) 554-1774. Newly built Victorian-style inn on 100 acres. $90 to $110.

**JR's Executive Inn,** One Executive Boulevard; (502) 443-8000 or 800-866-3636. Luxury riverside hotel. About $70.

**Trinity Hills Farm Bed and Breakfast,** 10455 Old Lovelace Road, Paducah; (502) 288-3999 or (800) 488-3998. New home on a seventeen-acre farm. Two rooms with private entrances, three suites; full breakfast plus evening dessert. $60 to $90.

#### MAYFIELD
**Super 8 Motel,** 1100 Links Lane; (502) 247-8899. $50 and up.

## MORE FUN PLACES TO EAT

#### BENTON
**Catfish Kitchen,** 136 Teal Run Circle; (502) 362-7306. Lakeside dining; great seafood and homemade desserts.

#### MURRAY
**Knoth's Bar-B-Que,** 3975 Highway 641 North; (502) 759-1712. Old-fashioned barbecue slow-cooked over wood charcoal.

#### PADUCAH
**Historic Oldtown Restaurant,** 701 Park Avenue; (502) 442-9616. Ribs, steaks, and seafood served in a renovated stagecoach stop.

**Ninth Street House,** 323 North Ninth Street; (502) 442-9019. Elegant dining in a restored 1886 mansion.

**The Pines and Café Maurice,** 900 North 32nd Street; (502) 442-9304. Gourmet steaks in an elegant setting, or soup and sandwiches in the adjoining bistro.

## PENNYROYAL REGION

Tennessee Valley Authority's (TVA) ✦ **Land Between the Lakes** national recreation area is considered the "crappie fishing capital of the world," not to mention the huge populations of largemouth and smallmouth bass—an angler's dream-come-true. The Tennessee River was dammed to make Kentucky Lake, and Lake Barkley was formed from the mighty Cumberland River. Together they comprise 220,000 acres of clean, safe water and form a 40-mile-long peninsula,

**TRUE BLUE**

The Jefferson Davis monument in Fairview is the fourth largest concrete obelisk in the world (351 feet).

which the TVA has developed for recreation and education.

For bird lovers, Land Between the Lakes, or LBL, is one of a scant handful of places where one can get a glimpse of wild bald eagles. In the 1960s poaching and the use of chemicals like DDT reduced the number of breeding eagles to fewer than 600 pairs, making our national mascot nearly extinct in this continent. The wildlife management people at LBL successfully got the numbers back up by returning raptors to a natural habitat with very little human contact. Ask about eagle and wildlife programs at the Woodlands Nature Center. During the winter, eagle field trips are scheduled for the weekends. Preregistration is necessary; call (502) 924-5602, extension 238 or 233. Photographers can get close-up pictures of these marvelous creatures in captivity at the nature center, or if you're lucky and very patient, in the wild. Throughout the year, there's plenty for nature enthusiasts to see and do. In addition to plenty of lake access ramps, there are great hiking trails, ranging from .2 to 65 miles in length. (The easy **Center Furnace Trail** goes past an historic iron furnace.) You can rent a bicycle or a canoe. One of the natural programs has been an effort to re-introduce endangered wildlife species. LBL is home to the nation's largest public herd of bison, and in 1996, elk were released into the area. You may be able to see these animals along a self-guided driving tour of **The Elk & Bison Prairie.** At the Golden Pond Welcome Center, there's a small planetarium. And if you drive to the southern end of LBL (actually in Tennessee), you can walk around **The Homeplace 1850,** set up as a working nineteenth-century homestead. Enter the park from any direction—Highways 68, 94, 641, 24, or in Tennessee, Highways 79 or 76—and go to the North, South, or Golden Pond Visitor Center for directions and information about the park.

> ## TRUE BLUE
>
> The Land Between the Lakes area was once known as the "Moonshine Capital of the World."

If you're not camping and are in favor of unusual lodging, try the **Round Oak Inn** off Highway 68, 1½ miles west of the Barkley State Park Lodge at Devils Elbow. It offers cozy "Western contemporary" bed-and-breakfast facilities for $54 per night. Call (502) 924-5850 for reservations.

If you're hungry and caught smack-dab between a lake and a wet place, pull in to **Patti's 1880's Settlement,** home of the Mile-high Meringue Pie, the two-inch-thick pork-chop, and bread baked in a flowerpot. With five gift shops, two restaurants, a miniature golf course, and an animal park, Patti's seems like a continuation of the dream that a young multimillionaire, Thomas Lawson, had for the town in the 1880s when he found it nestled between the Cumberland and Tennessee Rivers. Lawson changed the town's name from Nichols Landing to Grand Rivers and built himself a resort town with a theme of Southern hospitality. Now that the rivers have been dammed, it should be renamed Grand Lakes, but . . . Patti's Restaurant, owned by the Tullar family, and a perennial favorite with both seasonal and twelve-month diners, is open year-round from 10:30 A.M. to 8:00 P.M. every day. Other activities vary some. Call (502) 362-8844 for specifics.

The first major town east of the lakes on Highway 68 is **Cadiz** (pronounced *KAYD-eez*), named, perhaps, after the hometown of an early Spanish surveyor. Since the creation of Land Between the Lakes, people say that the name means "gateway" in Spanish, since Cadiz is at the southeastern entrance to the area. Saxophone lovers pay homage here to the inimitable Boots Randolph, who was born in Trigg County. (The question is, should a golf course be named after a musician? Poor guy.) Ham lovers must have a meal in town; prize-winning hams are served everywhere—try **Hamtown U.S.A. Restaurant** (502-522-3158), open every day from 6:00 A.M. to 8:00 P.M., or **Broadbent's Food and Gifts** (502-522-6674), a big place to buy take-home hams, bacon, sausage, and cheeses, located 5 miles east of town near I-24. During the second weekend in October, follow your nose to the Trigg County Country Ham Festival. Non-Southerners may learn that not all country ham can be safely compared to the salt-drenched tongue of your big brother's hiking boot.

There is something eerie and irresistible about stepping into a person's space and looking at the way that individual's daily life is shaped and revealed by his or her personal belongings. The ◆ **Adsmore Museum** in Princeton draws visitors into the lives of its turn-of-the-century residents in that almost-taboo way by presenting the house intact, changing detailed decorations and personal accessories seasonally, and building the tour around stories of the family. The interpretive staff reenacts weddings, birthday parties, and wakes (complete with wailing mourners dressed in period clothes). Details make this place a treat. That the Victorians in Europe were not morally able to utter the phrase "chicken thigh," for example, comes as no surprise when you find that the piano's legs, like a lady's, were always chastely covered with a shawl.

Built in grand late-Victorian style in 1857, Adsmore was fully restored in 1986 by the local library board to which Katharine Garrett, the last family resident, donated the building and its contents. Adsmore could have also been called "Collectsmore," for it is furnished lavishly with items from all over the world. Also on the grounds is the Ratliff Gun Shop, a restored 1844 cabin filled with antique tools. The museum and grounds are open Tuesday through Saturday from 11:00 A.M. to 4:00 P.M., and Sunday from 1:30 to 4:00 P.M. Admission ranges from $2.00 to $5.00, according to age category. Group rates are available. Call (502) 365-3114. Adsmore is at 304 North Jefferson Street in downtown Princeton, a town that has been called the Natchez of West Kentucky because of its grand homes. From Cadiz, the quickest route is Highway 139 north. From the Land Between the Lakes, take Highway 62, or take exit 12 from the Western Kentucky Parkway.

Princeton's oldest building, the circa-1817 Federal-style Champion-Shepherdson House at 115 East Main, has been renovated and is now home to the **Princeton Art Guild.** Like so many early settlements, Princeton began with a general store located near a big, dependable spring. A lean-to money-counting room, also used by fur traders, is now an artist-in-residence studio. The main building houses a gallery, a gift shop, and space for special events and workshops. Hours are 1:00 to 5:00 P.M. Tuesday through Saturday. For more information, write the guild at P.O. Box 451, Princeton 42445, or call (502) 365-3959.

For a historic picnic spot, stop just 1 block south of the Princeton courthouse at **Big Springs Park,** the original settlement's water source and a site where the Cherokees camped on the Trail of Tears. Also noteworthy is the Black Patch Festival, which Princeton hosts in early September to commemorate the times when dark-leaf tobacco was harvested in the area in massive quantities. Accompanying this event is a dark and touchy history involving tobacco price wars and the night riders, a movement of farmers (made nationally famous by writers such as Robert Penn Warren) who turned to a sophisticated form of organized violence to ensure the viability of their way of life. Local historians explain the events during the Black Patch tour.

Take Highway 91 south from Princeton to downtown **Hopkinsville.** In the grand old Federal-style post office building at the corner of East Ninth (Highway 68) and Liberty Streets is the ◆ **Pennyroyal Area Museum** (502-887-4270), an impressive regional history museum. The main display area is in the huge mail sorting room. Notice the enclosed catwalks overhead, secret vantage points from which postmasters watched postal workers handle the mail, not to enforce efficiency (it is after all, a federal institution), but to prevent workers from stealing cash from the envelopes in a pre-checking account era.

The museum's displays address many facets of the Pennyroyal region's history, from agriculture and the Black Patch wars to reconstructed pioneer bedrooms and an 1898 law office. In the middle of the room sits a beautifully preserved original Mogul wagon, made just 2 blocks away in a large factory that manufactured every imaginable type of wagon. Mogul Wagon Company's ads in the 1920s read EASY TO PULL, HARD TO BREAK and BUY A MOGUL and WILL IT TO YOUR GRANDSON. Railroad and early automobile artifacts compete for your attention with a miniature circus made by John Venable, which is said to have inspired Robert Penn Warren's *The Circus in the Attic,* the title piece of an early collection of short stories. Museum hours are 8:30 A.M. to 4:30 P.M. Monday through Friday and 10:00 A.M. to 3:00 P.M. Saturday. Admission is $1.00 for children under 12 and $2.00 for adults.

The Edgar Cayce exhibit is one of the most popular in the museum. The display case contains a few photographs and significant personal objects, like Cayce's dog-eared desk Bible. Cayce, who was born in

**TRUE BLUE**

Paducah was founded in 1827 by William Lewis (of Lewis and Clark).

1877 in southern Christian County near Beverly, was a "strange" child who preferred meditating on the Bible to playing baseball. In 1900 after a severe illness, Cayce mysteriously lost his voice. When put under hypnosis by "Hart-The Laugh Man" in 1901, Cayce diagnosed the problem and restored his own voice by using a treatment he discovered during hypnosis. That was the beginning of his career as an internationally known clairvoyant, "the sleeping prophet." He gave 14,256 psychic readings in which he diagnosed medical problems and predicted world affairs, including natural disasters and economic changes. Today the Association for Research and Enlightenment, based at Virginia Beach where Cayce spent the last twenty years of his life, continues "The Work," as Cayce called it, by providing a library and educational programs related to his readings.

Many of Hopkinsville's visitors from the west, passing through town en route to Virginia Beach, stop to see the place where Edgar Cayce and his wife, Gertrude Evans, are buried in the Riverside Cemetery on the north side of town, just east of North Virginia Street. Seven miles south of town on the Lafayette Road (Highway 107) in Beverly are Cayce's church, the Liberty Christian Church, which is open to the public at no charge, and his school, the Beverly Academy, which is now on private property. If you're a Cayce fan, ask at the museum about other significant sites.

Hopkinsville has done more than any other town in the state to pay tribute to the Native American people who were forced to move from their southeastern homelands across the Mississippi River to Oklahoma on the infamous Trail of Tears during the winter of 1838-1839. More than 13,000 Cherokee Indians camped in Hopkinsville and received provisions for their forced migration, during which thousands of people died.

The Trail of Tears Commission, Inc., has developed the **Trail of Tears Commemorative Park** on Pembroke Road (Highway 41) on the west edge of town. The park includes impressive, larger-than-life statues of Cherokee Chiefs White Path and Fly Smith, who are buried on the property. Near the banks of the Little River is a log cabin that serves as an education center. Although the Cherokee people fought alongside the colonists during the American Revolution and later with Andrew Jackson in the War of 1812, Jackson as president in the late 1820s insisted that Indians of numerous tribes yield to whites and leave their homelands east of the Mississippi. The forced removal spanned a decade, causing tremendous loss of lives in the process and leaving the survivors a legacy of hardship on barren reservations in the West. It should also be noted that gold was discovered on Cherokee land in Georgia in 1828, ten years prior to the Indians' forced migration. The center is open 10:00 A.M. to 5:00 P.M. daily, April through September.

◆ **The Trail of Tears Intertribal Indian Pow Wow** has become an annual event, held during the weekend after Labor Day. Although the recent history of the Native American peoples is tragic, this public festival is meant to commemorate the beauty and integrity of their culture. The pow wow features Native American crafts, food, storytelling, blow gun demonstrations, and a very competitive Indian dance contest. Contact the Trail of Tears Commission, Inc., P.O. Box 4027, Hopkinsville 42240, or call (502) 886-8033.

For lodging near Hopkinsville, Melissa and Gary Jones's bed and breakfast, the **Oakland Manor** (9210 Newstead Road; 502-885-6400) is a truly elegant restored 1857 antebellum mansion filled with period antiques. With its ninety-five trees, gazebo, flagstone walkway, and gracious Old South country setting, it looks like a scene from *Gone with the Wind*. From April through December three rooms are available for lodging at the rate of $45 per night. From downtown Hopkinsville, take Canton Pike (Highway 272) to the west, turn left on Newstead Road (Highway 164), and watch for the sign on the left side after about 3½ miles.

As soon as you drive east from Hopkinsville, you are in an area heavily populated by Amish and Mennonite people. Nationally there are about 85,000 Amish, many of whom live in Pennsylvania, Ohio, and Indiana in communities that are being encroached upon by rapidly widening urban edges. Rural Kentucky has become a popular place for Amish families to relocate because the land is beautiful, isolated, and relatively inexpensive. When you visit Amish and Mennonite businesses, keep in mind that they are committed to their way of life in part because they want isolation from the rest of the world. Respect their privacy. Observe their work practices, for they are good stewards of their land and of all their resources.

We could stand a little education.

About 6 miles east of town on Highway 68, at a big farmhouse with rock pillars by the driveway, Henry Hoover runs an unadvertised bulk food and farm supply business primarily meant to serve an orthodox community known as Horse and Buggy Mennonites, folks who have no cars or telephones. He will sell to the public, so stop in if you need flour, cereals, bread, cheese, and so forth. It's a great way to avoid excessive packaging and higher prices due to expensive advertising. Hours are by chance.

◈ **Pete's Custom Saddle Shop** is an orderly, productive (secular) one-man leather operation on Highway 68 about 8 miles east of Hopkinsville. In addition to making and refurbishing more than a hundred saddles a year, Russell (Pete) Harry makes holsters, halters, and bridles, not to mention guns, tomahawks, and an occasional painting. Although he's geared primarily to custom work, there are always a few items for sale in the shop that will knock your socks off. Pete's original saddle designs range from a sleek bird-hunting saddle to variations on Civil War styles to a western pleasure show saddle with special braces for a local woman who is paralyzed below the shoulders. Even if you are not in need of tack, his stunning work and positive spirit are unique and inspirational. Because his hours are not regular, call him at (502) 886-5448 before visiting.

Half a mile east of Pete Harry's place is an Amish harness shop called **Leather Works** (look for hand-painted signs by a road called Vaughns Grove on the north side of the highway), where a young farmer named Wayne Zimmerman makes and repairs leather tack of all kinds, except saddles. That his specialty is harnesses is no accident. Except for very heavy work like plowing, he and many Amish and Mennonite farmers in the area work with mule teams. The shop is small and he does not keep much in stock, but if you are interested in placing an order or just in seeing the operation, stop by. Hours are by chance.

One mile past the Leather Works place is Fairview, a tiny rural town you can't miss, thanks to the ◈ **Jefferson Davis Monument State Historic Site** looming overhead at the height of 351 feet. From miles away in any direction, the incongruous tower, said to be

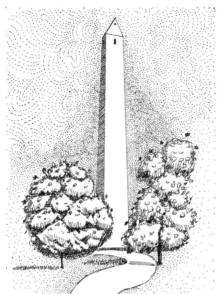

**Jefferson Davis Monument Historic Site**

the tallest concrete-cast obelisk in the world, is visible poking into the sky. During the summer you can ride an elevator to the top of the monument. Jefferson Davis, the first and only president of the Confederate States, was born in March 1886 in a house called Wayfarers Rest on the site of what is now the Bethel Baptist Church in Fairview.

Adjacent to the monument is the **Zimmerman Farms produce stand,** run by harness maker Wayne Zimmerman's brothers. From late May to mid-October, you can buy delicious, organically grown fruits and vegetables. You can trust the Amish when it comes to wholesome, flavorful produce.

At Elkton, 8 miles east of Fairview, take Highway 181 south for about 10 miles and look to the right for **Schlabach's Bakery,** an Amish bakery specializing in satisfaction. Their sourdough bread, sweet rolls, pies, cakes, cookies, and yes, even granola are delicious and always fresh. Hours are 8:00 A.M. to 5:00 P.M. every day but Thursday and Sunday. Although the owner is Abe Schlabach (502) 265-3459, you'll be more likely to meet one of his bakers who live nearby.

Just to illustrate how these Amish (there are many kinds of Amish communities) adjust their lives to both the community rules and the modern world, let me tell you how Betty Miller gets to work at the bakery every morning. Her community uses tractors and horse-and-buggy rigs, but not cars or bicycles. If she were male, she might hop on her Massey Ferguson and drive; if she were a child, she might sprint. Instead, she gets on her small tractor (a riding lawn mower) and commutes through yards and along the shoulder of the highway. Some churches won't allow use of any vehicle with rubber tires, so the members own steel-wheeled tractors. Other churches allow cars and trucks but insist they be painted black, even the chrome parts. Others allow their congregation to have cars and attend graduate school. And, at the other extreme, very orthodox communities use only horses and oxen.

**TRUE BLUE**

Musician Boots Randolph was born in Trigg County, Kentucky.

Another mile or so south, at the intersection of Highways 181 and 848, is the ◆ **Penchem Tack Store** (502-483-2314), a large Amish tack and farm supply store also used by the general public. John H. Yoders and his sons work in the leather shop in the basement while another family member tends to retail sales upstairs. It's a great place to browse, especially if you're in the market for good functional suspenders, straw work hats, Redwing shoes, veterinary supplies, tack (commercially and locally made), or just a soft drink and candy bar. Hours are 7:00 A.M. to 5:30 P.M. Monday through Saturday.

If Amish men are among the best leatherworkers, the women have always been known for the fine art of quilting. **Grandma's Cupboard** (502-483-2461) is an informal sales outlet for women who make quilts, hooked rugs, and woven runners. From Penchem's, go left (east) on Highway 848 to Highway 79; turn left (north) and stop at the second house on the right. Elmer and Mary Hochstetler have recently closed their large dairy business because none of the male children stayed on the family farm. What used to be the dairy barn is now the store where the family sells everything from homemade noodles, Amish cheese, soup mixes, and Mary's famous angel food cakes to Amish, Mennonite, and other Christian printed materials. The handmade quilts easily steal the show, however. With the help of other local quilters, Mary Hochstetler can make almost any type of quilt to order, and there are usually exquisite finished pieces for sale. Hours are 9:00 A.M. to 5:00 P.M. Monday through Saturday. Profits from quilt sales go, in part, to the Galilean Home Ministry, a Christian school in Liberty. Tell her and her daughters that I said hello.

If you are in the area in early summer and get that unbearable craving for strawberries (it's best to gorge), call the local **strawberry kings** Emmett Walton in Allensville (502-265-5597) or Tommy Borders near Elkton (502-265-5770) to see if they are open for picking. They'll direct you to the field on which you may sweetly graze.

Due south on either Highway 79 or 41, nestled right next to the Tennessee border, is the town of Guthrie, birthplace of Robert Penn Warren, poet laureate of the United States and Pulitzer prize winner for both poetry and fiction. For those who have read his work, it is enriching to walk the streets and drive by the endless fields, an environment that obviously influenced his writing. Once in town, if you want details or if you'd like to tour the **Robert Penn Warren Museum,** the house in which Penn Warren was born, contact Mrs. Dean Moore at (502) 483-2683. Tours are given 11:30 A.M. to 3:30 P.M. Tuesday through Saturday and 2:00 to 4:00 P.M. Sunday. The house is at the corner of Third and Cherry Streets.

**Libby's Steakhouse & Entertainment Center** is not only the biggest restaurant building you have probably ever seen, it's also bound to have the widest variety of entertainment you can imagine inside a restaurant—horse shows, professional Nashville country music performances, open dances, rodeos, thumb pickin' contests, parties, and even beauty pageants. Upcoming country musicians perform on stage Saturday night from 8:00 to 10:00 P.M. for "Live at Libby's," a syndicated FM radio show that has helped people such as Tracey Lawrence and Aaron Tippen get their starts. It's a "family" restaurant, so no alcohol is served, but they offer a full Southern menu. The three-pound "West Texas Slab" rib loin steak is yours free if you can clean your plate. Libby's opens at 5:00 P.M. on Friday and Saturday only (502-265-2630). Find the place on Highway 68 at its junction with Highway 1309 in Daysville, between Elkton and Russellville.

On Highway 79, about halfway between Guthrie and Russellville in Allensville, is **The Pepper Place.** Take Highway 102 east toward town and watch for the sign in front of a large, blue clapboard-sided house, circa 1864, with an inviting wraparound porch. The house is available for weddings, receptions, and catered meals. Many of the period antiques in The Pepper Place are for sale. Write Dr. Mack Craig, P.O. Box 95, Allensville 42204, or call (502) 265-9859 for reservations or a tour.

The **Southern Deposit Bank** in downtown Russellville on the corner of Main and Sixth Streets was the scene of a great crime, the Jesse James gang's first out-of-state robbery. Prior to that day the gang was just a handful of local hoodlums. On May 20, 1868, the gang held up the bank for $9,000, shot and wounded bank president N. Long, and galloped away to join the ranks of America's famous federal fugitives. (What old Jesse didn't know was that there were $50,000 more in the vault.) Today the building has been restored into a classy apartment building.

If you need a place to spend the night in Russellville, try the restored 1824 home of George Washington's third cousin, John Whiting Washington. The **Washington House** is a bed and breakfast with three lodging rooms, each fully furnished with antiques that are for sale. The first week in October is a great time to visit town and this B&B because of the Logan County Tobacco Festival; or try the weekend before Thanksgiving when gorgeous old houses in town participate in the Christmas Open House. Contact Roy Gill, 283 West Ninth Street, Russellville 42276, or call (502) 726-7608 or 726-3093.

Within shouting distance is the **Auburn Guest House,** a five-room bed and breakfast in a Colonial-style mansion (listed on the National Register of Historic Places) filled to the brim with antiques. A new carriage house in the back is also open as an antiques shop. Owners David and Joy Williams insist on serving a full (and I mean full) Southern-style morning meal. For reservations, write them at 421 West Main Street, Auburn 42206, or call

(502) 542-6019 after 3:00 P.M. The guest house is within walking distance of a number of antiques shops downtown.

Three miles east of Auburn on Highway 68 is ◈ **Shakertown at South Union,** now a wonderfully curated museum marking the site of a once-thriving village comprising more than 6,000 acres and 200 buildings. Members of the United Society of Believers in Christ's Second Appearing, more commonly known as Shakers, lived at the South Union community from 1807 until 1922. They supported themselves with sophisticated enterprises in garden seed, fruit preserves, fine colorful silk handkerchiefs, and farming. They also ran a large, steam-powered mill, hired out some of Kentucky's first purebred bulls for stud all over the state, and built and leased out (to the World) a train depot, post office/general store, and tavern.

The forty-room building that now serves as the main museum was the Center House, a dwelling complete with kitchen, communal dining room, and bedrooms—men on one side, women on the other. The structure fulfills your basic expectations of a Shaker building, but in a slightly showier way—some of the trim boards are beaded, there is a nook for a clock, the first-floor window casings flare, and arches abound. From the woodstoves to the cooking utensils to the hat molds, South Union is filled with original Shaker objects, not reproductions. Even the brick dust and mustard-ochre stains on the woodwork are original (let's hear it for organic paint!). This Shaker museum also boasts the largest collection of western Shaker furniture in the United States.

The museum and gift shop are open from March 1 through December 1 Monday through Friday from 9:00 A.M. to 5:00 P.M. and Sunday from 1:00 to 5:00 P.M. Admission is $4.00 for adults and $1.00 for children ages 6-12. Children age 5 and under are free. Call (502) 542-4167 for further information. One mile east of the museum is Highway 73. Turn left (south) and go half a mile to the **South Union Post Office** (501-542-6757), established April 1, 1826. This was the last building constructed in the Shaker community. For updated schedules of festivals and events, write Shakertown, South Union 42283.

Directly across the road from the post office is the **Shaker Tavern,** an ornate Victorian tavern the Shakers had built to house the

**Shakertown at South Union**

overflow of railroad travelers stopping at the village for lodging. The tavern was always run by non-Shakers and still is. Michael and Sharon Laster have turned the tavern into a combined restaurant and bed and breakfast and given this place the sparkle it deserves. Lunch is served Tuesday through Saturday from 11:30 A.M. to 2:00 P.M. On the first Sunday of every month from noon to 2:30 P.M. , an exquisite lunch is served to the accompaniment of a live classical guitarist. Special-occasion dinner reservations can be made for groups of up to one hundred. Five classy bed-and-breakfast rooms are available for between $55 and $70 per night, and the chefs guarantee a full Southern breakfast in the morning. Call (502) 542-6801 for reservations or more information.

# MORE GOOD LODGING

KUTTAWA

**Davis House,** 528 South Willow Way; (502) 388-4468. Two-story Victorian bed and breakfast on Lake Barkley. About $65 per night.

GRAND RIVERS

**Grand Rivers Inn,** downtown; (502) 362-4487. Rooms and cottages, 1/4 mile from lake. $54 and up.

GILBERTSVILLE

**Kentucky Dam Village State Resort Park,** Highway 62 at Highway 641 on Kentucky Lake; (502) 362-4271. Lodge and cottages, golf course. $70 and up.

CADIZ

**Lake Barkley State Resort Park,** Off Highway 68; (502) 924-1131. Two lodges and cottages with golf, and fitness center. $70 and up.

DAWSON SPRINGS

**Pennyrile Forest State Resort Park,** Highway 109; (502) 797-3421. Lodge and cottages. $55 and up.

# MORE FUN PLACES TO EAT

HOPKINSVILLE

**Bartholomew's,** 914 South Main Street; (502) 886-5768. Burgers, pasta dishes, and award-winning lemonade, served in a renovated turn-of-the-century grocery building.

**Kuttawa**

**Kuttawa Harbor Marina,** 1709 Lake Barkley Drive; (502) 388-9563. Famous for its "Rudyburger," with indoor and outdoor dining.

CADIZ

**Lake Barkley State Resort Park,** Off Highway 68; (502) 924-1131. Spacious dining room with fireplace, regional specialties.

GRAND RIVERS

**Miss Scarlett's Restaurant,** 708 Complex Drive; (502) 928-3126. Traditional Southern and regional fare, with homemade breads and soups.

**The Pelican,** 1006 Highway 62; (502) 362-8610. Homestyle dining (famous for its substantial breakfasts) in a casual atmosphere.

# YELLOW BANKS, GREEN RIVER

*Daddy, won't you take me back to Muhlenberg County,*
*Down by the Green River where Paradise lay.*
*I'm sorry my son but you're too late in askin',*
*Mr. Peabody's coal train has hauled it away.*

John Prine's famous lyrics give us a glimpse of Muhlenberg County's history, while traveling through the area gives us an update. "Paradise" is an enormous steam-generating power plant, the largest of its kind when it was built in the late 1950s. The county has not been all hauled away, but you may think they're trying to do so when you see some of the monstrous earth-moving machines in the surface mines visible from several major roads. (The term *strip mine* is taboo.) Even just driving through it, you'll believe that this county had been the largest coal-producing county in the United States for twenty-three consecutive years until Environmental Protection Agency (EPA) regulations reduced the market for the area's high-sulphur coal.

Aside from coal, great country music is this area's claim to fame. In front of the City Building in Central City is a monument to the town's native sons, Phil and Don Everly. Every Labor Day weekend the Everly Brothers and more than 10,000 fans come to town for a benefit concert called the **Everly Brothers Central City Music Festival,** the proceeds of which go to music scholarships and other community projects. One of the favorite events is the International Thumbpicking Contest in honor of Merle Travis. Call (502) 754-9603 for festival information.

Greenville, just south of the Western Kentucky Parkway on Highway 62 or 189, is home to several one-of-a-kinds. One is the **House of Onyx,** a megamart of gemstones that promotes investment in precious rocks and discourages trust in the banking system. Beyond inventory and prices, their literature consists of an odd combination of claims that theirs is a real, honest business and fortune-cookie-type moralistic quotes. One's curiosity is piqued. The business is primarily geared toward the wholesale and mail-order markets, but if you are in town on a weekday between 8:30 A.M. and

4:30 P.M., call ahead for a tour of the retail showroom. The mind boggles at the sight of rows of cases of rubies, sapphires, pearls, and myriad other stones. Though there is no sign, the office is in the Aaron Building at 120 North Main Street in downtown Greenville. Ring the doorbell and explain your interest, or call ahead for an appointment at (502) 338-2363.

A little known fact: Greenville is the home of the **State Championship Washer Pitching Playoffs.** Washer pitching is the rural American version of the ancient game of quoits and is related to horseshoes. In the heat of late summer, the playoffs are held at the Greenville Municipal Ball Park. You'll get a schedule for the event if and when you win a district blue ribbon.

If you plan to dine or spend a night in the area, take Highway 431 south from Central City to Highway 973 in Dunmor; take a right and go 4 miles through the countryside to ◆ **Everly's Lake Malone Inn** (502-657-2121). Don Everly recently purchased this hotel and big restaurant and redecorated it with Everly Brothers memorabilia.

Fishing is fantastic in the **Lake Malone State Park.** The 788-acre lake is surrounded by a 388-acre park laced with middle-aged pine forests and sandstone bluffs and caves where the Jesse James gang supposedly hid out. (Jesse James is to western Kentucky what Daniel Boone is to the central and eastern parts—both hid everywhere, carved their initials on every historic tree and building, and are still receiving royalties for their freely interpreted deeds.)

What do bluegrass music, Scotch taxidermy, and barbecued mutton have in common? The Owensboro area. If you are approaching the area by The Bluegrass Parkway and still need convincing that Kentucky is far from mundane, head north on the Green River parkway and take exit 69 to the tiny town of **Dundee.** When you get into town, keep your eyes to the sky. Standing stiffly above the Masonic lodge is a stuffed goat, imported almost one hundred years ago from Dundee, Scotland. The town, which was once called Hines Mill, changed its name to commemorate this oddity.

On to the self-proclaimed ◆ **Bar-B-Q Capital of the World** and the third-largest city in the state, Owensboro. In this town, where there's smoke, there's barbecue. Initiate yourself by eating at one of the many "smoking" restaurants, ranging from a humble joint called **George's Bar-B-Q** (1362 East Fourth Street; 502-926-9276), where you can sample one version of honest-to-goodness Kentucky Burgoo (a superhearty meat-and-veggie stew that originated in Wales and came here via Virginia with the pioneers), to the famous **Moonlite Bar-B-Q Inn** (502-684-8143), a huge restaurant west of town on Parrish Street where the barbecue is all hickory-pit cooked. George's is open 5:00 A.M. to 8:00 P.M. Monday through Thursday and 5:00 A.M. to 10:00 P.M. Friday and Saturday. Hours at Moonlite are 9:00 A.M. to 9:00 P.M. Monday through Saturday and 10:00 A.M. to 3:00 P.M. Sunday.

In mid-May Owensboro comes alive for the **International Bar-B-Q Festival,** during which time the local folks compete fiercely for culinary titles. A friend's father, "Pop Beers," concocted a darn good recipe for barbecued chicken that has won three festival championships. Because this generous soul has given me permission to pass on to you his secret recipe, I hereby command you to sensitize your palate before participating in the festival. I quote:

Bring the following ingredients to a rapid boil on medium high heat:

1 stick butter
1 big lemon
1 tablespoon Worcestershire sauce
1 tablespoon soy sauce
5 shakes Tabasco sauce
1 teaspoon black pepper
1 teaspoon paprika
1 teaspoon garlic powder
1 teaspoon Accent meat tenderizer
1 teaspoon poultry seasoning

Cook till a brown scum forms and then goes away. Let cool and use. Won't spoil if kept. Makes enough for three 3-pound chickens. To use, cut fat (NOT skin) off chicken. Grill chicken on one side for 30 minutes, turn and repeat, then turn again, baste, and grill for 15 minutes; turn again and repeat. Eat!

My favorite landmark in Owensboro is a ✦ **sassafras tree** in the front yard of E.M. Ford & Company on the corner of Frederica and Maple Streets. At a height of 100 feet and a circumference of 16 feet, this 250-300-year-old droopy-armed beauty is registered by the American Forestry Association as the largest of its kind in the country and probably in the world. A Mrs. Rash saved the tree from the merciless highway department by planting herself at the base of the trunk with a shotgun in hand. She then pulled political strings, and the governor immediately installed a retaining wall and lightning rod. (I'll bet Earth First! could use a Mrs. Rash.)

The ✦ **Owensboro Area Museum of Science and History** (220 Daviess Street; 502-687-2732) is a natural science and history extravaganza containing everything from live reptiles to a 100-plus-seat planetarium, a tobacco store figure of Punch, dinosaur replicas, and artifacts illustrating events in Kentucky history. Kids and uninhibited adults love the hands-on science exhibits called "Encounter" and "The Discovery Center." Though it is said that the museum started in a church building in 1966, the truth is that it began somewhat earlier in local storyteller and natural historian Joe Ford's backyard playhouse, where he stockpiled insects, rocks, and snakeskins, some of which are still in the museum collection. Open Tuesday through Saturday from 10:00 A.M. to 5:00 P.M. Admission is free.

Western Kentucky is almost as famous for bluegrass music as it is for barbecue. In fact, the "Father of Bluegrass Music," Bill Monroe, was born and is buried in the little town of Rosine, one county over from Owensboro. The **International Bluegrass Music Museum** (111 Daviess Street in Owensboro's RiverPark Center; 502-926-7891) honors Monroe and other bluegrass stars. The museum features interactive exhibits, vintage photographs, and film clips and memorabilia from a variety of performers. The museum is open from May to October. Hours are 1:00 to 5:00 P.M. Friday through Sunday.

The **Inter-Tribal Indian Festival,** open to the public and held annually in early October, is a cultural extravaganza that includes traditional food booths, Native American drummers and singers accompanying breathtaking dance performances, storytellers, medicine men lecturing on traditional uses of plants, and demonstrations of spear-throwing and flint-knapping. This event is held outdoors on the campus of Owensboro Community College, which is located just off Highway 231 on the southeast edge of town. Admission is a mere $2.00, or $1.00 for students, but no carload of people will be charged more than $4.00. For more information, call Libby Warren at (502) 686-4495.

One of Kentucky's largest fine art museums, ◆ **The Owensboro Museum of Fine Art** at 901 Frederica Street has an impressive permanent collection of works from eighteenth-, nineteenth-, and twentieth-century American, English, and French masters and a decorative arts collection of American, European, and Asian objects from the fifteenth to the nineteenth centuries. The museum has completed a $1.6 million expansion, which includes a new Exhibitions Wing; an Atrium Sculpture Court; a restored Civil War era mansion; the Kentucky Spirit Galleries, featuring rotating exhibitions of Kentucky folk art and crafts; and the Yellowbanks Gallery for works by regional artists. One highlight is a turn-of-the-century German stained glass collection displayed dramatically in 25-foot towers in an atrium gallery. The Mezzanine Gallery contains religious art. Hours are Tuesday through Friday from 10:00 A.M. to 4:00 P.M. and weekends from 1:00 to 4:00 P.M. Admission is free. Call (502) 685-3181.

There are times when rest can be found in activity. Do tennis (indoor and out), racquetball, swimming, horseback riding, fishing, canoeing, and weight lifting strike you as heavy labor? Joan Ramey, owner of Ramey Sports and Fitness Center and Ramey Riding Stables, has opened her **Friendly Farms** facilities to all appreciative visitors. Several cottages are now available for bed-and-breakfast lodging at $50 to $75 per night; this includes Ms. Ramey's athlete's breakfast. In addition to all these goodies, a masseuse is available. The Friendly Farms cottages are 3 miles east of Owensboro on Highway 56. Call (502) 771-5590 or fax (502) 771-4723.

**WeatherBerry Bed and Breakfast** at 2731 West Second Street offers country-style lodging very close to town. For $50 to $70 a night, depending on the size of the room, you get a private bath and a grand Kentucky-style breakfast, or a more moderate "healthful" repast. The previous residents of the impressive 1840 farm house had a vineyard and collected weather information for the national weather bureau, hence the name WeatherBerry. Call (502) 684-8760 for reservations.

In all cultures, people set time aside to make retreats, quiet time for contemplation away from the bustle of everyday life. Whether or not you are Catholic or connected to any church or creed in any way, ◆ **Mount Saint Joseph Center and Community of Ursuline Sisters** offers a quiet, respectful atmosphere to those of us yearning for space and time to absorb (or forget) life. Aside from retreats, the center offers all kinds of religious, cultural, and social programs. Call (502) 229-4103 for information. Take Parrish Avenue (Highway 81) west out of town until it turns due south; take Highway 56 to West Louisville, turn right (west) on Highway 815 and look for the sign within 2 miles. Go in the Maple Mount Farm entrance, find the Mother House, and ask to see the museum. Sister Emma Cecilia Busam

## TRUE BLUE

Both Civil War presidents—Abraham Lincoln and Jefferson Davis—were born in Kentucky, one year and 100 miles apart.

or Sister Mary Victor Rogers will guide you through the museum artifacts, which range from desks of the founders to gifts from foreign missions, musical instruments, religious articles, books, and displays, such as "The Madonna Room," which houses a collection of reproductions of famous European Madonna paintings. The non-Catholic visitor learns that *reliquaries* are saints' shrines of all sizes that can be displayed anywhere from behind an altar in a massive gold frame to behind a pendant in a tiny glass locket. The idea of wearing a first-degree relic, usually a chip of a saint's bone, hidden in the back of a ring has endless implications.

From Mount Saint Joseph, take a westward drive on Highway 56 for 11 miles to the ◆ **Diamond Lake Catfish Farm.** Statewide catfish farming is on the rise because reclaimed surface mines are required to have settling ponds, which are appropriate places for raising fish. This farm is a successful, sophisticated business whose owners are more than happy to show people around. During the summer visitors ride a tram to see the whole operation. Open daily during business hours. Call (502) 229-4961.

After the fish farm tour, you may be curious to know how the product tastes. The **Windy Hollow Restaurant and Museum** (502-785-4088) has a famous catfish buffet Friday and Saturday from 5:00 to 8:30 P.M. (and a big country ham breakfast buffet on Sunday from 7:00 A.M. to 1:30 P.M. if fish isn't your dish). Every day is your lucky day at the pay lakes, and you don't even need a fishing license! Windy Hollow wins the contest for having the most going on at once: drag racing, watersliding, camping, pay-lake fishing, barbecuing, golf, and even old Western movie viewing while you eat. Don't miss the cowboy museum. Yee-haw! From Owensboro, follow Highway 81 south to Old 81 and exit west. Follow the signs.

The ◆ **John James Audubon State Park** is about 20 miles west of Owensboro, along Highway 41 north of Henderson. Although Audubon is the most famous American painter of birds, he was a failure as a business executive. While he lived in this area, from 1810 to 1820, Audubon got involved in several entrepreneurial projects, all of which failed because instead of working, he spent his days in search of rare birds. With nothing left but his portfolio of bird paintings, his talent, and an idea, Audubon dragged his poor family all over the South while he painted and searched for a publisher. Eventually he found an engraver in London, England, who printed his 435 hand-colored plates as *The Birds of America*. A complete bound set of the original folios and numerous individual prints are on display in the Audubon Memorial and Nature Museum, as is the largest collection of Audubon memorabilia in existence, including many of his original paintings, journals, correspondence, and personal items. Another treasure in the museum is a rare 3-by-5-inch daguerreotype of the elderly Audubon taken by the famous early photographer Matthew Brady.

Adjacent to the museum is the Nature Center, which features a glass-enclosed Nature Observatory and a Discovery Center with exhibits on bird biology and psychology. Daily programs are offered in the summer, and special events are sprinkled throughout the rest of the year. Hours are 10:00 A.M. to 5:00 P.M. daily. Admission to the museum and nature center is $4.00 for adults, $2.50 for ages 6-12. Call (502) 826-2247 for more information.

The whole northern half of the park was donated as a nature preserve, with the stipulation that it be treated as a bird sanctuary and that the old-growth beech and sugar maple woods be preserved. Ask the park naturalist what wild and amazing flora and fauna can be seen. The park also sponsors spring and fall migration bird walks.

## MORE GOOD LODGING

### OWENSBORO

**Executive Inn Rivermont,** One Executive Boulevard; (502) 926-8000. $55 and up.

**Holiday Inn,** Highway 60 West; (502) 685-3941. Indoor pool, sauna, children's play area. $61 and up.

**Helton House Bed and Breakfast,** 103 East 23rd Street; (502) 926-7117. Mission-style home in a tree-lined neighborhood. $60 to $80.

### HENDERSON

**L&N Bed and Breakfast,** 327 North Main Street; (502) 831-1100. Historic home overlooking the river. $65 to $75.

**Super 8 Motel of Henderson,** 2030 Highway 41N; (502) 827-5611. About $45.

## MORE FUN PLACES TO EAT

### CENTRAL CITY

**Colonel's Grill,** 143 West Broad Street; (502) 754-4233. Hometown diner with fabulous fried chicken and pork chops, homemade breads, and desserts. Packed at lunchtime; closes at 3:00 P.M.

### HENDERSON

**The Mill Restaurant,** 526 South Main Street; (502) 831-2255. Decorated with antiques and stuffed animals; includes a microbrewery.

**Wolf's Restaurant and Tavern,** 31 North Green Street; (502) 826-5221. Henderson's local hangout since the late 1800s, famous for its bean soup and corn bread.

### OWENSBORO

**Old Hickory Pit,** 338 Washington Avenue; (502) 926-9000. Smoked mutton and great desserts.

**Shady Rest Barbecue Inn,** Highway 60 East; (502) 926-8234. Barbecue and burgoo (stew); fried pies for dessert.

# INDEX